T0329995

Entrepreneurial Growth in Industrial Districts

Entrepreneurial Growth in Industrial Districts

Four Italian Cases

Fernando G. Alberti

Assistant Professor of Strategic Entrepreneurship
LIUC University, Italy

Salvatore Sciascia

Assistant Professor of Business Administration
IULM University, Italy

Carmine Tripodi

Assistant Professor of Strategic Management
University of Valle d'Aosta, Italy
SDA Bocconi, Italy

Federico Visconti

Professor of Business Administration
University of Valle d'Aosta, Italy
SDA Bocconi, Italy

Edward Elgar
Cheltenham, UK • Northampton, MA, USA

Published by
Edward Elgar Publishing Limited
The Lypiatts
15 Lansdown Road
Cheltenham
Glos GL50 2JA
UK

Edward Elgar Publishing, Inc.
William Pratt House
9 Dewey Court
Northampton
Massachusetts 01060
USA

A catalogue record for this book
is available from the British Library

Library of Congress Control Number: 2008934705

ISBN 978 1 84720 085 3

Printed and bound in Great Britain by MPG Books Ltd, Bodmin, Cornwall

Contents

Figures

Tables

Acknowledgements

The writing of this book benefited from comments, suggestions and discussions coming from all the colleagues that took part to the series of seminars on the 'Evolution of industrial districts', held in 2006 and 2007 by EntEr (Centre for research on entrepreneurship and entrepreneurs), Bocconi University. We are also grateful to all our colleagues of ERDC (Entrepreneurship and Regional Development Center) of LIUC University, to the colleagues of the Department of Marketing and Management of IULM University and to those of the University of Valle d'Aosta, whose financial support is also gratefully acknowledged. Our gratitude also goes to the entrepreneurial and managerial team of Alessi, Geox, Illycaffè and Luxottica. Finally we would like to thank Terry Bland for language revisions and Francine O'Sullivan, editor of Edward Elgar Publishing, for her patience and support.

1. Introduction

F. G. Alberti, S. Sciascia and F. Visconti

In this chapter we introduce the purpose of the book, which is to explore what the antecedents of firm growth in industrial districts are, through the conceptual lenses of entrepreneurship theory. This chapter proceeds as follows; first we discuss the relevance of investigating the phenomenon of district firm growth and its implications. On the basis of that, we proceed to introduce the theoretical approach adopted in this book and we discuss the method chosen to approach our research question, together with the overall research design. The concluding section of this chapter outlines the entire structure of the book.

1.1. THE PURPOSE OF THE BOOK

Researchers and practitioners have long recognised geographically defined regional clusters of specialised firms as relevant socio-economic engines for the competitiveness and growth of regions and countries (Porter, 1998; 1990; Krugman, 1991). The notion of regional groupings of firms has been the subject of research for over a century, beginning with Marshall (1950), who first defined the concept of industrial districts. Concepts like innovative milieux (Camagni, 1991), regional innovation systems (Cooke, 2001), learning regions (Asheim, 1996) and regional clusters (Porter, 2000) have underlined the importance of the phenomenon. The general claim is that firms might enjoy advantages related to spatial juxtaposition. Italian industrial districts (Becattini, 1979), in particular, have proven to be a model for local socio-economic development (Piore and Sabel, 1984; Pyke et al., 1990). As several studies have shown, industrial districts are core in today's economies (Becattini, 2002). In studies of strategic management, whether of sources of international competitive advantage (Porter, 1990), or of the structure and dynamics of various industries (Malerba and Orsenigo, 1996;

Dosi et al., 1997), researchers have likewise found successful regional clustering of firms to be important for understanding patterns of competitiveness in many industries (Tallman et al., 2004). Thus, deepening our understanding on such socio-economic systems and how they transformed in time becomes crucial in facilitating their survival and renewal. This is especially true for the so-called 'made in Italy' industries, which vastly overlap with the model of the industrial district (Becattini, 1998) and contributed to popularise it all over the world.

Prior research on industrial districts (Piore and Sabel, 1984; Becattini, 1990; Saxenian, 1994; Markusen, 1996; Porter, 1998) suggests that they are the result of path-dependent agglomerations of small flexibly-specialised firms, together with external economies, local resources and local labour pools, supported by specialised institutions. Since the 1970s a growing number of scholars has dealt with the topic of industrial districts, observing them through the lenses of different theoretical frameworks: industrial organisation (e.g. Becattini, 1979; Brusco, 1989), sociology (e.g. Bagnasco 1977; 1988; Provasi, 1995), economic geography (e.g. Storper and Scott, 1989; Markusen, 1996; Cooke, 1999; Sforzi, 2002) and business history (e.g. Amatori and Colli, 2001). A core implication in most such studies is that all firms in a district were treated as being one and the same, performing similarly (Tallman et al., 2004). Piore and Sabel's (1984) popularisation of industrial district firms as organisationally homogeneous and identical, with similar functions and tasks has inaccurately represented industrial district firms. In other words, district firms were represented as homogeneous organisations, characterised as small and medium-sized and with equal access to local resources and competencies being 'in the air' (Boschma and Ter Wal, 2007). If Marshall could take a look at today's industrial districts, the first thing that he might notice would be that they have changed greatly over these last decades. As Lazerson and Lorenzoni (1999: 237) argued, if what Piore and Sabel described as homogeneous 'ever reflected the reality of industrial district firms, it certainly no longer does so'. Indeed, the idea that industrial districts were merely composed of homogeneous small and medium-sized firms contrasts with empirical evidence exhibiting heterogeneity in district firms size, performance, structure and strategy (see for example Porter, 1998; Lazerson and Lorenzoni, 1999; Rabellotti and Schmitz, 1999; Boschma and Lambooy, 2002). Further, in recent years, there has been increasing awareness – most strongly expressed by the literature on Italian industrial districts – that the traditional view on industrial districts tended to overlook the emergence of powerful leading firms (Visconti, 1996; 2002; Lipparini and Lomi, 1999, Lazerson and Lorenzoni, 1999; Staber, 2001; Minoja, 2002). As a matter of fact, several industrial districts have experienced the emergence of leading firms, which control the supply chain through their market power and orchestrate production phases and resources/knowledge flows in the district as well in global markets. In some cases, leading firms have grown through local mergers and acquisitions and/or takeovers by foreign multinational corporations (for example Dei Ottati, 1996; Boari and Lipparini, 1999; Albino et al., 1999; Whitford, 2001; Cainelli, Iacobucci and Moranti, 2006). In others, growth is mainly organic, thus driven by the productive opportunities of a single district firm (Penrose, 1959). To this regard, in recent years literature on industrial districts has increasingly reported evidence of district firm growth (see for example Lorenzoni and Baden-Fuller, 1995; Boari and Lipparini, 1999; Morrison, 2004; Malipiero et al., 2005), contrasting with the general assumption that being embedded in an industrial district restrains the possibility for firm growth in terms of attitude, opportunities and resources. Likewise, anecdotic evidence on district firm growth has acquired a central stage in the debate around industrial districts. We refer for instance to the cases of Benetton, Prada, Natuzzi, Filodoro, Zegna and Ducati, just to mention a few world-known cases of Italian district firms who experienced growth becoming global players.

However, despite the recent research interest on those district firms that have experienced growth, detaching from the industrial district cliché of being small, local and homogeneous, little is known on district firm growth. In this book we aim at filling such a research gap exploring the phenomenon of firm growth in industrial districts, looking at its antecedents. More precisely this book is guided by the following research question: 'what are the antecedents of firm growth in industrial districts?' This research question implies the use of proper conceptual and methodological lenses, which can allow a deep understanding of the phenomenon of firm growth in industrial districts. In order to do so, we propose a shift in the research approach from mainstream literature on industrial districts towards the conceptual lenses offered by firm-level entrepreneurship, given that growth may be a reasonable reflection of entrepreneurship (Davidsson et al., 2002). On the methodological side, we designed our study with the aim of building theory on the issue at hand. Thus, we used a comparative case study approach to explore the antecedents of district firm growth in four well-known cases of Italian district firms: Alessi, Geox, Illycaffè and Luxottica.

In the next sections, we introduce our theoretical approach, then we discuss the method we adopted to approach our research question and finally we outline the entire structure of the book.

1.2.   THEORETICAL FRAMEWORK OF ANALYSIS

The study of the antecedents of district firm growth calls for a plurality of possible approaches: growth is in fact a major theme both in economics and management studies (see for example Penrose, 1959; Greiner, 1972; Evans, 1987; Kazanjian and Drazin, 1989; Acs and Audretsch, 1990). Likewise, firm growth has become a major theme in the rapidly expanding field of entrepreneurship research.

Entrepreneurship theory suggests that a preoccupation with growth is the distinguishing feature that sets entrepreneurial businesses apart from other small firms (Penrose, 1959). As the field of entrepreneurship has developed, firm growth has been almost implicitly construed as a condition or assumption of entrepreneurship.

Many researchers associate 'growth' with 'entrepreneurship' and vice versa (Gartner, 1990; Livesay, 1995; Delmar, 1997; Wiklund, 1998). To this regard, Davidsson et al. (2002) debate upon the questions: 'is entrepreneurship growth?' and 'is growth entrepreneurship?' arriving at the conclusion that entrepreneurship is growth and vice versa under certain conditions, discussed hereafter.

First, there are several opposing views on what 'entrepreneurship' is. Sharma and Chrisman (1999) propose two main alternative views on the meaning of 'entrepreneurship'. The first holds that the major characteristic of entrepreneurship is the creation of organisations (Gartner, 1985) or new enterprises (Low and MacMillan, 1988). Along this view, there is no explicit consideration for innovation and new combinations (Schumpeter, 1934), neither the possibility of alternative ways of exploitation for a given opportunity (Shane and Venkataraman, 2000). Thus, setting the term 'entrepreneurship' equal to 'start-up of a new, independent business' reduces its empirical content so that it does not fully reflect contemporary theoretical definitions of entrepreneurship. The second view holds that entrepreneurship is the creation of new economic activity, that is, the pursuit of opportunity without regard to resources currently controlled (Stevenson et al., 1989), or the discovery and potential exploitation of profitable opportunities for creation of both private and social wealth (Venkataraman, 1997). According to this second view of entrepreneurship, opportunity is the central concept of entrepreneurship, and especially opportunities for new economic activities. Stevenson and Jarillo state that '[A]n opportunity is, by definition, something beyond the current activities of the firm...' (1990: 23). Moreover, Stevenson and Jarillo (1990) explicitly include growth, stating that 'Entrepreneurship is the function through which growth is achieved (thus not only the act of starting new businesses)' (1990: 21) and describe entrepreneurial behaviour as 'the quest for growth through innovation' (1990: 25). Venkataraman (1997) shares with Stevenson and Jarillo (1990) the strong focus on opportunity. Entrepreneurship deals with opportunities for future goods and services (Shane and Venkataraman, 2000: 220), that is, new economic activities. With respect to growth, it is important to note that Venkataraman (1997) includes not only discovery (or opportunity recognition) in his delineation of the field, but also exploitation. Davidsson et al. (2002: 332) suggest that 'If exploitation is included in the definition of entrepreneurship, it must logically follow that the growth that results from a better exploitation strategy of a given opportunity (relative to a worse exploitation strategy) is entrepreneurship manifested as growth'. Thus, according to this view of entrepreneurship as the creation of new economic activities – that is the recognition and exploitation of opportunities – an organisation grows as a result of developing new activities, therefore growth is a reflection of the firm's entrepreneurship (Davidsson et al., 2002). When new economic activities are added to old ones in existing organisations, this is entrepreneurship manifested as growth. Thus, entrepreneurship is growth, given that new economic activities add to the size of an established organisation.

Second, if it is accepted that entrepreneurship could be growth, then even the opposite must be true. This is clearly expressed by Davidsson (1989: 7) when he argues:

> [I]s growth entrepreneurship? The answer to that question is contingent on to which extent the manager is free to chose. If economic behaviour is discretionary, pursuing continued development of the firm is the more entrepreneurial choice when refraining from doing so is another feasible alternative, just like founding a firm is more entrepreneurial than not doing so.

But what kind of growth can justifiably be regarded as entrepreneurial growth, that is a manifestation of entrepreneurship? We know that firms come to grow through acquisition or by growing organically. To this regard, Penrose (1959) suggested that firms that exhibit organic growth have the ability to detect emerging expansion opportunities and to recombine existing resources in new ways so as to take advantage of these opportunities. In other words, organic growth could justifiably be considered as entrepreneurship and this is consistent with the idea that when a firm grows by adding new activities we have a case of entrepreneurship manifested as growth. Thus, the distinction between organic and acquired growth appears crucial for whether firm growth can be regarded as entrepreneurial or not. However, on the basis of empirically informed conceptual reasoning, Salvato, Lassini and Wiklund (2006) contend that even acquisition growth may generate entrepreneurial benefits over the long term.

Third, there are cases where growth does not involve addition of new activities, but only growth in volume of an existing activity of the firm. If we regard entrepreneurship not as a dichotomous but as a continuous phenomenon, that is continued entrepreneurship (Davidsson, 1991), we can find some justification for regarding growth as a reflection of entrepreneurship – even when it is only a volume growth based on the original activity – in the concept of opportunity recognition and exploitation (Venkataraman, 1997). In fact, Davidsson et al. (2002) suggest that the quality of the opportunity recognition determines the growth potential, and, in turn, the quality of the opportunity exploitation determines the actual volume of growth. They state: 'organic growth in volume can be regarded as a ... measure of the "amount" of entrepreneurship that a particular instance of new economic activity represents' (2002: 336).

In conclusion, firm growth – which represents either the introduction of new economic activity or the quality of the discovery and exploitation of opportunity for such activity – remains a proxy for entrepreneurship. There is, however, one last fundamental condition to consider when associating entrepreneurship with growth: a firm 'can only grow if it is successful' (Davidsson et al., 2002: 338).

1.3.   RESEARCH METHOD

If the aim of this book is to study what the antecedents of district firm growth are with the lenses of firm-level entrepreneurship – that is, to study the antecedents of entrepreneurial growth in district firms – we now have to define a proper research design. As argued by Yin (1989: 17), 'what' questions do not call for a specific research design if the nature of the study is exploratory, as in the case of the present book. Each research strategy is suitable (for example, an experiment, a survey, an archival analysis, a history, a case study). However, the study of the entrepreneurial growth of district firms needs direct and close observation of complex sequences of events. Opportunity recognition and exploitation occur in articulated contexts where several variables influence entrepreneurial growth over time. Hence, we decided to adopt a case study approach that allows obtaining a deep and rich empirical understanding of those research topics that received little attention by scholars, especially when they occur in dynamic settings (Eisenhardt, 1989; Yin, 1989).

1.3.1.   The Need for a Comparative-Case Design

Adopting a case study approach means to study a set of periods longitudinally in time (Pettigrew, 1979), in order to provide a transparent look on the evolution of the phenomenon of interest. Moreover, such an approach calls to rely on several methods and empirical sources to gather and construct empirical material in order to offer a holistic understanding of the phenomenon of interest. More precisely, we adopted a comparative-case studies method: we targeted four cases to be studied in depth and longitudinally in order to develop insights through a comparative logic.

Studies on firm-level entrepreneurship and growth have been mostly conducted adopting a quantitative approach. Surveys have been carried out in order to quantify the relative influence of different classes of constructs on the dependent variable. Quantitative studies achieve results that scholars can widely generalise at the expenses of the richness and concreteness of theories built. Areas of inquiries like the one we are approaching require qualitative studies in order to grasp higher levels of complexity in the generation of theory.

1.3.2.   Case Selection

When running a multiple-case study a core issue is the choice of the number of cases. Cases have not to be chosen to represent a larger pool of respondents, according to the sampling logic, thus the typical criteria regarding sample size are irrelevant (Yin, 1989). The replication logic is to be adopted instead, just like in multiple experiments; each case must be carefully selected so that it either predicts similar results (a literal replication) or produces contrary results but for predictable reasons (a theoretical replication). Moreover, the opportunity to learn is important, that means the possibility to access to the organisation and to the subject of inquiry (Pettigrew, 1990). The choice of the number of cases studies, thus, was also influenced by the possibility to follow the companies over an extended period of time and to get the necessary depth of analysis for a subject of such a complexity. Including more than four cases would have limited the possibility to reach the needed depth.

Cases were selected on a convenience basis, choosing among district firms operating within the so-called 'made in Italy' industries. Selected companies emerged as leading firms within the industrial district they are located: Alessi in the Verbano-Cusio-Ossola houseware district, Illycaffè in the Trieste coffee district, Luxottica in the Belluno eyewear district and Geox in the Montebelluna shoes district. We compared their growth rates with the average growth rates of the firms operating within their own industrial district. Growth was measured in terms of turnover and employees; details on such figures are included in Chapters 5 to 8, devoted to single cases analyses. The time span of reference, for both case selection and analysis, was variable on the basis of data availability and the fact that companies have different years of foundation. Cases were also selected looking at those district firms where growth was mostly a reflection of continued recognition and exploitation of opportunities, that is, there was a pre-understanding that they could be considered cases of entrepreneurial growth. Moreover, cases were selected only if growth was coupled with satisfactory financial results: we wanted to exclude those cases of firms growing at the expenses of their capacity to generate profits. Details on the financial results of the four companies, showing their positive returns on assets and equity, are reported in Chapters 5 to 8.

Despite an exploratory multiple-case study excluding the adoption of any sampling criteria, we tried to provide some kind of variety among case studies, in terms of industry, size, age and ownership. As shown in Table 1.1, although all four selected firms operate in the so-called 'made in Italy' sector (food, furniture and fashion), their specific industry differs; their company size varies considerably from 461 (Alessi) to 49 325 (Luxottica) employees; in terms of ownership, Geox and Luxottica are listed on the stock exchange, while Illycaffè and Alessi are family-owned companies; and as far as company age is concerned, selected cases include old firms like Alessi (founded in 1921) and younger firms like Geox (founded in 1989). We considered case heterogeneity as a way to generate as much variation as possible in the data, in order to grasp the complexity of the phenomenon of entrepreneurial growth in industrial districts.

Table 1.1 Cases comparison

Company	Industry	Year of Foundation	Ownership	Employees	Turnover (€M)
Alessi	Houseware	1921	Family	461	83
Geox	Shoes	1989	Listed	3 206	612
Illycaffè	Coffee	1933	Family	700	246
Luxottica	Eyewear	1961	Listed	49 325	4 676

Source: elaboration on annual reports of Alessi, Geox, Illycaffè and Luxottica, 2006

1.3.3.   Data Collection

Case studies typically combine different sources of evidence and data collection methods (Yin, 1989; Eisenhardt, 1989). Entrepreneurial growth is such a rich and complex phenomenon that multifaceted sources of evidence are needed to understand it. For these reasons, the present study relies on several sources of evidence.

Our primary sources include semi-structured interviews – that is, interviews with open questions focused on specific topics – we made to different interviewees at the managerial level. We carried on and transcribed interviews according to the most established methodologies (see for example

Miller and Glassner, 1997; Holstein and Gubrium, 1997; Bailey, 1982). At least six interviews were done per each case.

Secondary sources of data – gathered and written for purposes other than those of the present research – were used to corroborate and reinforce the evidence drawn from primary sources. Precautions in this sense were taken (Bailey, 1982) including several secondary sources of data:

– documentation, like a company's internal publications, articles from newspapers and magazines, administrative documents, written reports;
– archival records, like organisational charts and budgets, service records, lists of names, previously collected survey data, personal records;
– physical and cultural artefacts, observed and, when possible, gathered (for example, pictures, printouts, samples of products).

Data were collected between January 2000 and January 2007. A formal, retrievable database was produced per each case, organising data and evidentiary base. Each database comprised case study notes, transcripts, documents, files and records, available evidence of physical artefacts. We checked for triangulation of different data sources in order to obtain more robust evidence (Jick, 1979). Data collection was done at least by two researchers per each case: such couples were all different to each other.

1.3.4. Data Analysis

Data collected was analysed using the conceptual lenses offered by firm-level entrepreneurship. The unit of analysis was the district firm: a case study report was produced per each case by the same couple of researchers in charge of data collection. Although only two researchers wrote each case report, the remaining researchers read several draft versions in order to provide comments and share information. Chapters 5 to 8 report the main within-case analyses. Each case is contextualised within the industry and the district where the firm operates. Industry background and trends are analysed at both the Italian and the world level; industrial districts are analysed in terms of structure and dynamics. Finally, the entrepreneurial growth of each firm is analysed as a process of continuous recognition and exploitation of opportunities, along several stages.

Further, the complete team of researchers interpreted all four case studies in cross-sectional terms. Cross-case analysis enables the comparison of multiple cases in many divergent ways, which would not be possible within a single case analysis. Six meetings devoted to cross-case analysis were done between January and April 2007. According to Eisenhardt (1989), the overall idea of cross-case analysis is to force the researcher to go beyond the initial impressions using structured and diverse lenses on the data. Thus, we analysed data across all cases in order to identify the antecedents of firm growth through the lenses of firm-level entrepreneurship. The set of areas of inquiry is presented in Chapter 4. We reported on the different types of opportunities identified and exploited in the four district firms, the sources of entrepreneurial opportunities, the resources possessed by the firms that allowed the identification and exploitation of the entrepreneurial opportunities and the organisational mechanisms of resources acquisition and exploitation employed. We looked for within-group similarities coupled with inter-group differences so as to explore if any pattern could be identified concerning the process of entrepreneurial growth in industrial districts. We produced a cross-case report as a result of this activity, offering a holistic interpretation of the phenomena investigated.

1.3.5.   Theory Building

The cross-case analysis allowed us to build a logical chain of evidence (Yin, 1989; Miles and Huberman, 1994) for understanding the antecedents of district firm growth. Next, we conducted further analysis of consistencies identified across the cases (Miles and Huberman, 1994) in search of patterns (Eisenhardt, 1989) as characterised according to the theoretical lenses of firm-level entrepreneurship. Thus, we could answer our research question on the antecedents of district firms' growth, proposing a model. Our model was then developed into a theory that became the vehicle for generalisation to other cases of district firms not studied in this book. The process of generalising from one case to other cases that belong to the scope of the theory involved is called analytical generalisation (Yin, 1989) or theoretical generalisation (Seale, 2004).

On the basis of our theory of entrepreneurial growth within industrial districts, we examined the growth process according to specific combinations of antecedents. To this regard, we argued that varying the weight of these antecedents leads to different growth configurations. For this reason, we therefore discussed possible variations in the proposed model.

1.4.   MAIN CONTRIBUTIONS OF THE BOOK

This book is intended to stimulate entrepreneurs, managers and academic researchers to think of how firms in industrial districts can grow to become global players, offering the evidence drawn from four well-known cases of Italian district firms.

With this study, we aimed at contributing to the development of two fields of inquiry: entrepreneurship and industrial districts. In order to assess the theoretical contribution of the model, it could be helpful to take a definition of what a theory of entrepreneurship could be. As Amit argued in 1995, it should be a verifiable and logically coherent formulation of relationships or underlying principles that either predict entrepreneurial activity and performance or provide normative guidance. This definition is applicable also to the specific case of entrepreneurial growth. We believe that the model respects the above listed criteria. It could therefore be considered as a meaningful contribution to the study of entrepreneurial growth in industrial districts. Likewise, we believe our study is contributive to the field of industrial districts as well, since little is known on firm growth within the specific context of industrial districts. In conclusion, this book is intended to stimulate both academic researchers and practitioners to think of how firms in industrial districts can grow to become global players, adopting a different perspective on the phenomenon: growth as entrepreneurship.

1.5.   OUTLINE OF THE BOOK

The book is comprised of ten chapters. First, in Chapter 2 we introduce the reader to an overview of main contributions in the field of industrial districts research, from its inception to contemporary literature. After a review of the main contributions on the concept of industrial district and its main features, we focus on the so-called Italianate variant of the model, which is at central stage in our work. Finally, we offer a focus on the heterogeneity of district firms and the growth of district firms, in order to proceed towards our main arguments in the conclusion of the book. This part is followed by two chapters (Chapter 3 and 4), where we present and discuss the theoretical lenses used to explore the core issue of this book. With Chapter 3 we introduce firm-level entrepreneurship – or corporate entrepreneurship – as a key concept in interpreting the transformation process of industrial district firms, described in the previous chapter. The chapter has a threefold aim: to present the concepts of firm-level entrepreneurship; to justify the relevance of its adoption for the present study; and to review the relevant literature, looking particularly at the so-called knowledge-based approach to corporate entrepreneurship. In Chapter 4 we build on the literature on firm-level entrepreneurship introduced above in order to develop a framework of analysis, which is subsequently adopted in the rest of the book as a set of areas of inquiry to explore district firms' growth.

This first part of the book is followed by the four case study analyses. The aim of Chapters 5 to 8 is to describe the entrepreneurial growth processes of the four district firms studied in this book, setting each of them within the context of their respective industries and industrial districts, and providing a closer look at each case's history, growth and performance. In particular, Chapter 5 presents the case study of Alessi, a company based in the houseware district of Verbano-Cusio-Ossola (north-western Italy) and specialised in the manufacture of household articles, including design-based articles and objects with a high artistic-symbolic content. Chapter 6 presents the case study of Geox, a manufacturing company located in the area of Montebelluna (north-eastern Italy) and specialised in classic/casual leather shoes with a breathing impermeable membrane into the sole to eliminate the uncomfortable sensation of dampness in wet and rainy conditions. Chapter 7 is devoted to the case analysis of Illycaffè, a company based in the Trieste coffee district (north-eastern Italy) and specialised in the production of high quality coffee. Since the early 1930s Illycaffè revolutionised the coffee industry with the invention of the first espresso machine and the development of the technique of vacuum packing to maintain the freshness of the coffee for a longer time. Chapter 8 presents the case study of Luxottica, a company specialised in the manufacture and distribution of eyewear and based in the district of Belluno (north-eastern Italy). Luxottica – listed at the New York Stock Exchange (NYSE) and the Italian stock market – is world leader in the manufacture and distribution of prescription frames and sunglasses in the premium and luxury market segments.

Finally, in Chapters 9 and 10 we discuss within-case and cross-case analyses results and we build theory on the basis of the chain of evidence resulting from such analyses. In particular, in Chapter 9 we report the first group of results of the cross-case analysis, along the set of areas of inquiry presented in Chapter 4. We report on the different types of opportunities identified and exploited in the four companies, the sources of them, the resources possessed by the firms that allowed the identification and exploitation of the entrepreneurial opportunities and the organisational mechanisms of knowledge acquisition and exploitation employed. The chapter concludes with a discussion of the consistencies identified among cases regarding the antecedents of firm growth. On the basis of that, in Chapter 10 we discuss the antecedents of district firms' growth, identified in the four case studies. Then, we proceed to elaborate a framework of entrepreneurial growth of firms within industrial districts. The concluding section of this chapter summarizes and discusses the main findings of the study and examines implications, limitations and future research paths.

PART ONE

Industrial Districts and Firm-level Entrepreneurship

2. Industrial districts and firms

F. G. Alberti

The purpose of this chapter is to offer the reader an overview of main contributions in the field from its inception to contemporary literature, and to show its multi-voiced nature. After a review of the main contributions on the concept of industrial district and its main features, we focus on the so-called Italianate variant of the model, which is at central stage in our work. Finally, we show the reader narrower units of analysis in industrial districts' studies, focusing on district firms, in order to proceed towards our main arguments in the conclusion of the book.

2.1. INTRODUCTION

Industrial districts represent a fundamental basis for the economy of Italy, but they are also relevant economic phenomena for other different countries, where they may assume somewhat different socio-economical configurations (Markusen, 1996). A number of regions have been appointed as industrial districts, mainly because of their agglomeration patterns, growth and competitiveness, together with certain similarities to the model of industrial district provided by Marshall, or its Italianate variant. The most well known US examples are the regions of Hollywood, Silicon Valley and Orange County (see Hall and Markusen, 1985; Saxenian, 1994; Zagnoli, 1991) even if several others have been identified and studied (for example, Porter, 1998). Likewise, in the UK, districts have been identified in several areas, such as Lace Market, Leicester or Scotland; in France, Grenoble, Montpellier, Sophia-Antipolis, Roanne and the Haut Beaujolais are only a few examples, since some French institutes, such as Datar and Insee, count more than 140 clusters in the whole country; in Sweden the municipality of Gnosjö together with its surroundings have been described as an industrial district (Wigren, 2003); in Germany, Baden-Württemberg is the most famous area comprising districts, but also Solingen, Pirmasens, Pforzeim, Krefeld and Gottingen (for example, Herrigel, 1993; 1996); some areas of Spain, such as Valencia, Castellón   (for example,   Benton,   1992;   Castillo,   1989),   Northern Portugal, Denmark (for example, Illeris, 1992; Kristensen, 1994) and others outside Europe, such as Japan (Friedman, 1988), India (Cawthorne, 1995), Brazil (Schmitz, 1995) and Mexico (Rabellotti, 1997; Rabellotti and Schmitz, 1999).

Despite all these cases worldwide, industrial districts have typically characterised Italy since the 1970s, becoming a peculiar trait of its economy and a relevant source of socio-economic development and growth. The phenomenon may not have aroused so much attention if it had not coincided with a period of good results for Italian exports, especially of the goods that were in fact produced in industrial districts (textiles, clothing, shoes, furniture, and so on).

According to ISTAT, Italy comprises 199 industrial districts, mainly in fashion, furniture and food industries, that is, those industries which are conventionally labelled as the 'made in Italy'. In particular, industrial districts located in northern and northern-eastern Italy are considered models of economic efficiency, innovative output, and high employment levels (Benko and Dunford, 1991; Pyke et al., 1990; Sengenberger et al., 1990).

The relevance of this model for the Italian economy and society has also engendered an intense research production on the topic, contributing most in what has been addressed as the Italianate variant of the Marshallian industrial district. As argued by Becattini (1991: 83):

> What promoted studies and research was the 'shocking' fact that, while in the same period the major Italian firms (although much more prepared to operate on worldwide markets) were losing ground with respect to their foreign competitors, a myriad of small firms managed to increase their share of the domestic and international markets, to gain profits, and to create new jobs, despite their well-known disadvantages in sales facilities, scale of production, access to credit, and experience of foreign markets. This fact contradicted deeply rooted beliefs of economists of almost all schools, who were convinced that the chances of smaller firms were inherently weak and declining in time.

2.2.   TYPES OF GEOGRAPHIC AGGLOMERATIONS OF FIRMS

Many terms have been used to describe geographic agglomerations of firms in an industry or related industries, in addition to industrial districts. Terms with somewhat different meanings are sometimes used interchangeably, creating confusion and a need for more precise definitions. Nevertheless, only industrial districts have been indicated in literature as capable of enhancing trust-based cooperation, coordination, knowledge transfer, as well as producing collective strategies among firms. In particular, amongst the various concepts proposed in literature, it is important to distinguish between:

- 'unspecialised local productive systems', characterised by the agglomeration in a limited geographical area of a population of firms belonging to various industries. In some cases these areas might be urban or metropolitan, with the concurrent flourishing of professional services supporting manufacturing activities (Solinas and Baroni, 2001; Bellandi and Sforzi, 2001);
- 'industrial clusters', which Porter (1990; 1998) defines as a set of industries related through buyer–supplier and supplier–buyer relationships, or by common technologies, common buyers or distribution channels, or common labour pools. A cluster's boundaries are defined by the linkages and complementarities across industries and institutions that are most important to competition. Although industrial clusters often fit within political boundaries, they may cross state or even national borders. A cluster's roots can often be traced to historical circumstances (prior existence of supplier industries; related industries; entire related clusters; one or two innovative companies stimulating the growth of many others);
- 'local/regional industrial systems', described by Saxenian (1994) partly overlap with the concept of industrial cluster. They are agglomeration of firms belonging to one industry or more industries correlated together and localised in a small geographical area (a region or a part of it);
- 'regional clusters', according to Enright (1992; 1993) are industrial clusters in which member firms are in close geographic proximity to each other. A more inclusive definition would be: regional clusters are geographic agglomerations of firms in the same or closely related industries. Regional clusters, as defined here, include industrial districts of small and medium-sized craft firms, concentrations of high technology firms related through the development and use of common technologies, and production systems that contain large hub firms and their local suppliers and spin-offs;
- 'business networks' consist of several firms that have ongoing communication and interaction, and might have a certain level of interdependence, but that need not operate in related industries or be geographically concentrated in space (Staber, 1996).
- 'hub-and-spoke district', that is a local hierarchical network of firms, which revolves around one or more large leading firms locally embedded in a limited geographical area (Becattini and Rullani, 1993: 32–33).

Markusen (1996: 302) defines as: 'dominated by one or several large, vertically integrated firms, in one or more sectors, surrounded by smaller and less powerful suppliers'. Further, according to Markusen (1996: 302): 'hub-and-spoke districts may exhibit either a strongly linked form', that is, cases where smaller firms depend upon the large anchor firm or institution for either markets or supplies, or 'a weaker, more nucleated form', this is the case where small firms benefit from the agglomerative externalities of the larger organisation's presence without necessarily being linked to them. In the hub-and-spoke model, vertical relations prevail on horizontal ones; firms belonging to the network are predominantly small-sized or artisan, with a limited strategic choice, thus configuring the network as a 'putting-out' system (Lazerson, 1993);

- 'industrial districts' (such as the Italian industrial districts described in Brusco 1990; Piore and Sabel 1984; Becattini 1987, 1989a; Goodman and Bamford 1990; and Pyke et al., 1990) are concentrations of firms involved in interdependent production processes, often in the same industry or industry segment, that are embedded in the local community and delimited by daily travel to work distances (Sforzi, 1990).

These different kinds of geographical agglomerations of firms partially overlap. The industrial district might be interpreted as the Porter's cluster, even if the latter is characterised by a wider geographical area which prevents it to activate those social mechanisms which characterise industrial districts. According to Saxenian (1994) industrial districts are a case of local industrial systems characterised by density and intensity of relations between firms and firms and institutions. Markusen (1996) distinguishes among five kinds of industrial districts: the Marshallian industrial district; the Italianate industrial district; the hub-and-spoke district; the satellite industrial platform; and the state-centred district. Enright (1996) argues that the distinction between regional clusters and industrial districts (which he defines as a subset of regional clusters) resides in the fact that the focal point of an industrial district is often a single industry or even a single industry segment, whilst regional clusters generally involve a range of related industries.

Reading the phenomenon in dynamic terms, local productive systems may change their nature, assuming different characteristics through time. For instance, literature reports cases of hierarchical putting-out systems, which evolved in industrial districts through spin-off processes and the progressive disappearance of the large leading firm.

In addition, there are distinct similarities in the explanations for the development and persistence of the differently named agglomerations in the literature, particularly in the reliance on externalities and localised information flows. This is not to say that we should ignore the differences between different types of local productive systems, but rather that we should explore in detail both their similarities and differences and, in particular, wonder why only industrial districts proven to have that social stickiness that allows trust-based governance mechanisms, tacit knowledge transfers and dense inter-firm and inter-personal networks.

2.3. THE CONCEPT OF INDUSTRIAL DISTRICT

2.3.1. The Roots in External Economies and Spatial Proximity

Most references to the origin of industrial districts go back to the economist Alfred Marshall. In *The Principles of Economics* (1950) the development and features of industrial districts, or as the author labelled the phenomenon 'the concentration of specialised industries in particular localities', is discussed.

The notion that businesses might enjoy advantages related to spatial juxtaposition has been the subject of research for over a century, beginning with Marshall (1950) and Weber (1929) and continued by modern regional scientists' attempts to measure the link between productivity, productivity growth and innovation. The concept of scale underlies all theoretical perspectives on external economies, Marshallian or otherwise. Inter-firm proximity may be viewed on a continuum from production entirely concentrated in one establishment at a single location (the large plant) to production widely dispersed across multiple establishments at one location (the agglomeration or the industrial district, in Marshallian terms). The conventional theory of the firm suggests that the concentration of production within a single establishment may, under certain circumstances, generate cost savings up to some level of output; the well-known concept of internal returns to scale. Marshall casts his examination of industrial districts in terms of understanding how groups of collocated firms might take advantage of the same types of economies available to large manufacturers; the externalisation of internal economies was critical to the Marshallian view of the role of geographic proximity in economic development.

2.3.2. Marshall's Conceptualization of Industrial Districts

In clarifying the meaning between internal and external economies of scale, Marshall (1950: 266) identified the latter as dependent on 'the general development of the industry'. He argued that the efficiencies available to the large plant are also available to smaller plants located in what he termed an industrial district. These industrial districts are characterised by deep labour pools, a great number of specialised intermediate input and service suppliers, and what might be called technological or knowledge spill-overs. Marshall (1950: 271) asserted that a localised industry gains 'a great advantage from the fact that it offers a constant market for skill'. As an industry grows in a place, so does the pool of trained, specialised workers from which firms can draw. Likewise, the localisation of industry permits the growth of specialised input suppliers, granting cost efficiencies through a finer social division of labour.

Thus, in his original formulation of the concept of industrial district, he envisioned a region with a business structure comprised of small locally-owned firms making investment and production decisions locally. Within the district, substantial trade was meant to be transacted between buyers and sellers, often entailing long-term contracts or commitments. Reading through the lines in the seminal work by Marshall (1950), linkages and co-operation with firms located outside the industrial district appeared to be minimal. What made the industrial district model so special, in Marshall's account, was the nature and quality of the local labour market: internal to the district and highly flexible.

In his last book, *Industry and Trade*, Marshall added some new qualifications to the concept of industrial district, but without a clear rigorous formalisation of the notion. Notably, he introduced the notion of 'industrial atmosphere', which together with the existence of 'mutual knowledge and trust', already mentioned in *The Principles of Economics*, 'facilitates the generation of skills required by the industry, and promotes innovations and innovation diffusion among small firms within industrial districts' (Marshall, 1950: 96).

Individuals moved from firm to firm, and owners as well as workers lived in the same community, where they benefited from the fact that 'the secret of industry' was in the air, that is, there was an 'industrial atmosphere'. Workers appeared to be committed to the district rather than to the firm, and moreover labour out-migration was assumed to be minimal. The district was seen as a relatively stable community, which enabled the evolution of strong local cultural identity and shared industrial expertise.

Hence, the industrial district was originally conceived as a socio-economic mixing, where social forces cooperate with economic. Friendship linkages among local population and neighbourhood relations were meant to favour the diffusion of knowledge (Marshall, 1950: 271):

> The mysteries of the trade become non mysteries; but they are as it were in the air, children learn many of them unconsciously. Good work is rightly appreciated; inventions and improvements in machinery, in processes and the general organization of the business have their merits promptly discussed: if one man starts

a new idea, it is taken up by others and combines with suggestions of their own; and thus it becomes the source of further new ideas.

All of these features depicted by Marshall in the model of industrial district are subsumable under the notion of agglomeration, which suggests that the stickiness of a place resides not in the individual calculus of firms or workers on localising choices, but in the external economies available to each firm from its spatial conjunction with other firms and suppliers of services.

Marshall warned also of the diseconomies of industrial concentration: higher costs of labour of one kind of work or in the expensive cost of land.

It is therefore not surprising, after this overview of the industrial district concept, as elaborated by Marshall (1950), that many disciplines, from economics to sociology and geography, have investigated the topic of industrial districts, both in general terms and specific ones.

2.3.3. Back to Marshall: Flexible Specialisation and the New Industrial District

The notion of industrial district was highlighted again in economics when recession hit the world in the 1970s and 1980s. Despite the rising unemployment and the general economic decline, some regions prospered. These regions were to be found in different parts of the world, engaged in a variety of industries, including advanced industries as well as more traditional labour-intensive ones.

The examination of the link between micro-level business relations and regional economic change is the primary focus of the literature on new industrial districts (NIDs), which builds on Marshall's (1950) original analysis but also introduces theories of cooperation and trust, transaction costs, innovation diffusion and adoption of flexible production equipment and applied business organisation and management. The literature on NIDs owes much to the pioneering work of Piore and Sabel (1984), who argued that major capitalist economies are experiencing a crisis with respect to finding the appropriate path of technological development.

Scholars advocating the notion of industrial district considered the decline of the Fordist production model as the initiator of a new industrial organisation. The Fordist model was characterised by vertically integrated production systems. Due to the industrial development and new needs of customers on industrial markets, a more flexible organisation was requested. Industrial districts were characterised by such flexible specialisation, organising the production chain, vertically integrated, between independent small and medium-sized firms.

2.3.4.   Towards the Affirmation of the Italianate Variant

Behind the term industrial district, many different forms of organisation of labour and many different socio-cultural fabrics have been veiled. In what may be regarded as a common definition, industrial districts are taken as forms of organisation governed by trust and co-operation. What is striking in the extensive literature on industrial districts is the variety of approaches and the different phenomena that are taken into account.

The relevance of the model of industrial district for the Italian economy and society has also engendered an intense research production on the topic, contributing most in what has been addressed as the Italianate variant of the Marshallian industrial district (Markusen, 1996).

According to this variant, while in Marshall's formulation of industrial districts, it was not meant that each local actor should be consciously co-operating with each other in order for the district to exist and operate as such, in the Italian formulation grown in the 1970s researchers – Becattini (1979) among the first ones – argued that concerted efforts to co-operate among district members and to build governance structures would have improved the stickiness of the district (Markusen, 1996).

Becattini (1979; 1987; 1990), moving from Marshall's early writings, argued that in order for an industrial district to grow, it was necessary that the local population of firms would merge with the people living in the same territory and holding the social and cultural features (social values and institutions) appropriate for a bottom-up industrialisation process.

The key to this rediscovery of the Marshallian industrial district model consisted in the idea of a sort of congruence between the requirements of a specific kind of organisation of the production process, and the social and cultural characteristics of some group of people, which slowly developed in time. In other words, not just any system either of values or of local institutions is suitable to provide the 'historical' background for an industrial district as well as not just any kind of production process is suitable to provide the technical conditions for that particular form of symbiosis between production activity and community life, that characterises the industrial district (Becattini, 1989a). In other terms, '[the] concept of industrial district contains something that escapes traditional economic analysis and calls for another kind of analysis' (2000: 26–28).

2.3.5.   What is an Industrial District? A Classic Definition

Becattini, a fine scholar of Marshall, has revitalised the notion of an industrial district in a prolific and influential work written in the late 1970s (Becattini, 1979). In an influential and collective book published in 1990

(Pyke, Becattini and Sengenberger, 1990), Becattini and, to some extent, his collaborators, together with a small group of scholars, offer a systematisation of the concept of industrial districts with a comprehensive description of its distinctive features. Among the contributors are Becattini himself (1979, 1987, 1989a, 1990, 1997) and other scholars of his Florentine group, Piore and Sabel (1984), Piore (1990) and, to a lesser extent, Best (1990), Saxenian (1994) and Scott (1998a, 1998b).

Becattini (1990) provided a conceptualisation of the industrial district, defining it as: '... a socio-territorial entity which is characterised by the active presence of both a community of people and a population of firms in one naturally and historically bounded area'.

In the district, community and firms tend to merge. The fact that the dominant activity is an industrial one differentiates the industrial district from a generic economic region.

Several Italian scholars and colleagues of Becattini (Bellandi, 1989; 1992; Brusco, 1991; Trigilia, 1986; 1990) have adopted that definition, with each emphasising a different aspect of it. Dei Ottati (1996) has studied in-depth cooperative relations which – according to her studies – are responsible for decreases in transaction costs as well as a fundamental component of the balance between cooperation and competition which govern industrial districts. Brusco (1991) has put emphasis on the prevalence of the vertical division of labour among firms on the horizontal one, and argues that such division of labour is responsible for collaborative behaviours whilst the horizontal division of labour is responsible for competitive behaviours. In addition, Brusco (1991) emphasised the importance of tacit rules of the game in industrial districts and the sanctioning mechanisms that arise within them. Sforzi (1989) made a decisive contribution in translating the complexity and elusiveness of the concept of industrial district into parameters to qualify and measure industrial districts. In particular, Sforzi (1987; 1990) and Garofoli (1991a; 1991b) have vastly contributed in the identification of industrial districts in geographical terms.

2.3.6. The Currently Accepted Conceptualisation of Industrial Districts

As anticipated previously, the concept of industrial districts, referred to as classic, is the Italianate one, proposed by Becattini (1987, 1989b, 1990) and complemented by his scholars (Bellandi 1982, 1989; Dei Ottati 1986; Sforzi 1989, 1991). The sociologists Trigilia (1986) and Brusco (1982, 1989) can be included in the classic school as well.

Table 2.1 Marshallian and Italianate industrial district models

Marshallian Industrial District
- Business structure dominated by small, locally owned firms
- Scale economies relatively low
- Substantial intra-district trade among buyers and suppliers
- Key investment decisions made locally
- Long-term contracts and commitments between local buyers and suppliers
- Low degrees of co-operation or linkage with firms external to the district
- Labour market internal to the district, highly flexible
- Workers committed to district, rather than to firms
- High rates of labour in-migration, lower levels of out-migration
- Evolution of unique local cultural identity, bonds
- Specialized sources of finance, technical expertise, business services available in district outside of firms
- Existence of 'patient capital' within district
- Turmoil, but good long-term prospects for growth and employment

Italianate variant (in addition to the above)
- High incidence of exchanges of personnel between customers and suppliers
- High degree of co-operation among competitor firms to share risk, stabilise market, share innovation
- Disproportionate shares of workers engaged in design, innovation
- Strong trade associations that provide shared infrastructure, management training, marketing, technical or financial help
- Strong local government role in regulating and promoting core industries

Source: personal elaboration on Markusen (1996)

Analyzing the definition given by Becattini (1990) some stylised features of the industrial district model emerge. These aspects are also summarised in Table 2.1, where peculiarities of the Italianate variant of the industrial district model are separated from the original ones in the Marshallian formulation.

- 'The local community of people'. The 'community of people', as described by Becattini, is characterised by a relatively homogeneous system of values and views. 'The most important trait of the local community is its relatively homogeneous system of values and views, which is an expression of an ethic of work and activity, of the family, of reciprocity, and of change' (Becattini, 1990: 39). The beliefs system at the district level constitutes a fundamental requirement for the construction and development of a district as well as an essential condition for its reproduction. Such system of beliefs may engender through time a process of institutionalisation, capable of producing norms, rules and values, which are transmitted throughout the district and through generations. Such institutions may include the market, the firm, the family, the church, the school, local trade unions and other public and private, economic and political, cultural, religious bodies (as institutionalised arenas for social interaction, Wigren, 2003), as well as rules of conduct within firms and among them, business recipes and institutionalised strategic behaviours. All these may appear simply as the description of a closed community, while industrial districts have proven in many cases to be regions where such historical development has been functional to a consequent economic success. Undoubtedly, the cultural factors underpinning the phenomenon of the industrial district were already present in Marshall, but Becattini makes explicit the nature of the industrial district as an 'economic and social whole' and reintroduces the necessity for a multidisciplinary approach grouping together sociological, historical and economic contributions. To the extent that a population is geographically and historically bounded, face-to-face relationships are frequent and people tend to interact continually developing a shared culture and implicit rules of common behaviour. Nevertheless, according to Becattini (1990), the local system of beliefs and its change through time is still largely unexplored. In the 'canonical' literature, other attempts to qualify the combinations of values and general cultural traits compatible with the existence of the industrial district have been made. In particular, a climate of trust, solidarity and cooperation as a governance mechanism in inter-firm relations, have been emphasised by Italian and international scholars.

- 'The population of firms'. First of all, Becattini (1990) stressed the fact that an industrial district is not an accidental multiplicity of firms. 'Each of the many firms which constitute the local population tends to specialize in just one phase, or a few phases, of the production process typical of the district'. Thus, this localisation is 'other than an accidental concentration in one place of production processes, which have been attracted there by pre-existing localising factors. Rather the firms become rooted in the territory, and this result cannot be conceptualized independently of its historical development' (Becattini, 1990: 40). The firms of a district (Ferrucci and Varaldo, 1993) commonly operate in the same industry, including in same cases also what Marshall indicated as 'auxiliary' industries, thus related machinery industries and various business services. Moreover, Becattini (1990: 41) clearly states that only those industries whose production processes are spatially and temporally separable are suited for the industrial district model, since they 'allow for the formation of a local network of specialised transactions on phase products'. According to Becattini (1990), firms must be numerous; however their number is not clearly stated, even if certainly greater than that observed by Marshall. In order for such an extended specialisation to take place among a myriad of firms, the decomposability of the production process must be a prerequisite or, as Brusco makes explicit, sectors must be characterised by limited economies of vertical integration.

-   'Human resources'. 'There is an inner tendency of the district to constantly reallocate its human resources' (Becattini, 1990: 42), to sustain productivity and competitiveness. The specialisation of each worker, which is sometimes firm-specific and sometimes district-specific, loses its value only to a very limited extent, from the point of view of the district, when workers move from one firm to another. His/her specialisation becomes a sort of public good which Marshall (1950) labelled 'industrial atmosphere', indicating with this term both the set of local skills and competencies and the process of their transmission through spontaneous exchanges, the mobility of workers and the reorganization of notions and opinions by personal relationships. Each of these mechanisms also constitutes a factor of attraction to, and retention in, the industrial district of the most capable workers, whose skills and experiences are both acknowledged and strengthened within the district.

-   'The market'. 'The origin and the development of an industrial district is ... not simply the "local" result of a matching of some socio-cultural traits of a community (a system of values, attitudes, and institutions), of historical and natural characteristics of a geographical area and of technical characteristics of the production process...' (Becattini, 1990: 44), but – as Becattini suggests – an industrial district is 'also the result of a process of dynamic interaction between division-integration of labour in the district, a broadening of the market for its products, and the formation of a permanent linking network between the districts and the external markets'. Such a permanent link with external markets has been explored in industrial districts both for markets of finished goods as well as for markets of raw materials. The link with the former is usually guaranteed by the presence of either leading firms, who have developed through time not only a commercial brand (Ugolini, 1995), but also the internal competencies needed to interpret customer needs and arrange the production networks within the district, or intermediaries, such as the case of the 'converters' operating in the silk industry of Como, which play only a commercial role in the local filière (Alberti, Tomasetto and Sinatra, 2001). Since the district is also a big purchaser of raw materials, the link with the latter is often guaranteed by the presence of a number of specialised buyers.

-   'Competition and co-operation'. An important feature of industrial districts which has been particularly discussed is the balance between co-operation and competition (Staber, 1998; Dei Ottati, 1994). The main form of co-operation is the interaction concerning commissioning and subcontracting firms, thus, referring to inter-firm relations with organisations symbiotic to the focal one (suppliers, distributors and clients). Additionally, there are other forms of co-operation within the district. In particular, there is co-operation of a type that seeks economies of scale in some activities, such as selling, marketing and internationalising. Competition occurs among equal firms, that is, firms working on the same product or the same activity. Competitors in dense networks, such as industrial districts, are typically not linked to each other by exchange relations, rather, they occupy structurally equivalent positions, that is, they are linked vertically by similar exchange relations with comparable symbiotic organisations. Thus, in addition to a considerable degree of vertical co-operation, in industrial districts there is a great deal of horizontal competition. Finally, competitors operating within the same district are likely to forge certain inter-firm and social ties with each other, both through common arenas (for example, trade associations and co-coordinating councils) as well as direct relationships (joint projects, consortia and co-production), determining, thus, a form of horizontal co-operation. Cooperation and an extended division of labour distinguish canonical industrial districts from mere agglomerations of firms.
-   'An adaptive system'. 'The systematic and pervasive contrast of interests between all the agents in the district adapts itself quickly and accurately to the ever-changing shape of the production organisation, and operates a kind of automatic efficiency control of each single phase' (Becattini, 1990: 46).
-   'Technological changes'. Industrial districts are also characterised by the way technological progress is introduced. 'In a world of agents whose main capital is "human", technical change greatly impairs the value of that capital. Hence there is strong resistance to its introduction'. (Becattini, 1990: 46). In the district, the introduction of technological progress and major innovations is a social process, which gradually passes through a path of self-awareness by the local community. This occurs mainly because the introduction of technological progress is perceived neither as a decision to be suffered, nor as an external obligation, but rather as an occasion to defend an already acquired position.

- 'A local credit system'. One of the most diffused disadvantages of small firms as compared to large ones is the difficulty in accessing the credit system. This seems to be even more relevant for small district firms that, typically family owned and run, show a tendency towards growing only in relation to the equity of the family and the credit system, instead of looking for external investors. Given such relevance of credit for continuous development, industrial districts have promoted the flourishing of local banks, which could give greater importance to the personal qualities of whoever demands credit (Novello, 2000) rather than a bank not rooted in the local context.

- 'Sources of dynamism'. 'The dynamic and self-reproducing nature of the district consists of a continuous comparison between the cost of performing any given operation inside the firm and the cost of having it done outside' (Becattini, 1990: 48). This comparison is made building on a view of costs which is biased by the local culture. Historical and cultural factors as well as institutionalised beliefs are the bases for distinguishing what has to be considered or not a cost. Therefore, in industrial districts the decisions to put out or keep in a given phase of a production process are not purely economic, and this favours a continuous dynamism in their morphology. Whilst on one side the putting-out may favour the spin-off and development of new firms, outsourcing decisions may engender the creation not only of a tied subcontractor, but of a specialised firm inclined towards addressing a wider market and, thus, able to span the district boundaries or even disintegrate them (Becattini, 1990; Lazerson, 1993).

- 'The role of institutions'. In Becattini's view, social institutions (markets, firms, extended families, technical schools, churches, political parties, trade unions, employers' associations, and so on) arise spontaneously and reflect legitimate and reproduce dominant values (Becattini, 1989a). The relevant institutions in industrial districts are often depicted as 'intermediate' (Arrighetti and Seravalli, 1999) and include local employers' associations, trade unions, local councils, education structures, consortia and stable rules, which locally supply public goods for specific economic categories in order to relieve them of some costs. None of the studies reviewed in this analysis of the literature on industrial districts take institutions to be an unnecessary component of canonical industrial districts.

- 'Consciousness, class and locality'. 'Urged by ever-changing endogenous relationships (the relationships between local culture, society and economy), and exogenous ones (effects on the district of external markets, society and culture), the organisation of production and the social structure fluctuate continuously' (Becattini, 1990: 49). Such fluctuation occurs around a 'centre of gravity', that is supposed to bring a 'sense of belonging' to the local community. Despite the centrality of this element amongst the forging characteristics of an industrial district, it has been largely overlooked (Alberti et al., 2001) and only recently recovered through the conceptualizations of 'district identity and identification' (Sammarra and Biggiero, 2001a; 2001b) and the work by Cillo and Troilo (2002).

In addition to these features, Markusen (1996) underlined that the Italianate variant of the Marshallian industrial district model is mainly characterised by the fact that firms (often with the help of regional governments and trade associations) consciously network with each other to solve problems of cycles and over-capacity and to respond to new demands for flexibility.

Unlike the passivity of Marshallian firms, Italianate districts exhibit frequent and intensive exchanges of personnel between customers and suppliers and co-operation among competitors to share risk, stabilise markets and share innovation. Activist trade associations provide shared infrastructures as well as arenas to formulate collective strategies.

2.4.   INDUSTRIAL DISTRICTS RESEARCH: A MULTI-VOICED FIELD

Since the 1980s a growing number of scholars has dealt with the topic of industrial districts, observing them through the lenses of different theoretical frameworks (in particular, industrial organization, sociology, economic geography, economic history, political economy and economics of innovation), thus, contributing in making the field a multi-voiced one.

Economic geography, through the works of authors like Sforzi (1989), Storper and Scott (1989), Tinacci Mossello (1990), Vagaggini (1990), and Markusen (1996) have studied the spatial dimension of the district phenomenon, the 'Third Italy' as a geographical agglomeration of industries, the dynamics of firms' localisation as well as the diffusion and heterogeneity of district models amongst different countries. This discipline, in particular, helped to clarify how external economies and economies of agglomeration appear as the two basic pillars of the concept of an industrial district. Among this group of authors, the emphasis goes on the role of agglomeration or proximity of firms, for those scholars concerned with economic studies, and people, in urban studies, as the core factor able to produce positive effects in the district.

Geographers and theorists of technological innovation have emphasised how the proximity of firms fosters spill-overs of knowledge, and this explains the fast growth of a localised industry (that is, qualifying industrial districts as innovation systems).

Likewise, most of the Italian literature, pioneered by Becattini (1990), and supported by a number of contributions (for example, Piore and Sabel, 1984), claims that the mere agglomeration of firms is not enough to denote an industrial district, since other conditions referring to the attitudes and values of local population (such as, common values and culture) are also important to determine positive performance. Brusco (1982) requires an extended division of labour to recognise an industrial district. Piore and Sabel qualify industrial districts as 'flexible systems of production', putting emphasis on intra-firm and inter-firm relationships.

Industrial organisations' scholars have been concerned with the conditions for flexibility of companies; the structure and performance of industrial district; the competitiveness of the industrial district; local industrial policies. References go, in this case, to the seminal works of Vaccà (1986), Becattini (1979; 1987; 1989b; 1990) and Brusco (1989).

In Becattini's view, a main feature of an industrial district is cooperation. Dei Ottati (1987) – a colleague of Becattini – supports this view through her studies: cooperation economises on transaction costs and fosters flexibility and innovation, becoming the prevailing governance mechanism within industrial districts' networks. Additionally, industrial districts have been characterised by a particular balance between cooperation and competition (Staber, 1998; Dei Ottati, 1994) among firms.

Sociology scholars focus on the industrial district as a cultural-political entity, on the concept of industrial atmosphere, on family issues in local economies and on entrepreneurial values. Along this line, examples come from the contributions by Bagnasco (1977, 1988), Innocenti (1985), Provasi (1995), Parri (1993) and Viteritti (2000).

Sustainable development, regional issues, production factors, distribution of income and conditions for the birth of industrial districts are all topics investigated by political economists including Fuà and Zacchia (1983), Nuti (1992), Bramanti and Senn (1991), Ciciotti (1993), Garofoli (1991a, 1992), and Antonelli et al. (1988).

Economic history has fostered longitudinal studies of industrial districts, focusing on the dynamics of board members within district companies or the historical roots of local specialisation. Along this perspective, contributions come from Castronovo (1980), Sapelli (1989), Sapelli and Carnevali (1994), and Amatori and Colli (2001). Historians have highlighted the historical prerequisites of industrial districts. The contributions of Paci (1982) and others suggest that north-eastern Italian industrial districts arose from an artisan background where a widespread system of land tenure helped to train entrepreneurial skills.

Over the past twenty years, social scientists, both in Italy and abroad, have, thus, rediscovered industrial districts. Yet, despite their popularity, the contribution of organisation theory and strategic management in particular, is still less significant compared to the one of the other disciplines, which has vastly studied the field of industrial districts.

The entrenchment of resources in the district has legitimated organisational approaches based on 'cybernetic' concepts or on a competence-based theory of the firm. Some authors have recently looked at industrial districts' evolutionary paths, conceiving them as 'self-organised' systems; that is, as complex social and economic systems resulting from recursive interactions between their components and autonomy with regard to their environment (Biggiero, 1999; Corò and Rullani, 1998; Dematteis, 1994). Other organisation theorists have suggested applying to industrial districts the analytical tools of the competence theory of the firm (Lawson, 1998; Maskell, 2001; Maskell and Malberg, 1999). Other recent approaches apply ecological theory (Hannan and Freeman, 1989) to industrial districts (Lazzeretti and Storai, 2002; Staber, 1997, 1998) or the knowledge-based perspective (Nonaka, 1994), emphasising industrial districts as learning systems (Becattini and Rullani, 1993; Belussi and Pilotti, 2000; Pilotti, 1997).

2.5. INDUSTRIAL DISTRICT FIRMS

2.5.1. A Research Shift towards District Firms

During the 1980s a gap emerged between the theory on industrial districts and the reality of facts. It was mainly interpretable as a perspective gap, since, while the literature on industrial districts was still oriented towards giving an idyllic picture of them, industrial districts were facing limits and obstacles to their model. In that period, several industrial districts faced a strong decrease in their production and export that was not driven by pure market or industry crises. These phenomena proved, in fact, to have their roots in deeper limits of the district model: a certain delay in introducing new technologies; the inability to compete on research and development, marketing and logistics apart from manufacturing, the high fragmentation of the business system; the difficulty to control inputs critical for quality.

Exceptions to the approach of depicting industrial districts as industrial heavens have come both from economic historians and management scholars in recent times. In Carlo Poni's (1998) historical research on Bologna's silk industry – which prospered between the sixteenth and the seventeenth centuries only to virtually disappear by the end of the eighteenth century – all the disparate community interests from entrepreneurs, to workers, to the clergy, and the peasants joined together to preserve the city's silk-making monopoly. But in this case loyalty to community rules eventually foreclosed alternative choices or weak ties (Granovetter, 1973) external to the community that would have allowed Bologna either to compete with silk producers from other cities or develop new industries. The collapse of the silk industry left Bologna de-industrialised for almost one hundred years. Again, Grabher's (1993) account of the precipitous decline of the German Ruhr focused on the excessively closed nature of its business and social relationships, based exclusively on inner strong ties (Granovetter, 1973). Glasmeier (1994), too, attributed part of the blame for the Swiss watch industry's crisis to the limited information flows in the small towns of the Jura Mountains, which suffocated advances in technology and marketing. Dei Ottati (1996) reported that by the mid-1980s demand for carded wool, the main economic activity in the industrial districts of Prato, had declined precipitously. Fashion changes, climatic conditions and new competition from developing countries required ever lighter and more sophisticated textiles, but Prato's textile manufacturers lacked both the necessary skills and machinery. A few other papers, such as the one by Lazerson and Lorenzoni (1999), have presented a more realistic view of Italian industrial districts, even if the prevailing view was largely depicting them still as 'consensual islands of market harmony' (Lazerson and Lorenzoni, 1999: 259).

The classic approach to the study of industrial districts (Becattini, 1990) has undoubtedly put too much emphasis on industrial districts as a unit of analysis, leaving a more detailed analysis apart.

The result is that there has been a poor analysis of firms and inter-firm relationships, which are necessary to explain the division of labour across firms and the methods of organisational control and governance. In fact the contribution of firms to the development of industrial districts has too often been neglected in most of the existing literature.

According to Lazerson and Lorenzoni (1999), Piore and Sabel's (1984) popularisation of industrial district firms as organisationally homogenous and identical with similar functions and tasks has inaccurately represented the organisational structure of industrial districts. This has also discouraged any serious investigation into the nature of inter-firms relations. On the contrary, industrial district firms are increasingly heterogeneous and differentiated and merit attention on their own. Empirical evidence shows that there are no ideal-type organisations that have remained immutable since the Marshallian times. Thus, Lazerson and Lorenzoni (1999) condemn the widespread view conceiving industrial districts as an undifferentiated community of small firms.

The same argument is proposed by Rabellotti and Schmitz (1999) in their exploration of internal heterogeneity of industrial districts in Italy, Brazil and Mexico, where they apply both factor and cluster analysis to show that district firms vary a great deal in the strategies they employ and the growth they achieve. Even Sabel's more recent writings have recognised the complex and structured nature of subcontracting relationships. In a recent paper, Sabel (2001: 6) says:

> I was a partisan of something akin to the 'traditional' view of the districts when it seemed to many outlandish. I'm reasonably sure that the concept of flexible specialization that Michael Piore and I coined to capture the innovative responsiveness of district apparently bound by craft tradition is ambiguous enough to paper over the differences explored here.

This heterogeneity among different groups of firms has usually been disregarded in most of the literature on industrial districts, traditionally described as populated by a crowd of small, very similar firms. It is only the distant observer that assumes homogeneity and unity that rarely exists. Industrial district literature does not prepare us for this heterogeneity. Rabellotti and Schmitz (1999: 105) state:

> To be more precise what it prepares us for is the deepening division of labour between firms and, as a result, the differentiation of enterprises by process or product. It is however peculiarly quiet on the differentiation by size or by performance. There seems to be an inherent contradiction in the industrial district model. Small firm industrial districts, which are successful, are unlikely to remain populated by small firms only. Reinvested profits lead to expansion and increasing differentiation by size and performance.

The study of Rabellotti and Schmitz (1999) confirms considerable differences in performance and size among district firms and also stresses an existence of a diverse level of local embeddedness by firms.

Belussi and Pilotti (2002) have stressed that a process of diversification has emerged amongst district firms, in relation to: different models of knowledge production and utilization, different capacity of technological development, and different governance forms.

These organisational aspects have received little attention in most of the literature that has privileged discussion about local industrial policy and the role of private and public institutions in sustaining economic growth (Pyke and Sengenberger, 1992).

The approach of Piore and Sabel (1984) and Brusco (1982) can be summarised as follows: a) all the firms in the district are homogeneous; b) they interact uniformly with one another; c) institutions (associations, unions, local government, and so on) might matter more than individual firms in term of knowledge generation in industrial agglomerations.

Table 2.2 Main approaches to the study of industrial districts

Classic approach	Emergent approach
Similarities	
Industrial district as a population of firms located in an area Prevalence of small firms Networks based on personal relations and trust Agglomeration based on public knowledge Specialised work-force Centrality of the socio-historical background Creativity and innovation as strategic behaviours	
Differences	
• Unit of analysis: district • Small firms and large firms together is a problem to be avoided or regulated • Emphasis on economies of agglomeration and external economies at large • Governance mechanisms: only trust • Slow changes in the rules of the game • Glue: external economies • Fear for large firms	• Unit of analysis: firms and networks • Small firms and large firms together is beneficial in several districts • Emphasis on relational capabilities of firms, their relational influence and the governance of their network structure • Governance mechanisms: market, hierarchy, network (and so trust, too) • Continuous evolution of structures • Glue: social capital • Large firms operate as leaders

Source: personal elaboration on Lipparini (1995)

In summary, the traditional industrial district literature has paid little attention to the fact that district firms might differ. On the contrary, recent empirical evidence shows that many Italian industrial districts have been significantly shaped by individual entrepreneurial strategies (Lazerson and Lorenzoni, 1999; Viesti, 2000).

Table 2.2 shows the similarities and the differences between the classic approach to the study of industrial districts and the one suggested by scholars focusing on firms' heterogeneity and the variety of inter-firm relationships.

In this book, we adopt this second perspective on industrial districts, which leads to a very different view of the structure and nature of inter-firm relationships within geographical clusters. Without denying the role that institutions may play in the creation and development of industrial districts, we claim that: a) firms in the network are heterogeneous and not interchangeable in term of roles and tasks; and b) industrial districts are as much a product of the entrepreneurial agency of firms.

2.5.2. The Heterogeneity of District Firms

District scholars have increasingly addressed the kind of firm operating within industrial districts as a unit of analysis.

District firms belong to a production system that is characterised by a complex network of interactions. If all firms in the real world exhibit some linkages with their territory, district firms are 'entrapped' by high levels of territorial embeddedness. These peculiarities prevent to easy place these firms within the various traditional economic categories.

A first definition of district firms is given by Ferrucci and Varaldo (1993: 90). According to them, 'district companies are strictly embedded in the local socio-economic context with intense business relationships with the other local firms, small and medium-sized, typically lead by entrepreneurs with strong and influencing socio-cultural values and strongly affected by the industrial district as whole, from their start-up to their decline'.

Lipparini (1995), amongst the first ones, made the shift to firms as units of analysis explicit. In particular, Lipparini pointed out the role played by single firms in fostering industrial districts' growth and competitiveness. Bursi, Marchi and Nardin (1997) traced a research agenda for investigating industrial districts' firms, moving from the seminal works by Ferrucci and Varaldo (1993) and Visconti (1996).

Building on the considerations made above, the literature (Lipparini, 1995; Visconti, 1996; Lazerson and Lorenzoni, 1999) proposes a variety of district firms.

Flexible specialisation and the division of labour have mainly contributed to the creation and development of a plenty of micro and small companies, which act as capacity sub-contractors (Lorenzoni and Ornati, 1988) within an industrial district. These kinds of firm, especially when they provide mainly workforce to other companies, are anchored to a specific phase of the production process and therefore have not developed a broad view of the business system and of the competitive landscape. This type of firm shows very strong ties with some focal firms and in most of the cases this relation constitute a huge limit to its development. That is mainly the reason why these firms are labelled by scholars as 'stuck firms' (Visconti, 1996: 106), because their strategic freedom is very low.

A large number of small and medium-sized firms evolve from suppliers of simple parts, made to the specifications of the focal firms, into highly specialised manufacturers of components, groups of components and operations. These are firms that have developed specific competencies in the manufacturing area, where they base their competitive advantage. Their peculiarities are mainly based on technical capabilities and specialisation in one particular phase of the value system. The specialised firm often represents the only one in an entire local area, and sometimes also internationally, who is expert in producing a particular component or making a specific activity. Empirical evidence has shown that most industrial districts developed due to the presence of one or more specialised firms, holding strong core competencies that were spread to others. Some authors (Visconti, 1996) have depicted them as the heart of industrial districts. These firms are in a privileged position that permits them to develop relationships both within the district and outside it, offering a specialty subcontracting (Lorenzoni and Ornati, 1988). They typically develop strong ties with the leading firms of the district, with whom they have intense exchanges of know-how and intellectual capital.

The network structure of a district can evolve towards a situation in which one company can become the leader of a network (Lipparini, 1995; Visconti, 1996; Visconti, 2001; Ferrucci and Varaldo, 1993), where it outsources part of its activities previously kept internally. This process can originate both from the ability, resources, vision, contingency of a company towards the rest of the system or the district itself can elect one company to be its leader. Some literature has addressed this kind of leader as the 'locomotive' of the local business system (Lorenzoni and Ornati, 1988; Lorenzoni and Baden-Fuller, 1995). Leading firms may gradually shift their procurement strategy towards a greater dependence on the external network of suppliers and subcontractors. They concentrate on design and final assembly, outsourcing most operations and the production of parts and components. The presence of a leader produces a hierarchisation of the district where the asymmetry in relational influence is the main feature. In some cases such hierarchy originates partly from acquisitions and joint ventures and not only from a crystallisation of relationships.

Mimicking the path traced by leading firms (Boari, 2001) may bring some to become wagon firms (Visconti, 1996). As a matter of fact, there are cases of successful small firms that have been able to grow by imitating the leading firms. These firms operate in niches of the market that are generated by the industry structure or are abandoned by larger competitors. Wagon firms show a substantial weakness in innovation capabilities and design competencies, therefore their main strategy is to imitate other firms. Wagon firms are autonomous enough to move within the industry and the district, but only following the paths traced by the business system and their competitors. They are wagons moved by some locomotives that they assumed to be reference guides for the whole production activity. The problem with these types of firms, intensively concentrated in a few districts, is that their position within the district is hardly sustainable. They do not build their relationships on trust, since their behaviour discourages other firms to trust them. Only in districts where the network structure is dense enough to accept, use and drive these firms, their position can be sustained; otherwise they are induced to redirect their role or fail.

Some districts have encouraged the creation of firms that are not production oriented, but who have a consulting and service role, especially referring to machinery and production plants. These are called system integrators (Lipparini, 1995, 1997). The design of the production plant and the organisation of the business system as a whole is such a critical aspect of some industrial districts that technical experience plays a crucial role and requires a figure like the system integrator. The strength of this actor is based on the richness, variety and heterogeneity of the network where it developed. Its relational ability is at the base of its competitive advantage and assures it to be able to lower down costs and inefficiencies. Through its network it can exchange specific technical and managerial know-how.

Large firms (Lipparini, 1995; Lazerson and Lorenzoni, 1999; Ressico, 1999; Lipparini and Lomi, 1999) are a specific kind of leading firms. In most of the cases these are not firms originally born in the industrial district (since district firms, in general, do not show the tendency to grow internally) but they are multinational companies coming from outside the district. For some authors (Amin and Robins, 1991) this process that sums the hierarchisation of the district network with the presence of a large (multinational) company constitutes a threat for the district itself. On the contrary, empirical evidence (Lazerson and Lorenzoni, 1999) shows that the presence of multinational firms within industrial districts has a positive influence in pollinating local firms with fresh knowledge (Biggiero, 2002).

Schmitz (1995: 23) shows that it has been the large Brazilian shoe factories that have taken the greatest strides towards industrial districts: '[F]ordist expansion contributed significantly to the growth of the local supply industry'. In the Agra shoe-making district of India, Knorringa (1995) reached similar conclusions, pointing out how larger firms, often multinationals, imported new technology into the district and opened distribution channels for some of the local producers.

2.5.3.   Firms' Growth in Industrial Districts

Heterogeneity and in particular the emergence of leading firms seem to be a persistent feature of industrial districts.

In particular, the appearance of leading firms seems to have strongly affected districts' internal organisational structure; that is the way they compete, cooperate and access to inputs and external markets.

The traditional view on industrial districts tended to overlook the growing role of leading firms, now strongly expressed by the literature on Italian industrial districts (Visconti, 1996; 2002; Lipparini and Lomi, 1999; Lazerson and Lorenzoni, 1999; Boari and Lipparini, 1999; Minoja, 2002). Leading firms are not only bigger firms compared to small ones that traditionally populated the district landscape. They are firms able to promote competitive strategies based on a mix of commercial innovative proposals, investments in R&D or design-based innovation processes, and management of networks formed by specialised suppliers.

Leading firms in many cases have fostered internal cooperation and spurred the birth of subcontractors. More generally, leading firms have been depicted as actors that open gates to external markets and create channels to access external knowledge. These firms control the supply chain through their market power and orchestrate production phases and flows of resources in the district as well as in global markets. A leading firm displays relationships with other organisations and institutions outside the cluster and internationally. These ties are strategically pursued and used by leading firms to create business opportunities, to escape from inertia, and to foster change. Weak ties (that is, ties with firms outside the district) are as critical as strong ties (that is, ties with firms inside the cluster) to create and sustain its competitive advantage (Boari, 2001). As Malipiero et al. (2005) explain, leading firms have well-established contacts crossing the border of their own district. These loose attachments to distant networks help pollinate district firms with new ideas and concepts that are continually refined and sharpened because of the ubiquity of redundancy, proximity and transactional intensity.

Hence, those firms are dynamic players within the local systems, able to potentially couple local and global networks of innovation. Cases on leading firms have demonstrated that these actors may play a primary role in fostering entrepreneurship in the whole industrial district, facilitating the introduction of new technologies and the sharing of codified knowledge, sustaining the demand for workforce in sub-contracting companies, as well as modifying the organisational morphology of the industrial district, acting as boundary spanners. Leading firms can either be the core of renovation strategies at the local level or the driver for a negative transformation of the district through their growing investments abroad.

The role of leading firms is crucial in detecting emerging challenges to district survival promptly and pioneering new ways of tackling these threats, turning them into new opportunities for growth. The importance of imitative behaviours in district evolution explains why leading firms set out the path that other local players tend to follow. Leading firms show their positive roles as change agents even when a crisis destabilises the industrial district. These players act as strategic centres (Lorenzoni and Baden-Fuller, 1995), and lend momentum to processes of change towards higher levels of efficiency and competitiveness. The existence of firms with superior coordination skills and the ability to steer change in a given direction is a crucial factor for the survival – or at any rate the effectiveness – of a district formula based on extensive fragmentation of the production fabric.

Empirical studies highlighted that the presence of leading firms within industrial districts – and in more general terms within local economic systems – play a crucial role also for the transmission of technology and knowledge (Agrawal and Cockburn, 2002; Boari and Lipparini, 1999; Lazerson and Lorenzoni, 1999; Saxenian, 1991). They act as focal firms in the local innovation network, generating new knowledge and technologies, spinning out innovative companies, attracting researchers, investments and research facilities, enhancing other firms R&D activities, stimulating demand for new knowledge and creating and capturing externalities.

Recently the literature has focused on the role of leading firms as gatekeepers of knowledge, who search for and absorb non-local knowledge, and transmit it into the district (Morrison, 2004; Owen-Smith and Powell, 2004; Boschma and Ter Wal, 2007).

Hence, Italian industrial districts' dynamism is strongly indebted to a limited number of companies that were able to identify markets and products and to orchestrate and manage a large and differentiated set of relationships with firms and institutions within and outside districts.

The literature on industrial districts (Lazerson and Lorenzoni, 1999; Boari and Lipparini, 1999; Visconti, 1996; Morrison, 2004; Malipiero et al., 2005) has increasingly reported evidence of the growth of leading firms in industrial districts. Cases like Benetton, Brembo, Natuzzi, Prada, Filodoro, Zegna, Ducati and so on are just a few world-known Italian district firms who experienced growth.

District firms may grow either through local mergers or acquisitions and direct investments or takeovers by foreign corporations (Dei Ottati, 1996; Boari and Lipparini, 1999; Whitford, 2001; Cainelli et al., 2006) or organically. This last case contrasts with the general assumption that being embedded in an industrial district restrains the possibility for firm growth (Visconti, 1996).

Although leading firms usually start as very small firms, they are usually fast-growing firms that reach sizes larger than the other firms in their cluster.

These firms are locally embedded in that they have grown from small local firms to larger-sized firms by drawing on and contributing to the district. As a matter of fact, a question that arises from observing these cases is whether larger firms contribute to and draw on the district's collective resources as much as small or medium sized firms. The indications are mixed (Rabellotti and Schmitz, 1999).

Thus, growth of SMEs occurs in industrial districts (Boari, 2001), contrasting with the industrial district firm cliché of being small, locally embedded and homogeneous (Piore and Sabel, 1984). However, little is known on the phenomenon of district firms' growth, which is explored in the conclusion of the book.

3. The concept of firm-level entrepreneurship

F. Visconti and S. Sciascia

This chapter introduces firm-level entrepreneurship as a key concept in interpreting the phenomenon of firm growth in industrial districts. The chapter has a threefold aim: to present the concepts of firm-level entrepreneurship; to substantiate the relevance of its adoption for this study; and to review the relevant literature, looking particularly at the so-called knowledge-based approach to entrepreneurship. Thus, we provide an explanation of the relevance of firm-level entrepreneurship in the new competitive scenario. This is followed by a review of the literature on firm-level entrepreneurship, basing the discussion on earlier studies on entrepreneurship. Finally, we discuss the knowledge-based approach to entrepreneurship adopted in this book.

3.1. THE RELEVANCE OF FIRM-LEVEL ENTREPRENEURSHIP

3.1.1. The Need for Entrepreneurship in the New Competitive Landscape

Today's economic environment is characterised by increased risk, decreased ability to forecast and fluid industry boundaries. Uncertainty impacts markets and marketing practices. Markets shift, overlap and fragment as boundaries blur. Distribution channels reshape, reconfigure, and circumvent the status quo. Firms interact, compete, and collaborate for consumers whose demand is rapidly changing (Day and Montgomery, 1999; Kinnear, 1999). Surviving and prospering in such harsh conditions entail merely coping with rather than dealing fully with or managing complexity. Different names have been given to the complexity that companies have to face on the contemporary scene. The definitions of 'information era', 'global economy', 'new' or 'net economy', 'hypercompetition' and even the term 'third industrial revolution' have been used indifferently. It is evident that the economic context is characterised by phenomena of turbulence with a pace never seen before (Hamel and Prahalad, 1994; Zook and Allen, 2001; D'Aveni, 1994; Salaman and Asch, 2003; Kaplan and Norton, 2000).

Several changes, all related to each other, have occurred and have resulted in a totally new competitive landscape; consolidated managerial practices have lost their importance, even becoming a factor of inertia in the difficult process of change and transition determined by the new nature of the environment.

First of all, competition is now characterised by a process of globalisation. Operating at different levels, it changes the ideas at the basis of economic theory (Buckley and Casson, 1989) introducing new criteria for managing companies and developing new products (Vernon, 1989). Complexity arising from globalisation affects the activity of the company at different levels. It makes economies of scale and scope easier to achieve by firms located anywhere in the world.

Globalisation is considered one of the hardest challenges for the industrial districts model, in both developed and developing countries (Corò and Grandinetti, 1999; Humphrey and Schmitz, 2002; Guerrieri et al., 2001; Sammarra and Belussi, 2006). It creates the need for coordination of different structures operating in several countries; it also widens the context of the company's activities and increases the number of relations in which the firm is involved. On a general basis, industrial districts are experiencing a deep transformation in the geographical extension of manufacturing relations: most of district firms have extended their networks of suppliers as well as their manufacturing processes outside district and national boundaries. Finally globalisation opens the doors of domestic markets to new competitors, often characterised by lower production costs.

The phenomenon of deregulation operates as well, opening up new markets, which were previously inaccessible and therefore altering traditional competition rules. It forces those companies that have drawn benefits from operating in a regulated sector towards efficiency, increasing the intensity of competition.

In this sense deregulation is a force that contributes to generating a situation that D'Aveni (1994) defined as 'hypercompetition'. This is a battle between different companies that compete simultaneously on price, quality, know-how building, looking for first mover advantage, the creation of strategic alliances and the acquisition of financial resources. Competitors appear more quickly, come from unexpected directions and redefine entire industries. Resources are becoming more and more scarce.

In particular, the Italian experience of the 1990s shows that local manufacturing systems of SMEs – such as industrial districts – have to renovate their sources of competitive advantages in the context of globalisation and hypercompetition (Sciascia, Naldi and Alberti, 2008). This implies that the traditional core of knowledge and skills rooted in the local context may be unable to face the international competition of emerging countries if it is not constantly renewed. These processes lead some authors (Gereffi, 1999; Gereffi et al., 2005; Humphrey and Schmitz, 2002) to look at the development of industrial districts as depending on the global production chain, especially for the industries of standardised products and their connected supplier industries. Of course, this could also be seen as an opportunity for district firms to improve their competitive positions through the renovation of their products, processes and markets. The rising competitiveness of low cost economies makes relocation very convenient to countries, which can be entered a stage of low cost, and especially low labour cost accompanied by few and weak environmental and social rules and laws (for example, India and China).

Globalisation and hypercompetition are phenomena that the new technologies make possible and which accelerate companies' operating rhythm, allowing manufacturers to offer wider product ranges, increasing the ability to meet specific customer needs and desires, which in turn multiply and fragment.

The development of information and telecommunications technology has shifted competition to the management of knowledge and intangible assets; in this way it is possible to explain how even small companies can compete with the large incumbent companies that have ruled most industries for many years. Moreover, it has facilitated interrelations between companies, allowing business networks to arise and making competition more difficult to handle. This opens up to several opportunities for district firms to enhance interaction and communication processes as well as to increase their control on the efficiency of internal processes. Vice versa, if ICT could make computer-mediated communication easy, frequent, and so information-rich to become a closer substitute of face-to-face communication, then the advantage of spatial proximity would expire or at least heavily decrease. Firms would search its trade, productive or technological partners anywhere, crossing industrial district borders often and consistently for crucial activities.

The increase in technological change has been accompanied by a wider spread of technology (Hitt and Reed, 2000), and these two changes foster each other. Information is more widespread than ever as well. Competitive information is getting more accessible: patented inventions are imitated within an ever-shorter time, even in high-tech businesses.

The social environment, and consequently consumer behaviour have been changing with the same pace. The era of mass production is over, and individual consumers are developing different mindsets, leading to personalisation instead of standardisation. Consumers seem to be more rational and careful; at the same time they are losing their status-exhibiting attitudes; most of the basic human needs have been met in the developed world, so that new needs must be identified (Michael, Storey and Thomas, 2002). Moreover consumers show a strong interest in the firm's mission and beliefs. Respect for the environment, attention to ethical product contents, the quality of raw materials used and the transparency of companies' activities are becoming relevant factors in affecting competitive success.

Table 3.1 Innovation and renewal as a source of success

Strategy	Best Performers 1990-1999	Best Performers 1997-1999
Business Consolidation and Related Diversification	84%	49%
Core Business Renewal	4%	17%
New-to-world Business Model	12%	34%

Source: adapted from Zook and Allen, 2001

Under the pressure of globalisation and digitalisation, industrial district firms are passing a hard restructuring time, characterised by the erosion of traditional competitive advantages. In a word, this new competitive landscape is complex, characterised by uncertainty, unpredictability, dynamism and fragmentation, with a high number of actors and links between them. The current environment is an extremely powerful source of opportunities and threats, which only dynamic organisations can spot and exploit. Given the challenging nature of the present-day environment, district firms are called on to recognise the need to continuously change their business model, meaning the way they interface with the environment (Coda, 1988), at both competitive and social level.

While the need for change and innovation has been acknowledged, many firms have floundered through reductions in workforce, downsizing and budget cuts. Only those companies that have developed innovative products or processes have been able to build strong bases for success. The only way to cope with the new competitive landscape is to change the way we interface with it.

These arguments are justified by the results of research, such as that carried out by Zook and Allen in 2001. As Table 3.1 shows, best performance companies in the years of extreme environmental dynamism (1997–1999) have based their success on renewal and innovation much more than before (1992–1999).

3.1.2.   The Emergence of Firm-Level Entrepreneurship

Given these premises, studies on entrepreneurship, and above all on firm-level entrepreneurship, seem to have a high potential in terms of practical relevance; they could help companies to succeed in the present competitive scenario and therefore help entire national economies to be competitive.

Since the 1990s this research has emerged worldwide (Zahra, 2005). There seems to be widespread recognition that entrepreneurship is the engine driving the economy and society of most nations (Brock and Evans, 1989; Acs, 1992; Carree and Thurik, 2003). Although entrepreneurship is not a new concept, it has gained increasing interest and research attention over the past 15 years. Today entrepreneurship is considered the essential lever to cope with the new competitive landscape (Hitt and Reed, 2000).

Conferences, books, magazines and journals have been dedicated entirely or partially to entrepreneurship. At the beginning of this virtual journey through the entrepreneurship world we could define it as the process of creating value by bringing together a unique package of resources to exploit an opportunity (Stevenson et al., 1999). This means that entrepreneurship is much more than starting a business. The creation of a new organisation is not even a necessary condition, since entrepreneurial phenomena also occur in established companies.

Growing interest has been devoted to the study of firm-level entrepreneurship or corporate entrepreneurship (Dess et al., 2003). This field of studies is gaining ground in the management academy and could be seen as complementary to the better-established independent entrepreneurship field, exclusively devoted to the start-up of new businesses.

Corporate entrepreneurship can be defined as the entrepreneurial behaviour shown by existing organisations. It may manifest itself as the development of a new venture (internal venturing) or as organisational revitalisation (strategic renewal). Both the processes can encompass innovation, which is the introduction of something new to the marketplace (Sharma and Chrisman, 1999). Some studies have instead focused on the so-called 'Entrepreneurial Management', which considers firm-level entrepreneurship as a management approach rather than as a course of action, oriented to letting innovation arise in organisations (see Invernizzi, Molteni and Corbetta, 1990).

From these first sketches the complexity of the concept is obvious. It is not surprising that studies on firm-level entrepreneurship have been carried out by scholars with different backgrounds: Strategic Management, Marketing, Organization, R&D.

Before the early 1980s, apart from a few exceptions, entrepreneurship was still seen as being embodied in individual entrepreneurs (Schendel, 1990). Some writers even considered entrepreneurship as the opposite of 'corporate management' (Vesper, 1984); corporate entrepreneurship therefore sounded like a real oxymoron, a contradiction in terms (Stevenson and Jarillo, 1990). Nowadays firm-level entrepreneurship is at the core of management studies, and much research has been carried out, mainly focusing on identifying determinants and outcomes of the phenomenon.

3.2.   LITERATURE REVIEW ON ENTREPRENEURSHIP AND FIRM-LEVEL ENTREPRENEURSHIP

3.2.1.   A Literature Review on Entrepreneurship

For many years entrepreneurship studies have been conducted exclusively within the context of economics; entrepreneurship has been considered the heart of economic development and the unit of analysis of studies on it has basically been the individual.

The first definition of entrepreneur was given by Cantillon in 1755 in his *Essai sur la nature du commerce en general* and even Smith dealt with the issue in 1776 in his *An inquiry into the wealth of nations*. What first appeared as a link between economic activity and the role of the entrepreneur was his inclination to risk and his ability to manage situations of uncertainty. According to Cantillon, in fact, the entrepreneur is a speculator in search of profit from arbitrage, from buying at a certain price and selling at an uncertain price. Therefore the entrepreneur is different from the 'rentier', the other subject of the economic system identified by Cantillon, as his income cannot be predicted. On the base of this seminal work, almost two centuries later, Knight (1921) differentiated risk from uncertainty, considering that the first can be reduced through the creation of pools of risks that are not perfectly correlated, while uncertainty is never measurable, since it is not based on rational choice but on opinion.

Also Say (1971) introduced the concept of entrepreneur in his *Traite d'économie politique*, in the early 1800s. In his representation of the economic system, Say identifies entrepreneurial activity as the 'art of superintendence and administration'. According to Baumol (1993), in Say's theory the entrepreneur could also be seen as a speculator trying to resell different products. What differentiates this contribution from the previous ones is that the central aspect of the entrepreneurial function is no longer a risk but managerial skills and other moral qualities such as judgment and perseverance are (Say, 1971).

While developments were made by French scholars, in Britain, in his seminal work of 1776 *The Wealth of Nations*, Smith depicts the entrepreneur as: adventurer, since he is in search of hazard; projector, given that he is able to project and make plans anticipating the future; undertaker, since he takes wise risks, available for investments if properly remunerated. The function of the entrepreneur was conflated with that of the capitalist and profit was basically regarded as a reward for risking capital. The role of entrepreneur as innovator was almost ignored in the following work of Ricardo and neoclassical models, because the market was considered permanently close to the equilibrium and therefore, in the case of exogenous changes, the entrepreneur is called on to make new calculations for maximising profit. In 1890, Marshall (1930) defined the entrepreneurial function as providing innovation and consequently progress. It is important to underline how already in Marshall's formulation not all business players can be considered entrepreneurs in the sense just expressed. There are in fact business owners who cannot avoid taking risks and others who 'follow beaten tracks' (Lynskey, 2002). In order to belong to the first group, superintendence is not enough, but forecasting and leadership are also required (Marshall, 1930). Marshall's entrepreneur is innovative in operative terms, meaning that he innovates for efficiency more than efficacy, leaving to Schumpeter the possibility of developing his ideas in a fuller sense.

At the end of the 1800s, important research developments into these topics also came from the Austrian School, thanks to the work of important authors such as Menger, Von Mises and Von Wieser. The tradition of the Austrian School was subsequently revitalised by Hayek and Kirzner. It is of great significance to compare these studies to the neo-classical ones, as they start from an opposite point of view. According to the Austrian perspective, in fact, the market is far from equilibrium due to the effects of scarce awareness and asymmetric information, factors never taken into consideration by classical and neoclassical research. Market exchange occurs since individuals have different subjective evaluations of the same products. Given the above, the entrepreneur must have awareness and a superior ability to understand different phenomena, rather than an inclination to bear risk. All the contributions discussed above convey an idea of the entrepreneur as the first person with the ability to seize an opportunity of arbitrage in the market.

Nothing is said about the relationship between this asymmetry and the role of the entrepreneur. Schumpeter (1883–1950) was the first author to identify the role of the entrepreneur in creating these changes and disequilibrium in the market, through innovation and being proactive.

Schumpeter (1934) saw the entrepreneur as the major agent of economic development, defined by the 'carrying out of new combinations', which in turn means 'the competitive elimination of the old'. The concept of economic development covers the following five cases: 1) the introduction of a new good or of a new quality of a good; 2) the introduction of a new method of production; 3) the opening of a new market; 4) the conquest of a new source of supply of raw materials or semi-manufactured goods; 5) the carrying out of the new organisation of any industry. In his work, Schumpeter conceives the market as a system in equilibrium and entrepreneurship as the process of disrupting this equilibrium, a way of moving the market away from it. In the early ideas of Schumpeter two different worlds emerge. The first is the stationary equilibrium of the market, characterised by information symmetry, economic rationality and no uncertainty. In such a system, routines and experience play a fundamental role in orienting the behaviour of different actors. The second world is the one created by the entrepreneur, where changes are introduced in the circular flow of economy. These changes are the way identified by the entrepreneur to seek opportunity for profit. Considering the fact that changing the status quo would mean altering the existing relations in the market and destroying the pre-existing sources of advantage of incumbent firms (the idea of 'creative destruction' emerges here), innovation is generally carried out by new firms. Entrepreneurs appear as new agents using old resources; they are 'deviant' people, who are never satisfied by results obtained with existing innovation but are continuously looking for new opportunities for growth (Elster, 1983; Santarelli and Pesciarelli, 1990).

Later contributions of Schumpeter reduced the role of the entrepreneur as the agent of economic development. With the increasing importance of large companies, the roots of innovation were identified in this kind of integrated firm. They could in fact benefit from a larger amount of financial resources and shared knowledge, key inputs for the processes of innovation. Areas of uncertainty and potential discovery diminished due to the increasing commitment of big companies towards research. This change in position of the scholar is not at all a sign of incongruence, since it reflected the changes that the economic scenario faced in the 1900s. Combining the different views of Schumpeter it is possible to underline some particular characteristics of the entrepreneur: he is the one who transforms inventions into innovations, without any particular reference to any position in certain organisations or in general in the social context, and independently of any social values or beliefs. His representation as a deviant is due only to a strong need for achievement. Entrepreneurship is not a profession, nor a lasting condition. The entrepreneur is not just a risk taker or a capital provider: he is the agent of economic development.

Other relevant studies on entrepreneurship have been carried out by Kirzner (1973). The Austrian economist suggests that entrepreneurship is the consequence of innovation designed to exploit the opportunities afforded by economic disequilibrium. He therefore turns the Schumpeterian view upside-down, seeing the entrepreneur as an agent of equilibrium, taking advantage of disequilibrium. The work of Kirzner was strongly influenced by the theories of Von Mises. The role of the entrepreneur becomes, according to Kirzner, the identification of potential opportunities that are unexploited. The social function of this individual is also crucial: exploiting unseen opportunities means reallocating the resources available on the market in a more efficient way. In this sense the entrepreneur reduces 'social waste'. The core concept underpinning Kirzner's dissertation is 'alertness'. The entrepreneur is at all times scanning the horizon, ready to make discoveries. This could be the essence of 'alertness' that 'must, importantly, embrace the awareness of the ways in which the human agent can, by imaginative, bold leaps of faith, and determination, in fact create the future for which his present acts are designed' (Kirzner 1982: 150). The perspectives of Schumpeter and Kirzner can both be accepted if we consider that there are different kinds of entrepreneurial processes: the first one, Kirznerian, is oriented to incremental-continuous innovation, while the second one, Schumpeterian, results in any kind of innovation, even radical-discontinuous innovation.

Important contributions to the general understanding of entrepreneurial processes have been made by studies on innovation. Abernathy and Clark (1985) offer a classification of different types of entrepreneur according to the kind of innovation they introduce. Studies arising from the neo-Schumpeterian tradition offer important research insights into the entry of new firms into the market, such as the 'dominant design' one, which relates innovation to the product life cycle. One of the most important contributions in this perspective comes from Nelson and Winter (1982), who introduced the notion of 'technological regime' as the main determinant of the intensity of market competition. Technological regimes are defined by three main characteristics: opportunities, accessibility and cumulativeness. Innovation is therefore presented as the opportunity for new firms to enter the market and to compete with incumbent firms, but these opportunities for growth are structured by the dominant technology in the market. This idea is also accepted by Sutton (1998) within the industrial organisation field. Nelson and Winter (1982) focus on the role of technological opportunities and not on profit opportunities, distinguishing the 'entrepreneurial regime', which facilitates innovative entry into the market, from the 'routinised regime', where innovation is generally carried out by incumbents (Winter, 1984). They view firms as banks of knowledge, whose storage is instilled via organisational routines, defined as regular and predictable behaviour patterns. Innovation occurs when the 'search' activity changes routine; if routines are metaphorically considered as 'genes', search activities are procedures for 'mutations'. More recent contributions identify the crucial role played by knowledge in enhancing or hampering opportunities for entrepreneurship (Malerba and Orsenigo, 2000; Marsili, 2002).

Alongside the contributions from economic history and anthropology, much research on entrepreneurship has been carried out within the fields of sociology and psychology, all of them investigating the main traits of the entrepreneur. Sociological studies include those of Weber (1947), Gerschenkron (1965) and Granovetter (1995), while McClelland (1961), Hornaday and Aboud (1971), Timmons (1978) and Sexton (1980) may be mentioned in the field of psychology.

3.2.2.   Overcoming the Entrepreneurial Paradox

Ever since the work of Schumpeter, managers have been described as individuals who are different from entrepreneurs. 'We have seen that, normally, the modern businessman, whether entrepreneur or mere managing administrator, is of the executive type. From the logic of his position he acquires something of the psychology of the salaried employee working in a bureaucratic organization' (Schumpeter, 1942: 156). Chandler (1962: 11) also made a clear distinction between the two roles:

> The executives who actually allocate available resources are then the key men in any enterprise. Because of their critical role in the modern economy, they will be defined in this study as entrepreneurs. In contrast, those who coordinate, appraise, and plan within the means allocated to them will be termed managers. So entrepreneurial decisions and actions will refer to those which affect the allocation or reallocation of resources for the enterprise as a whole, and operating decisions and actions will refer to those which are carried out by using the resources already allocated.

On the basis of these differences, many studies have been carried out with the aim of clarifying the psychological aspects that distinguish the two categories. Besides a different level of risk aversion (McGrath et al., 1992), social behavioural aspects have been taken into consideration (Pettigrew, 1973; Shapero, 1975; Ginsberg and Buchholtz, 1989). After all these analyses, however, psychological differences are now considered minor or nonexistent (Brockhaus and Horwitz, 1986; Low and MacMillan, 1988). Nevertheless, risk-taking propensity is still considered fundamental in understanding entrepreneurial processes (Lynskey, 2002).

The failure of all this research has, however, generated the need to explain entrepreneurial phenomena from alternative perspectives and has reinforced the process of overcoming the separation between management and entrepreneurship. One of the fields that seems more likely to generate cross-fertilization processes in understanding entrepreneurship is Strategic Management. The growth in the connection between the two disciplines is witnessed by the increasing presence of entrepreneurship studies in strategy journals and among management researchers (Meyer and Heppard, 2000; Zahra and Dess, 2001).

Comparing the definitions of entrepreneurship collected by Gartner (1990) with Mintzberg, Ahlstrand and Lampel's taxonomy (1998) of Strategic Management's main contributions, Sandberg (1992) identified areas where entrepreneurship could benefit from strategic management studies. These are: 1) new business creation; 2) innovation; 3) opportunity seeking; 4) risk assumption; 5) top management teams; and 6) group processes in strategic decision.

The idea of 'Strategic Entrepreneurship' (Hitt, Ireland, Camp, Sexton, 2002) also witnesses how the two areas are linked. A firm's long-term survival implies two actions: strategic action, which is focused on developing the current competitive advantage, and an entrepreneurial action oriented to the research of continuously new opportunities (Hitt, Ireland, Camp, Sexton, 2001).

Entrepreneurship research has progressively moved from the study of individual traits to that of the features of the entrepreneurial organisation, seeing entrepreneurship as an entrepreneurial event within the organisation or as a managerial style (Morris and Kuratko, 2002). More recently the entrepreneurial phenomenon has been studied not only in relation to emerging ventures (Ucbasaran et al., 2001), but also to corporate ventures (McGrath et al., 1994), franchising (Shane, 1996) and the growth of firms (Davidsson et al., 2002), even within the family business (Church, 1993). Thus, many scholars have further investigated the nexus between organisational and management characteristics and firm-level entrepreneurship (Covin and Slevin, 1991; Zahra, 1993).

The removal of what had been presented in the literature under the label of 'entrepreneurial paradox' opened the space for communication between entrepreneurship and management. The idea that entrepreneurship is a phenomenon that goes beyond the individual level, producing outcome at the organisational level and even in the wider social context is now accepted. It is revealed by the most commonly accepted definition of entrepreneurship as a research domain (Shane and Venkataraman, 2000: 218):

> The scholarly examination of how, by whom, and with what effects opportunities to create future goods and services are discovered, evaluated and exploited. Consequently, the field involves the study of sources of opportunities; the process of discovery, evaluation and exploitation of opportunities; and the set of individuals who discover, evaluate and exploit them.

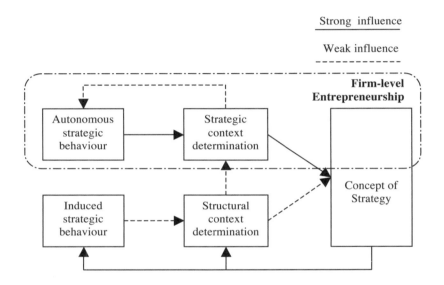

Source: adapted from Burgelman (1983)

Figure 3.1 Firm-level entrepreneurship according to Burgelman

3.2.3.   A Literature Review on Firm-Level Entrepreneurship

Starting with Peterson and Berger's (1971) study, research has sought to identify organisational and environmental factors that affect a company's entrepreneurial activities. Early research into corporate entrepreneurship paid great attention to the process by which established firms built up new business, discussing for example factors that influence its outcomes (Burgelman, 1983; Scholhammer, 1982). Likewise, Burgelman's (1983) contribution added considerable richness to the literature by analysing the interplay between autonomous and formal strategic behaviours existing in a firm's entrepreneurial activities. Burgelman (1983: 1349) defines corporate entrepreneurship as 'the process whereby firms engage in diversification through internal development. Such diversification requires new resource combinations to extend the firm's activities in areas unrelated, or marginally related, to its current domain of competence and corresponding opportunity set'. As emerges from these words, the author adopts a clear perspective in describing newness: innovation is something new for the company, regardless of market perspective. This way of thinking is typical of the strategic management scholars, who are more interested in the organisational dimension of firm-level entrepreneurship. As Figure 3.1 shows, the concept of strategy induces activity in the form of induced strategic behaviour, which comprises those activities that fit in with the current concept of strategy. The structural context comprises the various mechanisms that top management can use to keep the induced strategic behaviour in line with the current concept of strategy. It is aimed at influencing managers' strategic activities at both operational and middle levels, influencing their perceived interests. The direction of the arrows in the model clearly show that structural context mainly 'intervenes in the relationship between induced strategic behaviour and the concept of strategy, and operates as a selection mechanism – a diversity reduction mechanism – on the stream of induced strategic behaviour' (Burgelman, 1983: 1350). The entrepreneurial potential operates instead within a separate dimension of the strategic process, taking shape through autonomous strategic behaviour, meaning those strategic activities that do not fit in with the firm's current concept of strategy. As pointed out by Burgelman himself, corporate entrepreneurship will be identified with the autonomous strategic behaviour loop in the model (Burgelman, 1983). Autonomous strategic behaviour does not fit into the existing categories used in the strategic planning of the firm. To be successful, it must be accepted by the whole organisation – and not just by its proponents – and integrated into the current concept of strategy, which will be modified, as a result. The process by which this can happen is called strategic context determination and refers to the political mechanisms and activities used by proponents of autonomous strategic behaviour to question the current concept of strategy and, circumventing the selection mechanisms of the structural context, to obtain acceptance and integration of business innovations.

In the same year, Miller fixed a milestone in the field of study. As represented in Figure 3.2, Miller describes firm-level entrepreneurship as a multidimensional concept encompassing firm's innovative action (to which Burgelman's definition is limited), proactiveness and risk taking. Entrepreneurship is not restricted to diversification through internal development, but refers to any action relating to product-market and technological innovation (Miller, 1983). Over time this definition has become among one of the most commonly applied by scholars. Researchers in the US and other countries have been using Miller's theory and research instruments to examine the complex linkages between environmental, strategic, and organisational variables, and a company's entrepreneurial activities. In his study, Miller identified the main determinants of entrepreneurship in different organisational contexts, finding that in simple firms entrepreneurship is determined by the characteristics of the leader; in planning firms it would be facilitated by explicit and well integrated strategies; in organic firms it would be a function of environment and structure.

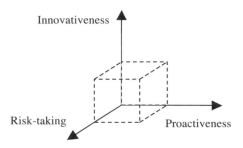

Source: personal elaboration Miller (1983)

Figure 3.2 Firm-level entrepreneurship in Miller's study

When Guth and Ginsberg (1990) reviewed the status of the field, they concluded that firm-level entrepreneurship encompasses two key phenomena: 1) new business creation through venturing; 2) transformation of the organisations through renewal of the key ideas on which they are built. They developed a framework for mapping firm-level entrepreneurship research, which identifies five classes of inquiry into corporate entrepreneurship: the environmental influences, the effects of strategic leader features, the organisational forms and conducts influencing firm-level entrepreneurship, the role of past performance and the effect of entrepreneurship on performance itself (see Figure 3.3).

At that time, firm-level entrepreneurship had been mainly identified with simple 'corporate venturing', according to a purely entrepreneurship perspective; it had also been defined as 'Intrapreneurship' by Pinchot (1985). Guth and Ginsberg (1990) made a claim for focusing corporate entrepreneurship studies on the 'strategic renewal' process. Zahra (1993) afterwards argued that very few studies captured both the dimensions and thus research into corporate venturing was not fully integrated, at that time, into discussions of firm-level entrepreneurship or entrepreneurial orientation.

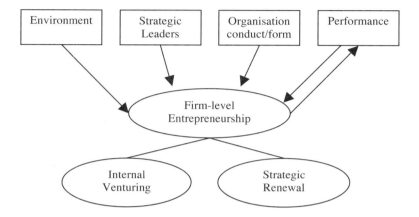

Source: adapted from Guth and Ginsberg, 1990

Figure 3.3 Guth and Ginsberg's framework for firm-level entrepreneurship

Among the studies on internal venturing conducted in the 1980s we position an Italian research carried on by Invernizzi et al. (1988). Invernizzi (1988) identified three main reasons in incepting corporate entrepreneurship: the need for developing new strategic business units, the need for renewing existing strategic business units and the necessity to reduce the risk related to the concentration of the entrepreneurial competencies just in one person (the entrepreneur). Behind these first level factors, other reasons could move the companies toward firm-level entrepreneurship: changes in the environment and unsatisfactory performances. The complexity of the process is influenced by the underlying strategic orientation (Coda, 1988), the perception of all these factors by the management and its willingness to change the status quo, which in turn depends on the power structures within the governance of the company (Sinatra, 1988). Given these contextual factors, Molteni (1988) identified five main steps in the internal venturing process, all aimed at developing a new business idea: generation, elaboration, implementation, consolidation and (in some cases) integration. Within each phase, the main critical roles, which are the main functions to be exerted for running the process successfully, were identified. In 1990, Stevenson and Jarillo stressed the need for studying the true nature of firm-level entrepreneurship, which they argued is 'Entrepreneurial Management'. They noticed that previous studies had focused on what happens when entrepreneurs act (the results of entrepreneurship) or why they act (the causes of entrepreneurship) instead of analysing how they act (the process of entrepreneurship). The authors proposed a view of corporate entrepreneurship that goes beyond 'corporate venturing' and the setting up of intra-firm 'venture capital' processes, mainly stating that firm-level entrepreneurship is the process by which organisations pursue opportunities without regard to the resources they currently control. In 1985, Stevenson and Gumpert (1985) had already treated entrepreneurship in these terms, stating that firm-level entrepreneurship is a behaviour in which:

1.   strategic orientation is driven by perception of opportunities;
2.   the commitment of resources is revolutionary, with short duration;
3.   resources are committed gradually, in many stages;
4.   resources are episodically used or rented more than totally controlled;
5.   the management structure is flat, with multiple informal networks.

Unlike Stevenson's studies, Invernizzi et al. (1990) did not conceive entrepreneurial management as the extreme of a continuum, as opposed to administrative management. It was seen as the proper mix between a certain degree of entrepreneurship and a certain degree of professionalism, which should coexist and cross-fertilize. Molteni (1990) studied the dangers of a wrong mix, which is represented by the first three squares of the matrix represented in Figure 3.4. He argued that the balance between entrepreneurship and professionalism depended on the phase of the company's life cycle. He therefore studied the right moves to make in order to get to the excellence square, that is to adopt an entrepreneurial management, in each of these phases.

Corbetta (1990) studied the role of strategic management systems in fostering entrepreneurial management. He identified three company archetypes on the basis of their balance between entrepreneurship and manageriality, corresponding to squares I, III and IV of the above-mentioned matrix. The majority of Italian district firms, given their small average size, are positioned in square I, and typically pass to square III in order to achieve sustainable development, due to the adoption of formal strategic management systems. The challenge consists in developing strategic management systems that allow the firm to reach the excellence square. According to Corbetta (1990) much emphasis should be put on the development of strategic diagnosis, since this can contribute to opportunity recognition. Strategic management practices could also offer models for selecting alternatives, for choosing the contents and methods of entrepreneurial development. Plans should be developed, but they have to be long-term oriented; a large base of individuals should be involved in strategy formation and the strategic system should be strictly linked to other systems, such as control and information systems and it should be submitted to continuous modifications.

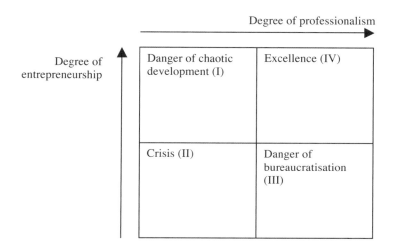

Source: adapted from Molteni, 1990

Figure 3.4 Entrepreneurial management

When developing the ideas of previous mentioned scholars, Covin and Slevin, in a later work (1991), coined the expression 'Entrepreneurial posture' underlining the need for a behavioural approach to the topic. Building on Miller's contribution, they represented entrepreneurial posture as a firm's risk-taking propensity, its tendency to act in a proactive manner and its reliance on frequent product innovation. They developed a conceptual model, which elicits the main variables affecting entrepreneurship in organisations. Their work was refined by Zahra (1993) two years later and this is represented in Figure 3.5. Forty-six propositions were completely developed. Four classes of variables influence firm-level entrepreneurship and vice-versa: external variables (dynamism, hostility and munificence), internal (management values, background values, structure, processes and culture), strategic variables (mission and competitive tactics) and performance (financial and non-financial). The first three classes also influence the relationship between entrepreneurship and performance and are therefore considered the most difficult to study.

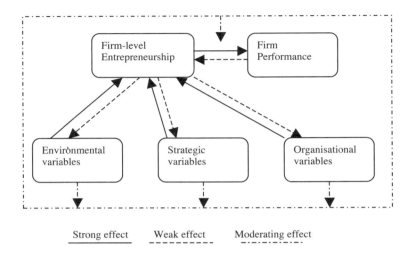

Strong effect   Weak effect   Moderating effect

Source: adapted from Zahra, 1993

Figure 3.5 Zahra's model of firm-level entrepreneurship

Stopford and Baden-Fuller (1994) identified three different types of corporate entrepreneurship: 1) the creation of new business within an existing organization; 2) the renewal of existing organizations; and 3) the changing of the rules of the competition within an industry due to the innovation introduced by an organisation. This third, apparently 'new' category, is nothing but the traditional Schumpeterian concept of entrepreneurship (Schumpeter, 1934). In such a definition, market-related innovation is seen as a sufficient condition for firm-level entrepreneurship but not a necessary one, since organisation creation or renewal can occur in the absence of innovation. This meaning is far from the original concept of entrepreneurship and has definitely enlarged the boundaries of the research domain.

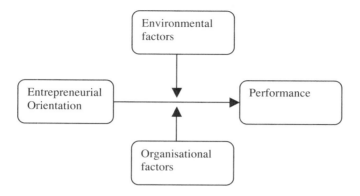

Source: Lumpkin and Dess, 1996

Figure 3.6 Lumpkin and Dess's conceptual framework for entrepreneurial orientation

In 1996, Lumpkin and Dess (1996) introduced the term 'Entrepreneurial orientation', basically referring to Stevenson and Jarillo's (1990) 'Entrepreneurial management'. While 'New entry' refers to what entrepreneurship consists of, 'Entrepreneurial orientation' describes how new entry is undertaken. They identify five dimensions characterising entrepreneurial orientation and added autonomy and competitive aggressiveness to the already established three dimensions identified by Miller (risk taking, pro-activeness and innovativeness) and argued their reciprocal independence. Their main concern was related to the study of the relationship between entrepreneurial orientation and performance, proposing that organisational and environmental variables affect this relationship, as shown in Figure 3.6. Among the former they include size, structure, strategy, strategic processes, firm resources, culture and top management characteristics. Among the latter they list dynamism, munificence, complexity and industry characteristics.

In the same year Morris and Sexton (1996) introduced the concept of 'Entrepreneurial intensity', as the combination of frequency of entrepreneurial events and the extent to which such events are innovative, risky and proactive.

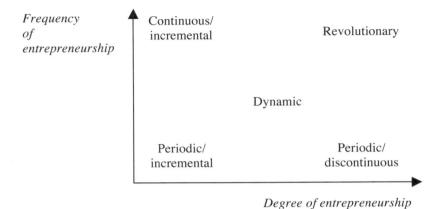

Source: Morris and Sexton, 1996

Figure 3.7 Five categories of entrepreneurial intensity

They gave the corporate entrepreneurship concept a dynamic meaning as no firm is entrepreneurial all the time and no firm can be solely entrepreneurial (Morris and Sexton, 1996). Moreover, several kinds of entrepreneurial intensity can be identified, depending on the frequency of entrepreneurial events and the degree of entrepreneurship and these are represented in Figure 3.7.

One of the most recent contributions towards a better understanding of corporate entrepreneurship comes from Sharma and Chrisman (1999). They provided a terminological framework that goes from a general to a specific point of view clarifying the existing boundaries of the field. First of all, Sharma and Chrisman distinguish between Independent Entrepreneurship and Corporate Entrepreneurship. Independent entrepreneurship is 'the process whereby an individual or group of individuals, acting independently of any association with an existing organisation, creates a new organisation' (1999: 18). Corporate entrepreneurship is 'the process whereby an individual or a group of individuals, in association with an existing organization, create a new organization or instigate renewal or innovation within that organization' (1999: 18). Corporate entrepreneurship encompasses two different phenomena: strategic renewal, prevalently studied by Strategic Management scholars, and corporate venturing, mainly referring to traditional entrepreneurship studies. The concepts both suggest changes in either the strategy or the structure of an existing corporation, which may involve innovation. On the one hand strategic renewal refers to 'corporate entrepreneurial efforts that result in significant changes to an organisation's business or corporate level strategy or structure' (1999: 19). On the other hand corporate venturing refers to 'corporate entrepreneurial efforts that lead to the creation of new business organizations within the corporate organization' (1999: 19). Corporate venturing can be classified either as external or internal. External corporate venturing refers to 'corporate venturing activities that result in the creation of semi-autonomous or autonomous organizational entities that reside outside the existing organizational domain' (1999: 19). Internal corporate venturing refers to 'corporate venturing activities that result in the creation of organizational entities that reside within an existing organizational domain' (1999: 20).

3.3. A KNOWLEDGE-BASED VIEW OF FIRM-LEVEL ENTREPRENEURSHIP

3.3.1. The Role of Knowledge in Firm-Level Entrepreneurship

There is increasing agreement around a view of entrepreneurship, at both individual and organisational level, as a process in which a creative recombination of resources and knowledge flows allows an organisation to meet a market need by introducing and selling a new good, service, raw material or organising method at greater than its cost of production, hence delivering superior value (Ardichvili et al., 2003; Casson, 1982; Kirzner, 1973, 1997; Schumpeter, 1934; Shane and Venkataraman, 2000).

According to the tradition of Austrian economics (see for example, Hayek, 1945, 1978; Kirzner, 1973), entrepreneurial opportunities are seen as existing because different economic agents have different beliefs about the relative value of resources, given the potential to transform them into a different state. In turn, these different beliefs depend on asymmetries of information available to economic agents, and on their different abilities to recognise the value of new information, assimilate it and apply it to entrepreneurship. According to this approach, the possession of idiosyncratic information allows some people to see opportunities that others cannot see: 'Differences in information lead people to see different value in a given good or service and offer different prices to obtain it. By buying or selling goods or services in response to the discovery of price misalignments, an individual can earn entrepreneurial profits or incur entrepreneurial losses' (Shane, 2000: 449). Therefore, recent conceptual frameworks place knowledge at centre stage in explaining the entrepreneurial process, which they interpret as being composed of the two separate phases of opportunity recognition and opportunity exploitation (Ardichvili et al., 2003; Denrell et al., 2003; Shane, 2000; Shane and Venkataraman, 2000).

This information and knowledge-based view of entrepreneurship suggests that individuals and organisations recognise opportunities related to information they already possess. According to Shane (2000), for example, prior knowledge influences the discovery of entrepreneurial opportunities based on the emergence of a new technology in at least three conceptually and empirically distinct ways. First, prior knowledge about markets will influence the discovery of which markets to enter to exploit the new technology. Second, prior knowledge about how to serve markets will influence the discovery of how to use the new technology to serve a market. Finally, prior knowledge of customer problems will influence the discovery of products and services to exploit the new technology. Shane and Venkataraman (2000) have conceptually refined this view, suggesting that individuals possess different stocks of information that, in turn, influence their ability to recognise particular opportunities. Stocks of information create mental schemes that provide a framework for recognising new information. To recognise an entrepreneurial opportunity, an individual needs prior knowledge that is complementary to newly accessed knowledge, and which triggers an entrepreneurial conjecture (Shane and Venkataraman, 2000: 222).

As Figure 3.8 illustrates, prior knowledge not only has an impact on the recognition process, but also on the choice of methods to exploit identified opportunities. Since entrepreneurship consists of combining resources in innovative ways (Schumpeter, 1934), and since knowledge is recognised as the most valuable resource in the new competitive landscape (Bettis and Hitt, 1995), prior knowledge plays a critical role in the exploitation of entrepreneurial opportunities.

This approach is taken up in several recent contributions. Ardichvili et al. (2003), for instance, explicitly refer to Shane's (2000) propositions in building a model of the opportunity recognition and exploitation process. In line with existing theory, they suggest that prior knowledge of markets, customer problems and ways to serve markets increases the likelihood of a successful entrepreneurial process. The effect of prior knowledge on entrepreneurship is mediated by the positive impact of entrepreneurial alertness and social network relationships, which are hinted at but not formally developed in their model.

The central role of prior knowledge in these contributions is also evident in the concept of 'information/knowledge corridor', given by an individual's or organisation's idiosyncratic prior knowledge (Hayek, 1978; Ronstadt, 1988). Differentiated knowledge corridors exist because of the specialisation of information in society. Specialisation, in turn, is a result of the higher value of specialised versus all-purpose knowledge (Becker and Murphy, 1992; Hayek, 1945), and of the often-stochastic distribution of information in society (Nelson and Winter, 1982).

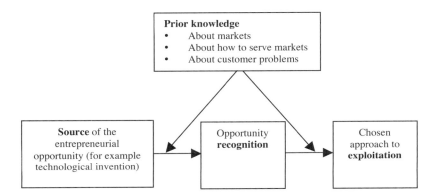

Source: adapted from Shane (2000)

Figure 3.8 A conceptual model of entrepreneurial opportunity recognition and exploitation

With the exception of these references, however, existing models of firm-level entrepreneurship pay but scant attention to the mechanisms of knowledge acquisition, storage, retrieval and exploitation – and to their role in opportunity recognition and exploitation. Hence, they miss the chance of explaining how successful entrepreneurship may be enhanced by purposefully manipulating such activities through the use of organisational levers.

In these models prior knowledge is always treated as an exogenous variable that is accessed and transformed by individuals. This characteristic may result in a major weakness of existing conceptualisations of entrepreneurial processes. Failing to understand how knowledge corridors develop over time, how multiple actors' knowledge interacts in co-creating entrepreneurial outcomes, and how knowledge stratification may be purposefully directed towards improving the entrepreneurial process, may hinder these models' power in explaining the actual drivers of entrepreneurship. Once knowledge endowments are given, there is not much a firm can do to enhance its chances of spotting entrepreneurial opportunities. Hence, incorporating insights into how knowledge corridors develop and are built and how multiple actors' knowledge flows interweave in yielding entrepreneurial outcomes into existing opportunity-recognition models may significantly enhance both their explanatory and their prescriptive power.

A step in this direction is attempted by Denrell et al. (2003), although with reference only to the opportunity recognition phase. Moving from an applied economics perspective, they posit a central role of prior knowledge within the opportunity recognition process. According to Denrell et al. (2003), the view of each firm is shaped by its own set of resources and information, including its ability to assess the resources owned by other firms. To that extent, such a view is unique. The more distinctive the view, the more likely it is to encompass valuable opportunities not visible to other companies, ensuring at least a temporary advantage to the firm that identifies the opportunity (Denrell et al., 2003: 978).

In a similar vein, Ardichvili et al. (2003) suggest that the opportunity identification process results both in enriching the entrepreneur's knowledge base and in increasing his/her alertness. This may lead to the identification of further entrepreneurial opportunities. Thus, they propose that the probability of future successful opportunity identification is positively related to the number of previous ones (Ardichvili et al., 2003: 120).

However, they do not speculate further about how cumulated experience may actually improve the chance of subsequent opportunity identification. Entrepreneurs are left wondering how these mechanisms actually function and, above all, how they can be enhanced. We suggest the concept of absorptive capacity as having a significant potential in bridging these conceptual and empirical gaps. In particular, we build on the assumption that the ability to spot and pursue entrepreneurial opportunities is facilitated by the routines and processes composing an organisation's absorptive capacity (Zahra and George, 2002).

3.3.2.   The Concept of Absorptive Capacity

The central role of knowledge within innovation processes has encouraged some authors to focus on those organisational capabilities that are explicitly aimed at accessing and storing knowledge, and at recombining it in novel ways. In their studies, these capabilities are labelled as organisational absorptive capacity. The concept of absorptive capacity (Cohen and Levinthal, 1990) has attracted increasing attention, given its potential to connect insights from cognitive psychology literature focusing on learning and creativity to the stream of managerial studies on organisational capabilities and innovation (Jansen et al., 2005; Lane and Lubatkin, 1998; Tsai, 2001). Absorptive capacity explicitly recognises the role of existing knowledge within innovative processes, which can be considered akin to entrepreneurial processes within entrepreneurship literature: 'The prior possession of relevant knowledge and skill is what gives rise to creativity, permitting the sorts of associations and linkages that may have never been considered before' (Cohen and Levinthal, 1990: 130).

Conceptualisations of absorptive capacity explicitly recognise and develop organisational-level mechanisms of knowledge access, integration and use. Hence, they offer potentially valuable insights to complement existing entrepreneurship models of opportunity recognition and exploitation, which currently overemphasise access and transformation of knowledge by individuals.

Absorptive capacity (ACAP) is usually interpreted as an organisational capability for storing, retrieving and applying externally accessed knowledge. According to the original formulation offered by Cohen and Levinthal (1990: 128), ACAP is 'an ability to recognize the value of new information, assimilate it, and apply it to commercial ends'. Subsequent conceptualisations have developed specific aspects of this initial definition. According to Mowery and Oxley (1995), for example, ACAP is a broad set of individual skills through which an organisation manages the tacit component of transferred knowledge, modifying it for its internal purposes. Kim (1998) offers a definition of ACAP as a capacity to assimilate knowledge for imitation (a 'learning' capability), and to create new knowledge for innovation (a 'problem-solving' capability). In an effort to build an all-encompassing re-conceptualisation of ACAP, Zahra and George (2002: 186) define it as 'a set of organizational routines and processes by which firms acquire, assimilate, transform and exploit knowledge to produce a dynamic organizational capability'.

ACAP may thus provide a suitable starting point for trying to understand why organisations differ in this capability and how this capability can be purposefully improved by their management.

ACAP has two components. The first consists of processes aimed at accessing and assimilating external knowledge. This is seen by Zahra and George (2002: 189) as comprising the two sub-processes of acquisition (a firm's capability to single out and to access externally generated knowledge considered relevant to its purposes), and assimilation (a firm's capability to analyse, process, interpret, and understand knowledge acquired from external sources). Together, these two dimensions constitute what Zahra and George (2002) label Potential Absorptive Capacity (PACAP).

Clearly, PACAP is crucial in firm-level entrepreneurship. Organisations need prior related knowledge to assimilate and use new knowledge. Therefore, a firm's ability to recognise the value of new external knowledge in developing innovative business ideas will be significantly shaped by its available existing knowledge. New, externally accessed knowledge is therefore the building block of opportunity recognition. As a result, any organisational arrangement aimed at improving a firm's access to and assimilation of external knowledge will significantly improve its prospects of successfully identifying new and unexplored entrepreneurial opportunities.

The second component of ACAP embodies processes aimed at transforming and exploiting accessed external knowledge. Transformation of knowledge refers to 'a firm's capability to develop and refine the routines that facilitate combining existing knowledge and the newly acquired and assimilated knowledge' (Zahra and George, 2002: 190). In turn, knowledge exploitation refers to a firm's capability 'to refine, extend, and leverage existing competencies or to create new ones by incorporating acquired and transformed knowledge into its operations' (Zahra and George, 2002: 190). Together, transformation and exploitation constitute what Zahra and George (2002) label Realised Absorptive Capacity (RACAP).

RACAP – which is responsible for knowledge transformation and exploitation processes – is at the core of firm-level entrepreneurship. Transformation involves adding, deleting or reinterpreting existing knowledge, in order to yield novel insights; a process, which is frequently referred to as bisociation (Koestler, 1966). RACAP shapes the entrepreneurial mindset (McGrath and MacMillan, 1992) and fosters entrepreneurial action (Smith and DeGregorio, 2002).

4.   Firm-level entrepreneurship as a framework of analysis

F. G. Alberti and S. Sciascia

This chapter aims at developing a framework of analysis for firm-level entrepreneurship, to be subsequently adopted in the rest of the book in order to interpret the entrepreneurial growth of district firms. On the basis of previous studies on entrepreneurship, we present a set of areas of inquiry addressed to the analysis of entrepreneurial growth in industrial districts. The main determinants of firm-level entrepreneurship will be identified within several domains that can explain the phenomenon.

4.1.   DIRECTIONS OF FIRM-LEVEL ENTREPRENEURSHIP

Firm-level entrepreneurship occurs when an entrepreneurial opportunity is recognised and exploited within an existing company (Morris and Kuratko, 2002). Recent theorising within the field of entrepreneurship has increasingly revolved around the concept of entrepreneurial opportunity. Entrepreneurial opportunities can be defined as those situations in which new products, services, raw materials, and organising methods can be introduced and sold at greater than their cost of production (Casson, 1982; Schumpeter, 1934; Shane and Venkataraman, 2000; Venkataraman, 1997).

As shown in Figure 4.1, there are three main directions of firm-level entrepreneurship. They are named on the basis of the nature of the entrepreneurial opportunity identified and exploited:

1.   the introduction of a new product or service;
2.   the adoption of new processes (in terms of purchasing, production, selling or organising);
3.   the entrance in a new market.

We underline that firm-level entrepreneurship can be represented by more than one of the above listed points. This means that, for example, a company can be entrepreneurial by introducing a new product without changing its markets and its processes. At the same time, a company can be entrepreneurial by introducing a new product and, parallel to this, entering new markets and/or adopting new processes. In other words, corporate entrepreneurship can be reached following one or more directions.

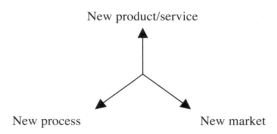

New product/service

New process   New market

Source: personal elaboration

Figure 4.1 Directions of firm-level entrepreneurship

Moreover, the newness of each of the above-mentioned objects (product, technology, market, raw materials) refers to the company, not to the market (Sathe, 2003). Innovation could be part of firm-level entrepreneurship, but it is not a necessary condition. Innovativeness, as well as proactiveness and risk-taking, is a variable for measuring the degree of entrepreneurship (Morris and Kuratko, 2002). Some entrepreneurial events can be so disruptive as to change even the organisation of an entire industry; these are the events with the highest level of entrepreneurship.

Firm-level entrepreneurship can be defined as such when it changes the business model of a company, meaning the way of interfacing with the environment (Coda, 1988), at both competitive and social level. This means that a change within a company can be considered entrepreneurial only if it affects a firm strategy, not just its operations.

In some cases firm-level entrepreneurship consists simply in a strategic renewal of the company. In others it can consist in the creation of a new organisational unit, with different possible levels of control by the parent company (Sharma and Chrisman, 1999).

As stated before, firm-level entrepreneurship occurs when an entrepreneurial opportunity is recognised and exploited. Building on the tradition of Austrian economics (for example, Hayek, 1945; Kirzner, 1973), entrepreneurial opportunities are seen as existing because different economic agents have different beliefs about the relative value of resources, given the potential to transform them into a different state. In turn, these different beliefs depend on asymmetries of information available to economic agents, and on their different abilities to recognise the value of new information, assimilate it and apply it to the entrepreneurial process. Resources, knowledge and abilities are therefore at the basis of the opportunity recognition and exploitation, at both individual and organisational level. The following sections are dedicated to these concepts, which can be considered as determinants of firm-level entrepreneurship.

4.2. A RESOURCE- AND KNOWLEDGE-BASED APPROACH TO FIRM-LEVEL ENTREPRENEURSHIP

The determinants of firm-level entrepreneurship are classified and represented in Figure 4.2, and subsequently reviewed in the remainder of the present section. The models represent a broad initial framework to guide research activities. Determinants of firm-level entrepreneurship are classified as follows.

1. Sources of opportunities.
2. Resources and competencies, classified in tangible resources, human capital and intellectual capital.
3. Organisational mechanisms of resources and competencies' acquisition and recombination.

This classification reflects the theoretical perspective adopted; following the most recent approach to entrepreneurship we adopt a resource and knowledge perspective of firm-level entrepreneurship (Alvarez and Barney, 2002; Kazanjian et al., 2002).

The resource-based view suggests that firms can be seen as bundles of heterogeneously distributed resources; it therefore holds that a firm can obtain economic rents from the stock of resources it has, and from the ability to actively exploit them in different business settings, instead of passively submitting to environmental pressures (Barney, 1986; Eisenhardt and Martin, 2000; McGrath and MacMillan, 2000; Wernerfelt, 1984).

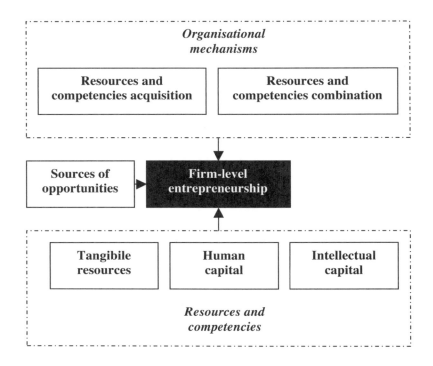

Source: personal elaboration

Figure 4.2 Determinants of firm-level entrepreneurship

The resource-based view of the firm has then witnessed a shift in its focus. Recent works (for example, Amit and Schoemaker, 1993; Iansiti and Clark, 1994; Grant 1996; Teece et al., 1997; Galunic and Rodan, 1998; Helfat, 1997) have focused attention on how resources may be internally generated and used by firms, usually stressing the role of resource re-combinations in determining strategic innovation. Hence, innovation 'consists to a substantial extent of re-combinations of conceptual and physical materials that were previously in existence' (Nelson and Winter, 1982: 130). Therefore, the resource-based view has assumed a more dynamic turn, from which the dynamic capability approach emerged. According to established conceptualisations, dynamic capabilities can be seen as the firm's ability to integrate, build, and reconfigure internal and external knowledge and competencies to address rapidly changing environments (Teece et al. 1997). More concretely, dynamic capabilities are organisational and strategic routines by which managers alter their resource base to generate innovative strategies. Hence, they allow an organisation to access and re-combine other resources into new sources of competitive advantage (Eisenhardt and Martin, 2000).

Clearly, the resource-based view of the firm, including the dynamic capability approach, is evolving in the direction of seeing knowledge as the major determinant of resource and competence re-combinations and, therefore, of firm growth and performance (Teece et al., 1997; Galunic and Rodan, 1998). From this point of view, the perspective benefits from recent developments of the knowledge-based view of the firm (see for example, Kogut and Zander, 1996; Nelson and Winter, 1982; Spender, 1996), which considers firms as entities characterised by knowledge and competencies. Already, according to Penrose, what drives the recognition of new potential uses of existing resources, that is, new services, is knowledge: 'The possibilities of using services change with changes in knowledge. More services become available, previously unused services become employed and employed services become unused as knowledge increases about the physical characteristics of resources, about ways of using them, or about products it would be profitable to use them for' (Penrose, 1959: 76). Hence, knowledge can be considered as the major determinant of resource re-combinations and growth.

All these reflections explain how the resource and knowledge approach could be a valuable framework for understanding firm-level entrepreneurship. This idea is much more solid if we consider that even in entrepreneurship literature there seems to be agreement on the fact that the pursuing of opportunities consists in combining resources in innovative ways (Stevenson and Jarrillo, 1990). This idea, discussed at the end of the previous chapter, can be traced back to Schumpeter, who defined entrepreneurial innovation as the carrying out of new combinations (1934).

4.3. SOURCES OF OPPORTUNITIES

Firm-level entrepreneurship cannot occur if there is no opportunity to exploit. According to Drucker (1985) sources of opportunities can be classified into two groups: sources existing within a company or industry and sources residing outside the company, in its social and intellectual environment. As shown in Figure 4.3, the former are unexpected occurrences, incongruities, process needs and industry changes. The latter are demographic changes, changes in perceptions and new knowledge.

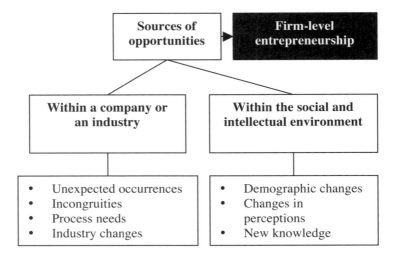

Source: personal elaboration

Figure 4.3 Sources of opportunities

Unexpected successes and failures are productive sources of opportunities. Companies tend to treat the unexpected as a problem, as can be read in corporate reports; what you do not expect is perceived as leading the company out of control. Nevertheless, some innovations and strategic renewals start from recognising opportunities from unexpected events. Incongruities are dissonances between what is and what everybody assumes it to be. They can exist between economic realities, or between expectations and results. When they lie within the logic or rhythm of a process, they can be called process needs. Incongruities and process needs create windows of opportunities, so that incongruities disappear and process needs are satisfied.

Industry changes are situations occurring again and again in the current scenario, because of markets' quantitative and qualitative changes, regulatory changes, globalisation and ICT developments. These changes offer the opportunity to develop new products, markets and processes. Demographic changes are the most reliable sources of opportunities. In the current scenario people change frequently and intensively in numbers, age distribution, education, occupation and geographical location. Often things do not change, but the perception that people have about things do change. These changes are faster and determine changes in customer needs, processes and even let incongruities emerge. Last but not least, new knowledge is the source of the most known entrepreneurial opportunities. Innovations arising from new knowledge need longer lead time and carry higher risk. Usually, they need the integration of different kinds of knowledge and this makes them more difficult to implement.

4.4. RESOURCES AND COMPETENCIES

Resources and competencies can be classified into three groups: human capital, intellectual capital and tangible capital. The first group refers to resources and competencies at individual level, mainly referring to knowledge-based resources; that is, information and capabilities (see Figure 4.4). The second and the third groups refer to resources and competencies at organisational level, referring to both physical and knowledge-based resources (see Figure 4.5).

4.4.1. Human Capital: Knowledge and Capabilities of Individuals

With the term 'human capital' we refer to the information and capabilities of those people working in the company, from the owner to the employees. Thus, we refer not only to the number of people working, but mainly to their quality. Knowledge and capabilities of organisational members affect the possibility of firm-level entrepreneurship occurring. On the one hand, opportunity identification and exploitation are influenced by prior individual knowledge; on the other, they are influenced by the capabilities of the individual.

As a matter of fact, individuals recognise opportunities related to information they already possess. To recognise an entrepreneurial opportunity, an individual needs prior knowledge that is complementary to newly accessed knowledge, which triggers an entrepreneurial conjecture (Shane and Venkataraman, 2000: 222). Prior knowledge derives from working experience, personal experience and observation, social ties and even hobbies (Shane, 2003). As discussed in Chapter 3 the discovery of entrepreneurial opportunities is related to the possession of three types of prior knowledge: knowledge about markets, knowledge about how to serve markets and knowledge of customer problems (Shane, 2000).

Individuals recognise and exploit entrepreneurial opportunities also on the basis of their capabilities, mainly at cognitive level. Studies by Barron and Harrington (1981) and Amabile (1988) show how individuals who are more able to recognise and exploit entrepreneurial opportunities are characterised by energy, need for autonomy, intuition, curiosity and richness in interests. According to Basadur et al. (1990) they are skilled in problem finding and problem solving, keen to generate various possible solutions and to implement at least one of them. Baron (2000) found that they tend to act instead of thinking, they are focused on their objective with no counterfactual thinking and overcome the failures more easily then others. Generally speaking, they see opportunities even where other persons just see threats (Sarasvathy et al., 1998). Beside cognitive capabilities, individual capabilities related to business functions (marketing, production, purchasing, finance and so on) may help in the exploitation of entrepreneurial opportunities.

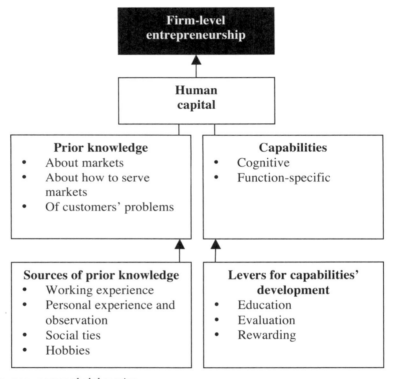

Source: personal elaboration

Figure 4.4 Resources and competencies at individual level in firm-level
         entrepreneurship

The hiring of people with a large knowledge base and well-developed cognitive capabilities oriented towards entrepreneurship is a lever to adopt for enhancing firm-level entrepreneurship. Education towards entrepreneurship can be fruitful in this sense (Alberti et al. 2005). Evaluation and reward systems are organisational levers used to promote firm-level entrepreneurship through the development of human capital. A policy of evaluating and rewarding employees in proportion to the recognition and development of entrepreneurial opportunities, through appropriate bonuses or personal equity stakes, is compliant with the will to foster entrepreneurial orientation within an organisation (Wall, 2005). Rewarding people for performance rather than responsibility or tasks induces them to adopt a long-term perspective in action (Stevenson and Gumpert, 1985), where entrepreneurship has its own domain. The afore-mentioned Figure 4.4 summarises this discussion on the role of human capital in firm-level entrepreneurship.

4.4.2. Intellectual Capital: Knowledge and Capabilities at Organisational Level

Already according to Penrose (1959), what drives the recognition of new potential uses of existing resources and their innovative recombination for growth is knowledge. As well as individuals, organisations have their own knowledge base, that is commonly labelled as 'intellectual capital' (Nahapiet and Ghoshal, 1998). Although some scholars deny the possibility of an organisation having a knowledge base that is conceptually distinct from the information of its members (Simon, 1991), the presence of collective knowledge in organisations has been empirically proved (Weick and Roberts, 1993). Intellectual capital is more than the aggregation of the human capital of the individuals; it is a result of the interplay of the knowledge base of all the organisational members within teams.

Know-how, on the other hand, is the skill or expertise that allows an organisation to do something efficiently (Von Hippel, 1988). It refers to the ability to conduct an activity, utilising and organising available resources. As well as individuals, organisations are able to carry on different activities, and these abilities are called competencies or capabilities (Kogut and Zander, 1992). Organisational capabilities that are at the core of the organisational success are generally called core competencies (Prahalad and Hamel, 1990). Competencies can be function specific (for example, marketing, production) or cross-functional, and may be fundamental in the exploitation of entrepreneurial opportunities.

4.4.3. Tangible Capital

Undoubtly, material resources, such as physical and financial ones, are necessary for firm-level entrepreneurship to occur. More precisely, they are necessary for exploiting entrepreneurial opportunities, not for identifying them. This implies that those contexts characterised by the availability of these resources are more likely to foster firm-level entrepreneurship.

This position is in line with the resource-based view. This strategic perspective suggests that firms can be seen as heterogeneously distributed bundles of resources; therefore it holds that a firm can obtain economic rents from the stock of resources it has, and from the ability to actively exploit them in different business settings, instead of passively submitting to environmental pressures.

Entrepreneurial postures are resource-consuming (Shane, 2003), therefore an organisation's entrepreneurial capacity will be, to some extent, limited by its resource base. With specific reference to tangible resources, growth through entrepreneurship needs financial resources, in order to make investments, and physical resources, to be recombined and to be further exploited. The afore-mentioned Figure 4.5 summarises the role of organisational level resources and competencies (intellectual capital and tangible resources) in firm-level entrepreneurship.

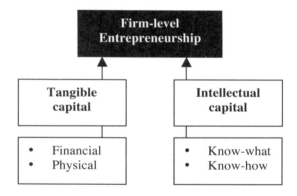

Source: personal elaboration

*Figure 4.5 Resources and competencies at organisational level in firm-level
      entrepreneurship*

4.5. ORGANISATIONAL MECHANISMS OF RESOURCES AND COMPETENCIES ACQUISITION

As mentioned in Chapter 3, absorptive capacity (ACAP) is the organisational capability referring to the acquisition of external knowledge and its combination with the existing knowledge base. These processes are at the core of firm-level entrepreneurship. In this section the organisational mechanisms that enable potential absorptive capacity are discussed. The next section is devoted to those mechanisms that enhance realised absorptive capacity.

There are several mechanisms for acquiring external resources and competencies in organisations; they are represented and synthesised in Figure 4.6. First of all, since organisational knowledge comes from the interplay among individual knowledge bases, the acquisition of external knowledge can be achieved by hiring knowledgeable personnel from other organisations, or training them adequately.

Organisations can learn from their competitors. This can be done at both product and process level, using mechanisms such as reverse engineering and benchmarking (Mansfield, 1985). In this sense, industry specific journals and participation at industry fairs can be helpful (Appleyard, 1996).

Organisations often acquire knowledge from suppliers and customers; the interplay with commercial interlocutors lead them to get new information and often to the learning of new techniques and processes (Von Hippel, 1988). More generally speaking, inter-organisational relationships can represent mechanisms for resources and competencies acquisition when alliances and networks as well as joint-ventures and acquisitions can guarantee access to information and capabilities that in turn can be useful for opportunity recognition and exploitation. An increase in the number of contacts an organisation has with the environment, coupled with an increase in the intensity and frequency of such contacts, results in an improvement of organisational members' social capital. Social capital can be defined as the ability of actors to secure benefits by virtue of membership in social networks (Portes, 1998). Social capital facilitates the acquisition of resources and competencies by promoting a constant flow of information from diverse sources (Blyler and Coff, 2003), with positive effects on opportunity recognition. Coleman (1988) suggests that social relations reduce the amount of time and investment required to gather information, and Burt (1992) argues that such a benefit increases as the social network of an organisation increases. Frequent, various and intensive contacts with customers, research and development centres, partners, suppliers permit companies to increase the understanding of their market thus raising the likelihood of anticipating nascent market needs.

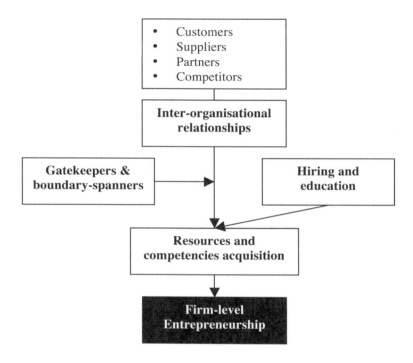

Source: personal elaboration

Figure 4.6 Organisational mechanisms enabling resources and competencies acquisition

Knowledge acquisition will be favoured when the relationships are characterised by high levels of trust, cooperation, frequency of contacts, access to documents and data, frequency of personnel transfer, geographical proximity and similarity among organisations (Argote, 1999). Of course, the transfer of explicit, codified knowledge will be easier than the transfer of tacit, non-codified knowledge. We underline that the role of networks in firm-level entrepreneurship goes beyond the possibility to acquire knowledge; even tangible capital, needed for opportunity exploitation, can be more easily accessible if the company is part of a network.

The presence of such arrangements as 'Gatekeeping' or 'boundary-spanning' roles facilitate the acquisition of knowledge. They consist of individuals standing at the interface between the firm and its environment, facilitating the acquisition of valuable information and its transfer into a form understandable to the firm (Allen, 1977; Tushman, 1977). Their relevance in facilitating knowledge flows is contingent upon the extent to which shared knowledge within the organisation differs from external knowledge considered relevant to the opportunity recognition process. Whenever such difference is high, gatekeepers and boundary-spanners are expected to play a central role in the transfer of knowledge from external sources. On the contrary, when this difference is limited, organisational actors will be able to autonomously assess the content and significance of external information to the innovative process (Cohen and Levinthal, 1990).

4.6. ORGANISATIONAL MECHANISMS OF RESOURCES AND COMPETENCIES COMBINATION

If the heart of entrepreneurship lies in the capacity to combine resources and competencies in new ways, the potential of entrepreneurship occurring within a company resides in the capability of the firm to combine different pieces of information and capabilities in new schemas. Such a combination process is often known as 'creative problem solving'.

Entrepreneurial companies adopt, intentionally or not, organisational routines to exploit their knowledge base for new uses. These routines consist first of all of recalling existing pieces of knowledge, already created or acquired and then assimilated. Then, the information related to existing ends-means relationships is applied to different means or different ends. Technologies, components and solutions applied in the past are recognised to be potentially adopted in different contexts. This cognitive process is called 'analogical thinking' (Neustadt and May, 1986).

Although it occurs in individuals, it is more likely to be successfully carried out within companies. As a matter of fact, creative processes through analogical thinking need high levels of familiarity with the knowledge to be recombined, several types of knowledge sources and a deep awareness of a company's needs. It is hard for a single person to be extremely familiar with several sources of knowledge, at the same time as being completely aware of company's needs. For this reason these processes are more likely to occur within companies where team-work is promoted and adopted.

Organisational mechanisms of resources and competencies combination can be present at the functional level, meaning within and across functions, as well as at strategic level, depending on the features of strategic processes. All the organisational mechanisms are represented and synthesised in Figure 4.7.

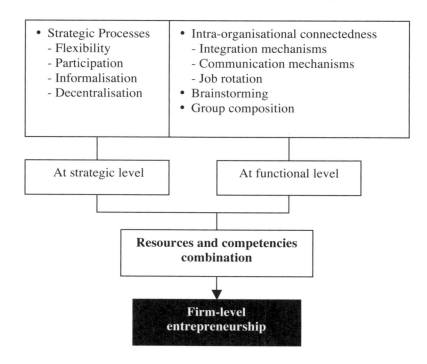

Source: personal elaboration

Figure 4.7 Organisational mechanisms enabling resources and competencies combination

4.6.1. Organisational Mechanisms at Functional Level

In order to maximise the capacity to re-combine knowledge, there is a need to share knowledge among individuals. Intense intra-organisational relationships among organisational actors permit organisational members to share and effectively combine different sources of knowledge for the exploitation of opportunities (Jaworski and Kholi, 1993). Social interactions among different business units blur the boundaries of those units and stimulate the formation of common interests, understandings, view-points and orientations, hence increasing the opportunity to combine knowledge (Tsai and Ghoshal, 1998). 'Intra-organizational connectedness' is the label that can be used for referring to the presence of intense intra-organisational relationships (Jansen et al., 2005). The development of a dense network of internal relationships fosters trust, cooperation and encourages communication, reducing the likelihood of conflicts related to the implementation of decisions (Rindfleisch and Moorman, 2001). Building a dense network of relationships between individuals also leads to the congruence of values and beliefs, which foster commitment to exploiting knowledge and opportunities (Adler and Kwon, 2002).

Thus, it can be said that entrepreneurial companies are those that favour knowledge sharing: organisations are more likely to develop entrepreneurship when a systematic collaboration among all organisational members is promoted. The more people collaborate, the more knowledge can be shared and re-combined. Such a situation is typical when a company is small and young (Mintzberg, 1973) and requires the adoption of specific mechanisms when the organisation has grown. Collaboration for knowledge sharing and re-combination should be promoted both at managerial and technical level. This could be done by organising frequent meetings in which division managers share their experiences, problems, solutions, with specific interest given to those situations in which they introduced something new (Drucker, 1985). Personal and more open communication increases the richness of those communication channels that facilitate knowledge sharing and combination (Gupta and Govindarajan, 2000). Discussion and exchange of viewpoints reduce information equivocality and favour mutual understanding in decision-making processes.

Intra-organisational connectedness can be enhanced by integration mechanisms that facilitate the necessary knowledge exchange (Kanter, 1985) and generate support for entrepreneurial projects from different positions in the firm (Zahra, 1991). Integration can be carried out both horizontally (across functions) and vertically (across hierarchical levels). Among integration mechanisms we mention task forces, project teams, liaison personnel and the so-called 'information providers', meaning those managers responsible for administering information from a central knowledge repository to organisational subunits (Lenox and King, 2004). Product managers and brand managers can be considered integration mechanisms as well (Daft and Lengel, 1986). Their presence can facilitate knowledge sharing, since they are present in lateral forms of communication that improve knowledge flows across lines of authority and functional boundaries (Jansen et al., 2005). They contribute to overcoming differences in interpreting issues and favour mutual understanding among individuals, hence reducing the level of information equivocality (Daft and Lengel, 1986). Integration mechanisms regulate mutual adjustments between individuals, increasing the possibility of integrating diverse knowledge components. They are beneficial in supporting individuals in rethinking company products, services and activities and subsequently revisiting the ways in which their components are integrated (Henderson and Cockburn, 1994).

Similarly to integration systems, communication systems enhance entrepreneurship, given that they favour knowledge sharing for opportunity recognition and for overcoming the problems related to its exploitation. Zahra (1991) and Miller (1983) found empirical support for the positive relation between well-developed communication systems and firm-level entrepreneurship. Communication systems help employees to scan more effectively for opportunities that increase company value, making the whole organisation more adaptive (Miller, 1983).

Another way to increase the intra-organisational connectedness is job rotation; it develops those organisational contacts that build a coalition needed for knowledge transformation and opportunity exploitation (Mumford, 2000).

Beside the intra-organisational connectedness, the capability to combine knowledge in new ways can be increased by the adoption of techniques as 'brainstorming' at functional level (Osborn, 1957). It consists of encouraging group members to produce as many ideas as they can, avoiding reciprocal criticism and favouring the mutual development of ideas.

Finally, group composition has been studied as a factor affecting the capability to combine knowledge in new ways. Organisational actors characterised by different knowledge endowments seem most beneficial in creative tasks. Previous studies (for example, Eisenhardt and Tabrizi, 1995; Moorman and Miner, 1997) suggest that whenever there is uncertainty about the external repositories of knowledge from which useful information may emerge – which is almost always the case in firm-level entrepreneurship – a varied knowledge base of organisational actors increases the prospect that acquired information will relate to existing internal knowledge (Simon, 1985), and will hence facilitate innovative processes by enabling actors to build novel associations and linkages (Cohen and Levinthal, 1990; Hargadon and Sutton, 1997). Organisations can therefore deliberately improve the odds of recognising novel opportunities through recruitment policies oriented to hiring people with different backgrounds, work experiences, education and cultural origins.

4.6.2. Organisational Mechanisms at Strategic Level

By strategic processes we mean all those practises related to strategic management, from planning to control. They act as mechanisms of resources and competencies combination as well, thus being responsible of realised absorptive capacity and consequent entrepreneurship.

According to Normann (1977), there are two main perspectives in strategy making: the objective perspective and the process one. The first leads to strategic plans generated through formalised processes, implemented only after their completion. The latter leads instead to strategic visions, long-term plans, not completely extensive and detailed, to be gradually implemented over time since they can be changed. They are generated in less formalised ways. The process perspective is expected to be more suitable for identifying and exploiting entrepreneurial opportunities. According to Corbetta (1990), entrepreneurial companies develop strategic plans, but they are long-term oriented; a large base of individuals is involved in strategy formation; the strategic system is strictly linked to other systems such as control and information systems and it is submitted to continuous modifications. In other words, strategic planning should be flexible, participative and informal.

It has been found that low levels of centralisation are correlated with firm-level entrepreneurship (Jennings and Lumpkin, 1989), meaning that high involvement of employees in decision-making makes the companies more entrepreneurial (Barringer and Bluedorn 1999). This can be explained by two arguments; it is decentralisation that allows the most knowledgeable people to help the firm to innovate (Miller, 1983); and it is dispersed power that enables the existence of a large variety of innovation supporting coalitions (Jennings and Lumpkin, 1989).

Entrepreneurship is enhanced within firms by low levels of formalisation in strategic planning. If people within the organisation feel more free to choose how to go about solving problems, then experimentation and novel ideas are more likely to emerge. Low formalisation permits the company to involve employees in the planning process, avoiding good ideas being overlooked (Burgelman, 1983). Moreover the absence of formal constraints allows people to compare their different viewpoints. Innovation is more likely to appear in contexts like this (Dutton and Duncan, 1987).

Barringer and Bluedorn (1999) argue that corporate entrepreneurship requires the development of strategic control practices, but entrepreneurial activities cannot be conducted within a context based on command; they require control systems based on mutual adjustment, which in turn calls for overlapping responsibilities (Kanter, 1985). Strategic control systems should be as flexible as the planning system. Discretion is allowed, budget deviations are more tolerated and success measures include both financial and non-financial indicators (Morris and Kuratko, 2002).

4.7. CONCLUSIONS

As suggested in Chapter 1, firm growth – represented by either the introduction of new economic activities or the quality of the discovery and exploitation of opportunities for such activities – can be interpreted through a firm-level entrepreneurship approach. Hence, growth is seen as a reflection of the firm's entrepreneurship (Davidsson et al., 2002).

Along these lines, this chapter has proposed a framework derived from the literature on firm-level entrepreneurship for studying this phenomenon. Drawing from a resource- and knowledge-based approach, we have presented a set of determinants of firm-level entrepreneurship, which represent areas of inquiry to be addressed in the analysis of entrepreneurial growth in industrial districts. Namely, we suggest focusing on subsequent case analyses: the sources of entrepreneurial opportunities (new products, new markets or new processes); the resources and competencies a firm can rely on (tangible resources, human capital and intellectual capital); and the organisational mechanisms devoted to resource and competence acquisition and combination.

In the rest of the book, we will rely upon the framework of analysis proposed here to act as the conceptual lenses to be used in exploring the entrepreneurial growth of four district firms.

PART TWO

Four Italian Cases

5. Alessi

F. G. Alberti

This chapter presents the case study of Alessi, a company based in the houseware district of Verbano-Cusio-Ossola that specialises in the manufacture of household articles, including design-based articles and objects with a high symbolic value. The aim of this chapter is to describe the entrepreneurial growth process of the firm, setting it within the context of the sector and the industrial district and presenting the economic–financial consequences of this growth. The chapter is divided into four parts: the background of the houseware sector and its development; a focus on the history and trends in the houseware district of Verbano-Cusio-Ossola, which accounts for one third of the whole Italian sector; the milestones in the history of Alessi, the chief player in the district; a closer look at Alessi's growth and performance.

5.1. THE HOUSEWARE INDUSTRY

5.1.1. The Market and Industry at World Level

The houseware industry is very varied both in terms of products and of materials and technology used. As far as materials are concerned houseware can be divided into articles made in metal (pots, cutlery and knives), in plastic, ceramic or china and those made of glass. In terms of products, the houseware industry is generally divided into tableware, kitchenware and other household articles. The tableware sector can be broken down into three product categories; dinnerware (plates, bowls, cups, saucers, dishes), glassware (glasses, stemware and barware of glass and crystal); flatware (cutlery, knives and other eating utensils); and kitchenware (cookware, cleaning and storage utensils and ovenware). Thus, kitchenware products include a range of kitchen utensils used for cooking and various other purposes. Other household articles include in particular small domestic appliances: kitchen appliances (blender, mixer, microwave oven, coffee machine, toaster, and so on; personal-care products (electric toothbrush, hairdryer, shaker, and so on) and household appliances (humidifier, iron, vacuum cleaner, and so on).

The sector is dominated by well-known European brands, while the market tends to be fragmented, with some leaders in specific market segments. Nevertheless the number of mergers, acquisitions and joint ventures with American companies is growing and this is leading to some consolidation within the sector.

On an international scale there is growing competition from low labour cost countries (China in first place), who can manufacture household goods of an inferior quality but sufficiently valid to take a large share of the market away from western firms. Taking the Far East as an example; over the last 50 years several countries have in turn subjected the traditional European manufacturers to increasingly cut-throat competition, thanks to the opening up of the international market and low labour costs. Hong Kong (1950–70), Japan (1980–90), South Korea (1990s) and China (1995 to now) have been the main competitors among the emerging economies in that area of the world. Today China is the main competitor in the houseware sector, while the European countries are going through a stagnation phase or even slight recession in terms of output and turnover as well as levels of employment and number of firms. The market in western countries is substantially saturated and purchases tend to be made to substitute products rather than add new ones to those already acquired. There are some positive signs from the entry into the world market of new purchasers (from Eastern Europe) and market expansion and increasing loyalty in other countries (USA). Global demand in the sector was more or less static in 2006 (+0.2 per cent). Sales in the pots, pans and tableware segments showed a slightly positive trend except for aluminium pans, which fell slightly after having grown over recent years. Sales of pressure cookers have recovered, while in cutlery and knives only the cutlery segment had positive results with the other segments falling slightly or remaining stable. Forecasts for 2007 indicated a general stability in sales with further contraction in cutlery and knives.

Italy continues to occupy an important position in the global market thanks to high quality, know-how, design and product innovation with products that are often radical inventions. The strong points are those that have always marked 'Made in Italy' production: creativity combined with style and excellent quality. Weak points remain the high labour costs and the lack of raw materials.

5.1.2. Trends in the Italian Industry

In Italy metal household articles account for 60.4 per cent of turnover, while 39.5 per cent comes from plastic household goods. Almost 5000 people are employed in the metal houseware sector, which today has an annual turnover of almost 1 billion euros with a consolidated export share of 60 per cent. Italy is the biggest producer of metal houseware, followed by Germany (€286 million) and France (€253 million). Some of the most important and best-known companies with the 'Made in Italy' label operate in this sector, mainly in the manufacture of six types of article: coffee makers, pots and pans, knives, cutlery, china and gift articles for the home.

Table 5.1 The Italian houseware industry 2001–2006

Variables	2001	2002	2003	2004	2005	2006
Production (€M)	954	925	865	880	862	890
Exports (€M)	575	535	475	500	500	520
Investment (€M)	n.a.	n.a.	10	10	9,5	9,5
Use of plant capacity	n.a.	n.a.	73%	75%	72%	72%
Number of employees	6 000	5 700	5 500	5 300	5 000	4 800
Producer prices	n.a.	n.a.	+1,0%	+3,0%	0%	+5%

Notes: The above figures refer to the following products: cutlery, knives, pots and pans, coffee makers and metal dishes (Ateco codes 28.61- 28.75.1).

Source: based on ISTAT data

As reported by FIAC (Italian Federation of Houseware Manufacturers), since the beginning of the 2000s the economic results in the metal household article sector have offered little satisfaction to the houseware manufacturers, confirming the stagnant to downwards trend in the sector. In fact, despite the total sector growth of 54 per cent between 1996 and 2004, the period 2004–2008 has seen the positive trend diminish with revenue almost stable at the 2002 level and a continuing decrease in operating results.

As Table 5.1 shows, between 2001 and 2002 production fell by 3 per cent, employment by 5 per cent and exports by 7 per cent. The only positive result was the increase in demand for non-stick pans, while the sector for stainless steel articles, such as cutlery and pots and pans, was stagnant. In 2003 activity in the sector fell by about 8 per cent. Domestic demand was negative, as were exports, penalised by the strengthening of the euro against the dollar and the growing competition from Asian manufacturers. Employment levels fell by 3.5 per cent. In 2004 production saw a slight increase of 1.7 per cent in terms of value compared to the previous year, following three negative years. This was the effect of increased sales in the foreign markets, which grew by 5.3 per cent. The revaluation of the euro against the dollar, however, continued to penalise Italian companies both in terms of exports towards the dollar area and of purchase of raw materials, the increase in price of which was partially responsible for the increase in producer prices of approximately 3 per cent. Meanwhile, competition from Asian manufacturers on the international market was becoming tougher. Employment in the sector fell by 3.6 per cent, while investment remained stationary. According to FIAC data, in terms of production, 2005 saw a decrease (-2 per cent) compared to 2004, while there was an increase of 3.2 per cent in 2006, due to strong growth, sustained by a constant demand for technological innovation on the part of the consumer. Of the average total production of approximately €870 million over the last three years, 14 per cent is destined to the hotel and catering sector, while 86 per cent to household use.

Table 5.2 International trade in houseware by geographical area (2005)

	exports	imports	balance
EU25	302 058 029	39 716 004	262 342 025
France	57 122 344	8 113 240	49 009 104
Germany	84 409 035	17 341 152	67 067 883
UK	17 789 341	1 430 653	16 358 688
Spain	37 859 727	4 851 806	33 007 921
Africa	10 894 095	1 230 819	9 663 276
North America	85 181 535	398 846	84 782 689
USA	79 296 424	396 959	78 899 465
Central and South America	9 612 994	247 127	9 365 867
Asia	30 808 389	70 890 043	-40 081 654
India	486 144	11 476 321	-10 990 177
China	1 136 329	51 446 075	-50 309 746
Australia & Oceania	6 097 927	15504	6 082 423

Source: personal elaboration on Coeweb data

In Italy overall employment in the sector fell by approximately 6 per cent in 2005 and 4 per cent in 2006, to below 5000 units. Investment remained stable after falling by 5 per cent during 2005. Finally average prices remained stable between 2004 and 2005 and rose 5 per cent in 2006.

5.1.3.   The Italian Houseware Industry Today

Over the last year foreign sales showed an increase of 4 per cent to stand at €520 million and continue to sustain production in the sector with a stable export share of 57–58 per cent. The main foreign markets for Italian metal household appliances (Table 5.2) are the EU (approx. 56 per cent), the rest of Europe (17 per cent), North America (16 per cent) and Asia (6 per cent). Exports are increasing to Turkey (by over 33 per cent in 2005) and to Africa (+ 25 per cent approx.) while those to India have fallen sharply (-74 per cent approx.). The North American market has lost 0.7 per cent, the EU 2.6. per cent, Asia 1.9 per cent and Oceania 2.8 per cent, confirming the general trend of a contraction in the export market of around -1.2 per cent. On the other hand the domestic market is generally stable, although there is a continuing trend towards consolidation in the sector with growing emphasis on medium to large firms.

5.1.4.   The Main Dynamics in the Industry

The metal household appliance industry is mature and characterised by falling demand. The sector is going through a period of recession caused by the competition and growth in production of the low cost countries as well as by the change in purchasing habits of the end user, represented by a reduction in spending on household articles. Average profitability in the sector has fallen to relatively low levels as a result of fierce price competition, above all in the low and medium-low segments, and to the growth in sales through promotional channels and mass distribution.

   The intense pressure of competition within the sector is due, on the one hand, to the progressive globalisation of the trade and supply channels and, on the other, to the consolidation that is typical of the sector. A succession of mergers and takeovers that have taken place over the last few years has, in fact, led to the dominance of big companies with brands that are well-known nationally and internationally. Two of the most significant takeovers in the last year were the acquisition of Aeternum – a traditional brand famous above all for its pressure cookers – by the Bialetti group (which in 2004 had already taken over Girmi, a firm that specialised in small household appliances) and that of Lagostina – leader in stainless steel pans and pressure cookers – by the French multinational Seb (which already owns the Tefal, Moulinex, Rowenta and Krups brands).

This intense internal pressure is matched by the aggressive competition on the part of Asian manufacturers, who produce low price, low quality goods which tend to disorient the purchasers. This has a particularly negative effect on the small product-oriented firms, who have not developed an adequate brand strategy to face the low cost competition.

In order to put up an effective defence against the serious threat of Asian competitors, whose production went up from €4.4 million to €41 million in just ten years from 1994–2004 (as reported by FIAC), the Italian firms in the sector must be able to count on the exclusive difference of the product and a distinctive brand identity that is well-known enough to keep others out. Thus, fundamental importance is taken on by factors such as brand image; the careful selection of distribution channels and communication strategies that are coherent with the product policies adopted; product innovation; enhancement of the production process, above all in terms of flexibility and reduction of fixed costs; logistics management, understood both as organisation of flow of incoming raw materials and/or finished products and as organisation of the finished product warehouse in order to provide optimum customer service.

In a mature sector there is little interest on the part of the purchasers who find such a vast offer that the majority of the products are rapidly considered obsolete. Today's purchasers can be divided into two categories: those who are strongly price-oriented and those who look for quality. For this reason, the manufacturers in the Italian houseware sector have moved towards making their offer more appealing by using alternative materials and exploiting innovation and design. Alessi is certainly the precursor of this trend.

Imports cover nearly half of domestic demand. The share of imports handled by the manufacturers themselves is growing, as are purchases destined for foreign mass distribution chains and wholesalers.

There has also been an increase in the cost of raw materials, such as steel, brass, nickel and silver; this increases the contractual power of suppliers and forces firms to make continuous adjustments to their price lists with an impact on profitability from sales.

As far as distribution is concerned, there has been an inversion of trend compared to recent years, when the mass distribution chains were accused of ignoring quality household articles to focus mainly on an aggressive pricing policy. The present trend is to give more space to products that are slightly different in an attempt to extend the sales of household articles beyond basic low cost products. The main distribution channels are wholesalers both in Italy (36 per cent) and abroad (49 per cent), with retail sales in second place in Italy (24 per cent) and mass distribution abroad (22 per cent).

The main firms in the sector are trying to meet retailers' needs by providing point-of-purchase materials, such as displays, leaflets, and so on, which help point-of-sale merchandising and give greater visibility to the product. The strategic importance of cooperation between the manufacturers and the main operators in mass distribution is now evident; mass distribution can be considered an innovative means to create opportunity in a sector with stable demand, such as that of household goods.

The catering sector is more dynamic, being less subject to fluctuations in the domestic market and having a much higher and more constant product replacement rate.

From what has been said so far, it is clear that the houseware sector in Italy is going through a phase of growing maturity and hostility, characterised by structural and developmental constraints, such as high costs, the development of essentially price-based forms of competition and the market entry of increasingly cut-throat new competitors. Critical success factors, thus, lie in the enhancement of skills and resources, the focus on tradition by means of historical brands with a worldwide reputation, the firm's high production and technological capacity, the presence of a solid industrial structure and, finally, the high product quality level both in terms of manufacture and design.

Given the widespread recession and the difficulty in getting out of it, our analysis so far would seem to indicate that the houseware sector has managed to maintain a relatively satisfactory level. The firms in the sector have had to face two essential problems: the desperate race to cut prices on the part of Asian competitors and the general economic situation in Italy marked by a drop in consumption. The continuing economic recession, which has lasted since 2004, has had a negative effect on the consumption of Italian families, particularly in terms of those products which are not seen as essential, such as household articles. Looking at other European markets, the situation is more worrying still inasmuch as Italy is losing competitiveness in terms of product policy, innovation and use of communication means compared to countries like France, Spain and Germany. In order to react to this situation, Italian firms have started to move towards product and process research and development and to focus on Italian quality products. Market research shows, in fact, that despite the economic recession, Italians are not willing to give up quality. Thus, the main players in the sector are moving towards excellence in the whole range of offers with a decided emphasis on design. The other threat hanging over the sector and which has caused a serious shock is represented by the arrival on the market from the 1990s onwards of low cost low quality Asian products, mainly from China. Before this the houseware sector in Italy had been principally made up of small family firms with a traditional approach to business and was extremely fragmented with

few entry barriers and low investment. The only element that guaranteed
survival was a good product system and thus a high quality offer. Most firms
were thus unprepared to face the new competition.

Initiatives were taken to move production to Eastern European countries,
which were geographically and culturally close and had a good industrial
culture. Joint ventures and more structured joint production ventures were
also undertaken with countries in the Far East. At the same time steps were
taken to globalise production by setting up production plants abroad, not just
to reduce production costs but also with a view to being present in the most
promising markets, which were accessible to the larger companies with a
consolidated image and sufficiently strong financial and organisational
structure. Today, many Italian firms rely on offshoring their production
processes, manufacturing their products in Asian factories, or implementing
price reduction strategies, cutting costs that are considered superfluous –
cutting investment in marketing and communication, for example – thereby
worsening their product offer system and reducing their competitiveness
within the sector. Other braver and more far-sighted firms have sought to
position their products in the high-quality high-price market range thus being
able to offer a top-of-the-range product. Alberto Alessi emphasises non-
standard working, small batches, stylistic innovation; a type of production
that is somewhere between craftsmanship and industry and a strong brand to
impose on the market by means of continuous investment in marketing. In
spite of the recession, some firms have managed to face up to the sector and
market situation, regaining profitability and setting off new growth cycles. A
survey carried out by the FIAC in 2005 underlines how these firms have
chosen to embark on the path of research, style and product and materials
innovation, moving away from the sector of metal household articles and
entering the wider design industry. These dynamic firms renew their product
range due to the use of new materials, innovative design and attractive
styling, emphasising the customised aspect of the offer, adapting it more and
more to customer needs. In other words the firms that have reacted better to
the crisis are those that have been able to specialise, differentiating their offer
due to a superior know-how and a strong brand. They have emphasised
continuous   product   innovation   and   have   communicated   better   with
distribution channels and the end user by means of advertising and
promotion. In short, the way in which the key players in the sector have been
able to effectively face up to and stave off the invasion of Asian products is
to remain faithful to the values that are typical of 'Made in Italy' products;
that is the ability to combine style and quality, functionality and creativity.
The distinguishing features that leading firms in the houseware sector have
exploited to face competition and to avoid the price war are, in fact, a strong

emphasis on design and innovation, starting from the roots of the culture and local tradition of the product and the strength of the brand.

5.2.   THE VERBANO-CUSIO-OSSOLA HOUSEWARE DISTRICT

5.2.1.   Origins and Specialisations

The district, which extends across the provinces of Novara, Vercelli and Verbania, is one of the best known and in many ways most fascinating of the industrial districts officially recognised by the Piedmont Regional Council in application of Law no. 317/91. On the map the Omegna, Varallo Sesia, Stresa district extends from Lake Maggiore (also called Verbano), to the lake of Orta (or Cusio) and the Ossola valley. On the boundary between two countries (Italy and Switzerland) and two regions (Piedmont and Lombardy), the Verbano-Cusio-Ossola area, from which the district takes its name, has always been at the crossroads of important ways of communication across Central-Southern Europe. Altogether there are 41 municipalities with a total of 60 000 inhabitants in an area of 975 square kilometres.

Morphologically speaking the area is not uniform, being made up of plain (20 per cent), hills (50 per cent) and mountains (30 per cent). This partly explains the lower population density (61 residents per square kilometres) compared to most other manufacturing districts. This figure is much higher in the towns, however, and at Omegna, on the banks of the lake of Orta, about 50 kilometres from Novara, population density reaches 150 inhabitants per square kilometre. Most of the manufacturing activities in the district are based in Omegna, so much so that the district is also known as the 'Omegna district'. The centre of gravity of production in the district is the Alto Cusio, north of the lake of Orta, encompassing the municipalities of Omegna, Gravellona Toce and Casale Corte Cerro, all situated on the banks of the River Toce, going upstream towards the Val d'Ossola.

This district is famous above all for the manufacture of metal kitchenware and tableware. Its influence on the local economy is shown by the fact that household articles represent 60 per cent of the exports of the metal and mechanical engineering industry in the province. There is a long tradition of the production of these articles in the Verbano-Cusio-Ossola area. Specialisation in metal household article manufacturing in the area of Omegna began with Carlo Calderoni and Baldassarre Cane. In 1851 on his return from Germany, where he had gained experience working in pewter, Calderoni started to make household articles in brass copper and tin-plated metal, going on to the production of cutlery in brass and nickel-silver. In

1853 Cane left the Strona valley and, after a period in Paris where he learned how to make soda siphons, he moved to Omegna to set up the first real workshop in the district. Initially dedicated to the working of tin, lead and brass, this workshop became an important aluminium working factory in the early 1900s, before closing down some years later. In the following decades the example of Cane and Calderoni was imitated by dozens of artisan craftsmen, some of whom had trained as skilled workers in these two factories and then set up on their own as spin-offs. In 1901 Carlo Lagostina, who had worked in Calderoni's factory, set up his own firm together with his son, who was a mechanical engineer, and about ten workers. Initially the firm manufactured iron cutlery, aimed at a lower market segment than Calderoni, but then went on to produce pans with an aluminium base, which resulted in the firm being included in the 1933 catalogue of the famous MOMA in New York. In 1919 six craftsmen set up a working cooperative, La Subalpina, which at first produced tin articles for perfumeries and hairdressers and then moved on to develop the household appliance sector with the Girmi brand. In 1918 Alfonso Bialetti set up a workshop applying the technique of aluminium die casting, which he had learned in Paris and at FIAT. In 1921 – as we will see in more detail later in the chapter – a small turning workshop was set up by the Alessi family, who also came from the Strona valley but moved to the district following the entrepreneurial initiative of Cane. Initially they worked tinplate, then moved on to brass, silver- and chrome-plated nickel silver and steel.

The development model for the district has always been based on small firms (today they represent 88 per cent of the total), alongside some medium-large companies. Unlike the traditional industrial district, a two-track structure grew up in Omegna with, on the one hand, a few large companies known all over the world and, on the other, many small firms working mainly as suppliers or sub-suppliers to the large companies.

The first modern industrial firms were born out of local craft traditions and many are still run today by the same family as the founders. Over time other metals took the place of the pewter originally used by local craftsmen to make household articles; brass, nickel silver, aluminium and finally stainless steel are the raw materials that have been used by the firms in the district over the last 150 years. The houseware district with its solid tradition in metal-working (stainless steel in particular) expanded greatly in the 1950s. The first TV commercials for Lagostina and Bialetti date from that period, as do some technological product innovations (for example, the thermoplan bases and pressure cookers). The case of Bialetti is emblematic of the development of the district in that period. The 'Moka Express' coffee maker had been introduced without success in 1935; Alfonso's son, Renato Bialetti decided to re-launch it in 1953 with a massive advertising campaign, which introduced the now famous 'moustached figure' as the brand logo. It was at this time that Carlo Alessi started to show an interest in industrial design and began to involve well-known designers from outside the company. The Subalpina cooperative reconverted to a small domestic appliance manufacturer and launched the successful 'Girmi' mixer, which became the new name of the company in 1961.

The 1970s marked the peak of growth in the VCO district; all the main firms reached their maximum employment levels in this decade. Lagostina and Bialetti had 700 employees each, Girmi had 400, Alessi with over 300 and Calderoni had 200. A few years later the sector reached maturity and the first signs of labour trouble appeared. The 1980s saw the first signs of recession. In many cases the founding families withdrew from the ownership and management of the firms and were substituted by big international groups.

The district's decline was blamed on lack of investment in innovation, the emergence of new competitors (in first place the district of Lumezzane, near Brescia) and the slowdown in market demand for steel household articles.

In the 1990s it even became difficult to define the district of household article manufacture. In fact, firms continued to diversify product and materials used, moving further and further away from the traditional production of metal household articles.

Table 5.3 Structure and performance in the district over a 10 year period (1997–2006)

	1997	2006	Δ 1997-2006
Firms	440	180	-59%
Employees	6 000	2 000	-67%
Turnover (€M)	491	300	-39%
Share of turnover represented by exports	19%	40%	+21

Source: estimate based on data from Largo Consumo and Sole 24 Ore

5.2.2. Trends in Structure and Performance

There are 1260 manufacturing firms in the VCO area (23 per cent of the total) and half of these firms manufacture metal products. Some 180 firms carry out the typical district production: metal household article manufacture. Today the houseware district provides employment for approximately 2000 people (including induced activities) and represents approximately 26.9 per cent of national production of steel pans. The total annual turnover of metal household articles is approximately 300 million euros, equal to 30 per cent of the national total. Forty per cent of turnover for the district comes from

exports, mostly to European countries and USA. Historically Germany is the
most important European purchaser, even if the share has been falling in
recent years. Most imports come from Russia and China; Chinese imports
have increased by 100 per cent every year since 2000. While production in
the sector is divided between a myriad of small firms manufacturing metal
pans and household articles, turnover for the sector is highly concentrated.
Data regarding the 30 most important Italian firms in the metal pan and
kitchenware manufacturing sector show 8 firms from the district in top
positions with a total turnover of €200 million. The first five firms in the
district account for over 70 per cent of total turnover for the sector but only
35 per cent of employment. Against this the small firms employ together just
under 1000 people (approximately 60 per cent of total employment for the
sector in the area). A summary of these figures is shown in Table 5.3. The
last ten years have seen a steady reduction in turnover as well as in the
number of employees and number of firms. Exports make up a significant
part of turnover, increasing from 19 per cent in 1998 to 40 per cent in 2007.
Moreover, the main destinations for exports are other European countries, as
is the case for the entire Italian household article sector. The result is
undoubtedly a district that is getting structurally weaker and weaker but
which has an enormous symbolic value coming from the names of the
famous firms in the area, whose products have entered everyday life as
symbols of Italian creativity and *savoir faire*.

Even the geographical distribution within the area is far from uniform; the
firms are mainly concentrated in the municipalities of Omegna (30 per cent),
Gravellona Toce (23 per cent), Casale Corte Cerro (11 per cent), Ornavasso
(6 per cent). 70 per cent of firms are therefore based in the upper Cusio, to
the north of Lake Orta, where we find the five largest firms in terms of
employees and turnover. The more one moves away from the town of
Omegna, the smaller the firms become – usually working as specialised sub-
contractors for other companies – and the less they specialise in the
houseware sector, turning instead to the production of taps and valves,
mainly in the Cusio area.

The industrial structure of VCO is typical of Italian industrial districts:
most firms comprise of artisan craftsmen.

The manufacture of household articles is the main form of production
carried out in the district; the manufacture of machine tools for their
production grew up alongside.

The supply chain involves the local network in the whole production
process. The area is historically linked to the working of stainless steel, used
in the manufacture of kitchen pots, and aluminium for coffee makers and
non-stick pans. There are thus two different production processes: cold-
forging (by deformation) and rough machining (by shaving). After working

the metal must be polished and this is sub-contracted to specialised local craftsmen, who make up the vast majority of the firms in the district.

The large firms in the district have specialised more and more in marketing functions at the expense of production, with a reduction in the number of employees and in local production. The small and micro firms, at greater risk given their lack of market power, can take advantage of the positive external effects, in terms of image and innovative capacity, of the big companies in the district. The main links between the small and large firms are through decentralised production, even if there are cases where smaller firms have imitated the larger ones and exploited their innovations.

The growth of the big manufacturers has encouraged the birth of sub-suppliers, which are often spin-offs of the big firms. This growth model fits well into the provincial socio-economic microcosm and is unanimously considered one of the district's big competitive advantages, above all because of the quality provided by the sub-suppliers, which is still vastly superior to that of the Far East and other emerging countries.

From time to time the relationship between the large and small firms is consolidated with the signing of joint ventures or acquisition of shares, with the aim of guaranteeing quality control and maintaining continuity in production. As well as phases in the actual manufacturing process, such as press-forging or drawing, the sub-suppliers often handle the final buffing and polishing. A few firms carry out highly specialised activities, such as laser stamping, tool-making, gilding details, and so on. External contractors and sub-contractors are used mainly during the manufacturing phase.

Competition from China and the Far East in general is a serious threat for the whole VCO houseware district. In the 1980s Asian manufacturing had already eroded part of the market but without causing serious difficulties to the district. The loss was compensated for by raising product quality. Since 2002, Asian competition (Chinese in particular) and counterfeiting have become the most pressing problems to deal with, while at the same time the district seems to have lost the general capacity to innovate and carry out research into processes and materials.

The offshoring of parts of the production process is another important trend, which is typical of Italian industrial districts over the last few years. This is linked to the need both to reduce costs and to enter new markets. The firms in the VCO district tend to maintain the knowledge-intensive activities and the skilled services in the local area, relocating the parts of production with low technological content, in order to keep control over the final product.

The supply chain has undergone gradual change: some medium-large companies stopped using local production capacity in favour of outsourcing first to neighbouring provinces and then overseas. In some cases the complete finished product is manufactured in low cost countries, especially in the case of articles subject to greater price competition. These changes in the supply chain have particularly affected the small firms who have seen their share of sub-contract work diminish since the 1990s. The larger companies, on the other hand, have undergone a series of mergers and acquisitions. In 2005 Lagostina was sold to SEB, a French multinational working in the sector of small household appliances, pressure cookers and non-stick pans, and who already owned the Tefal, Rowenta, Moulinex and Krups brands. In 2002 the present-day Bialetti Industrie was formed from the merger of Alfonso Bialetti & Co. with Rondine Italia, a firm from Brescia, that specialised in the manufacture of aluminium pans. Although Bialetti has changed hands, part of it still manufactures coffee makers in the VCO district. Following a long period of economic difficulty, Girmi stopped trading in 2005 and became a brand of Bialetti Industrie, who also took over CEM (a firm that produced and sold cooking utensils in non-stick aluminium with a strong brand and tradition in Turkey) and in 2006 Aeternum (a leading Italian brand in steel production). Alessi has also made changes over the years.

Different strategies have been followed by the main firms in the district; for some time Alessi has been focusing on design and product diversification rather than production, developing a strong network of suppliers in various parts of the world, including the Far East. Lagostina continues to concentrate on quality and occupies the medium-high market segment within the SEB group. Bialetti has invested in the innovation of a product-icon, the octagonal coffee maker – innovating technology, functionality and design – and alongside it has developed a wide range of non-stick aluminium and steel cooking utensils and small household appliances. Piazza Effepi has gradually moved production away from the consumer to the business segment, specialising in household articles for hotels and catering events.

5.2.3. The Main Dynamics in the District

The Omegna houseware district can boast of world-famous high-quality brands. Alessi, Lagostina, Bialetti, Girmi, Calderoni and Piazza are all brands that come from the Verbano-Cusio-Ossola district and it is due to some of these that the district has been able to make a real qualitative leap, changing in terms of structure and way of working and at the same time bringing about changes in the wider houseware sector. The Bialetti coffee maker and the Lagostina pressure cooker in particular have been able to affirm their position in the world market owing to the aesthetic value of these 'classic' articles from the sector. The biggest break with history and tradition however has been made by Alessi with the emphasis on design, gradually moving away from the manufacture of metal household goods in favour of new materials (glass, china, wood, plastic) and then expanding into the realm of furnishing accessories and then actual interior design.

The strong and weak points of the district highlight the positive district structure, which still maintains industrial and market competitiveness despite structural and developmental limitations. The strong points are the world-famous brands, the high qualitative level of production (both in terms of materials and design) and the presence of a solid industrial structure with close collaboration between the big firms and the top quality highly specialised local induced activities. The weak points are the lack of horizontal cooperation between firms (where competition rather than cooperation is the order of the day, although this is improving), the lack of a single consolidated image for the district and the fact that innovative initiatives are not uniformly taken up throughout the sector, although they are a fundamental competitive lever to guarantee survival in a mature sector.

The increasingly aggressive competition on the part of the emerging countries in the whole sector, as described above, also applies to the houseware district, raising the issue of competitive strategies and the economic situation of the sector. The phenomenon of counterfeiting is cause for alarm in the district; 40 per cent of local firms say their products and/or brands have been faked or their patents copied and only 40 per cent of these have started legal actions to protect themselves.

The key success factors lie above all in the district's ability to emphasis skills, traditions, manufacturing and technological capacity and the high quality of the products. Investment therefore becomes a number one priority in order to safeguard the specificity of the firms working on the production of the end product and belonging to the supply chain and to add value to the district. The aims are to: involve local firms in a network system; make the houseware sector more competitive at an international level and identify new markets; emphasise quality and the specificity of the production to become more competitive within the global system and face up to competition from the Far East; safeguard production (for example, from counterfeiting); and emphasise product value both in tangible (qualitative) and intangible (sustainability, innovation, design, ethics, environment) terms.

Over the last few years the main players in the district have made an effort to improve communications at a local level by bringing firms together and also closer to the local population. The involvement of workers is considered a necessary condition to guarantee high quality performance and to create a favourable context for the development of new companies. A certain number of meta-management structures have been created in the district to this end: the 'Lake Maggiore Tecnoparco' (which carries out research and provides technological support for product and materials innovation); the 'Omegna

Forum' (which promotes the image of the city and its entrepreneurial spirit, also by means of a 'History of local industry' museum); Ars.Uni.VCO (which promotes the setting up of specialisation courses for the area on the part of Italian and overseas universities); a local brand for the district 'Lago Maggiore Casalinghi' (to emphasise the culture, tradition and creativity of the area, guaranteeing the origin of production and safeguarding from possible counterfeiting); an internet portal for the district (to strengthen synergies between the firms in terms of services, business opportunities and communication); the 'Sistema Casa VCO' project (which has encouraged the search for production and trade synergies between firms in the district and similar firms in Hungary); and the energy supply consortium 'Co-Ver Energy Trading'.

5.3.   THE HISTORY OF ALESSI

The well-known firm of Alessi, based in Crusinallo di Omegna, grew up within the VCO houseware district and accounts for a quarter of the total exports from the area. The company was founded by Giovanni Alessi Anghini in 1921 and its first products were coffee pots, trays and accessories for the table. In 1938, the method of turning metal was gradually substituted by press-forging and experimentation began with stainless steel, which took the place of traditional raw materials (silver- and chrome-plated brass) after World War II. The second generation, represented by Carlo and Ettore Alessi developed the company further, emphasising the role of design and launching new products for the home (baskets, fruit bowls) and for the hotel trade. In the 1970s to 1990s Alessi diversified production further. Famous designers were invited to collaborate and the firm courageously embarked on the route of elegant and innovative design, which won it worldwide recognition. Alessi, now under the guidance of the third generation (Michele and Alberto) launched new lines of products for the kitchen and the home, which soon became cult objects, receiving many prizes (for example, 'Compasso d'Oro', ADI) and being shown at the MOMA in New York and at the Victoria and Albert Museum in London. Recently Alessi has expanded its vast network of suppliers and partners in various parts of the world and in particular in the Far East. The various phases in the history of Alessi are analysed in the following paragraphs.

5.3.1.   From 1921 to 1955: the Origins

In 1921 Giovanni Alessi Anghini, artisan entrepreneur, skilled in turning sheet metal and brass knobs, purchased a piece of land in Omegna and began the manufacture by hand of goods for the house and table, such as coffee pots and trays, in brass, nickel silver and copper. At first the production was exclusively to order for private customers. The firm was set up under the name of FAO (Fratelli Alessi Omegna); this was changed in 1924 to ALFRA (ALessi FRAtelli) and again in 1967 to Ceselleria Alessi. Since 1971 the company has traded under the name of Alessi Spa. From the start the emphasis was on quality production and from this, the Alessi name soon became known to be synonymous with high quality.

In 1928 the company moved from Omegna to larger premises in the Crusinallo area, where there was also a river to provide water power. The river still flows through the company headquarters today.

In the 1930s Carlo's eldest son, Giovanni, joined the company, following studies in industrial design in Novara. His first role within the company was as designer, before taking over the general direction from his father. Carlo Alessi was responsible for most of the products in the catalogue between the mid-1930s and 1945. Archetypes of the first era of Italian design – such as the Bombè and Cilindrica coffee makers designed by Carlo Alessi – date from this period and marked the beginning of the distinctive Alessi style, which is today recognisable in most of the production, even when products are designed by external designers.

In the 1930s Alessi also began to export products abroad and experiment with the use of stainless steel instead of the metals traditionally used in the district. During the same period the cold forging of metals was introduced to replace the traditional turning.

In the 1940s Alessi was obliged to convert part of the production of household articles into military production (stars for uniforms, mechanical parts for Savoia Marchetti aeroplanes, and so on) At this time Ettore – Carlo's younger brother – entered the company and began to make a significant contribution to improving techniques in the cold forging and pressing of metals, leading the name of Alessi to become synonymous with standards of excellence. After 1945, faced with the huge demand for brass ladles from the US army, Alessi decided to double the machinery and begin large-scale production. At this time Giovanni Alessi's 1930s intuition was confirmed and stainless steel began to take over from chromed metals and silver-plated alloys. Giovanni retired in the 1950s, leaving the running of the company to Carlo, who definitively gave up the design side of the business. The firm became a limited company and began to take on an industrial dimension; the premises were enlarged, machinery increased, mass production begun and new markets were sought abroad.

5.3.2.   From 1955 to 1970: the First Steps towards a Design-based Company

In 1955 Ettore Alessi was in charge of the technical office and decided to bring further innovation into the way of working by using external designers. In this way the design part of the activity was outsourced to independent designers, for example the architects Carlo Mazzeri, Luigi Massoni and Anselmo Vitale. Several ranges of products were designed in particular for the hotel sector, many of which are still in the catalogue today. However, the first relations with external designers were not problem-free on the management side and particularly on the technical side. In fact many brilliant original projects led to technical problems in terms of production and were abandoned. Ettore Alessi also strengthened the design team in the internal technical office, leading to the launch of some products that became best sellers, like the metal wire baskets and fruit bowls. At this point brass and nickel silver definitively left the scene and stainless steel took over. The hotel sector was very important for Alessi and favourites such as stainless steel serving dishes or the wide range of soup tureens, vegetable dishes and sauce boats came onto the market.

Alessi soon began to classify the production and collections into programmes, in other words into sets of products for the end market that were homogenous in terms of style and type. It was the so-called 'Programma 4' – designed by Massoni and Mazzeri – that represented a cultural turning point for Alessi, introducing the concept of 'author', 'project' and 'design' to the world of household goods. In 1957, the 'Programma 4' shaker, ice bucket and ice tongs were selected for the XI Triennale in Milan. It was the first time that Alessi objects had appeared in an exhibition of products of industrial design and it was the beginning of what was to become Alessi's mission: working in the sector of applied arts. The 1960s saw further expansion of the plant and increased presence abroad.

5.3.3.   From 1970 to 1983: the Great Divide

In the 1970s the third generation of the Alessi family entered the company. In 1970, just after graduating in Law, Carlo's eldest son, Alberto, started working in the marketing and sale of new products. The second son, Michele, joined the company in 1975, looking after administration, finance and organisation. Finally, Alessio started working for the company in 1980 and in 1984 Ettore Alessi's elder son, Stefano, also joined the organisation. The corporate structure was soon divided into various departments and areas of responsibility: Alberto took care of new product development, marketing and communication; Michele was in charge of finance and business organisation; Alessio dealt with distribution; and Stefano with purchasing.

When Alberto entered the company there was a radical change in the way they worked with designers; in fact alongside the industrial designers, architects and artists were asked to contribute ideas. These artists and architects included Michael Graves, Aldo Rossi, Ettore Sottsass and Achille Castiglioni. The idea to open up to new ideas – in particular from the art world – was based on the desire to turn Alessi production more towards design. The concept was in fact soon extended from the product itself to packaging, graphics, the work space, stands at fairs and merchandising.

The first two programmes that Alberto set up were radically innovative both for the company and for the sector and district. The first, called 'Alessi d'après', was based on the utopian idea of mass consumption of art replicas designed by artists like Giò Pomodoro and Salvador Dalì. This programme only lasted three years due to serious production problems and lack of success on the market. If, on the one hand artists were little inclined to design objects destined for production on an industrial scale, on the other the market found it difficult to accept objects that were so far removed from the usual perception of 'household articles'. The second programme set up by Alberto Alessi at this time was the famous 'Programma 8', a vast and complex design process, which gradually developed a coordinated system of objects with the help of designers, Franco Sargiani and Eija Helander, who were asked to design just one oil cruet. With 'Programma 8', Alessi introduced a series of articles that were highly adaptable and flexible in use. They were made in stainless steel to underline further the fact that they were functional and practical, as well as being aimed at the new working class. The new smaller working class homes demanded a more efficient use of domestic space, thus modular household articles that were square or rectangular in shape. 'Programma 8' – which was in production until 1985–1987 although some articles remained in the catalogue for decades after – marked the firm's passage from metalworking plant to 'Italian Design Factory'. The key feature of Italian design is the ability to use traditional materials and to constantly renew product quality focusing on the research and quality of the finishing.

In the following years many other designers started to work with Alessi; Munari, Coppola, Grignani, Tovaglia and Confalonieri put together 'Programma 7' in 1972; Sottsass extended 'Programma 5' and became one of Alessi's most prolific collaborators, designing articles in different materials: steel, glass, plastic, wood and china. In 1977 Sottsass introduced Richard Sapper, who began to work with Alessi, putting his name to objects and projects that were met with great success, including the famous '9090' coffee maker, of which over 1.3 million pieces have been made and which won the 'Golden Compass' in 1979 and was exhibited at the MOMA in New York.

Important figures in the design world worked with Alessi in this period: Sapper, Sargiani Helander, Pomodoro, Cascella, Coppola, Confalonieri, Sottsass, Mendini. From 1979 Mendini became the Alessi family's consultant and partner in defining the firm's design strategy (responsible for the designer network, composition of product portfolio, and so on). From now on the company was seen as a 'research laboratory in the field of applied arts' positioning itself halfway between industry and art.

5.3.4. From 1983 to the present: towards New Entrepreneurial Opportunities

In its relentless drive for research and invention, Alessi began in the 1980s to experiment with production in new materials and new technologies: wood, china and ceramic, glass, electricity and electronics. A new internal function – 'Edizione' – was created with the objective of paying special attention to the growing role of the external designer network, defining an area of competence that was distinct from that of the Technical Office. Alessi thus defined its function as that of product 'publisher', giving the external designers total freedom over the actual design. However, this activity soon became so much a part of the way of working that the distinction between the two functions was made redundant.

In 1983 the 'Officina Alessi' brand was created alongside the Alessi brand. The objective of the new brand was to experiment with innovative shapes, new materials, functions and production methods that went beyond the logic of mass production. At the same time a reorganisation of international product distribution was started in order to identify potential subsidiaries or exclusive agents in some strategic markets (Germany, France, UK and USA) and to reduce drastically the number of sales outlets. In Italy alone the number of outlets was reduced from 4000 to 1200 (Moon et al., 2004).

The next few years saw the start of a number of successful strategic ventures. Up to then Alessi had used only local suppliers belonging to the VCO houseware district, with which the company maintained generally informal relationships.

In 1988 Alessi took over Piazza Battista, a company founded in 1865 and specialised in the production of small wooden articles for the kitchen and table, production of which had ceased 20 years earlier. In 1989 Alessi published the first catalogue of wooden articles under the 'Twergi' brand name and acquired another small firm, 'Tendentse', founded in 1985, to develop the manufacture of household articles in china and ceramic. In the case of both 'Twergi' and 'Tendentse', the objects were designed by Alessi's external network of designers.

At the beginning of the 1990s, Alessi set up some 'meta-projects', to explore the emotional structure of the objects and developed the first range of articles made in plastic. In fact the designers Alberto Alessi was working with started to propose ideas that were brilliant but difficult to realise in steel. In this sense, plastic was the ideal solution to continue to innovate the world of household articles in the most varied shapes and colours. In the words of Alberto Alessi: 'The image that we want to convey with our products is not just linked to the material used but also to the project, the design, the capacity to communicate. Manufacturing in plastic has enabled us to expand the range and possibility of products considerably, maintaining however our solid traditions'. The introduction of plastic products – above all with the 'Family Follows Fiction' meta-project, started in 1993 and aimed at reproducing childhood images – caused some perplexity and scepticism amongst sector observers and opinion leaders but allowed Alessi to achieve a considerable increase in turnover as well as to reach a new market segment.

Alessi did not only change materials in order to encourage research and experimenting with the notions of emotion, play and irony, but also set up the 'Centro Studi Alessi' (CSA), dedicated to coordinating the work of young designers and a wide range of other professional figures (designers, sociologists, semiologists, anthropologists and opinion leaders), coordinated by Laura Polinoro. The CSA also organised workshops – planning seminars – around the world to study the significance and perception of the objects.

With the developing product catalogue, Alessi moved the manufacture of some articles to European suppliers and acquired a Brazilian company dedicated to cutlery production. In 1992, Alessi and Philips set up a partnership – which ended in 1994 – for the manufacture of four household appliances (an electric toaster, an electric kettle, a juice squeezer and an espresso coffee machine), which did not completely meet with the favour of the market.

In 1998 the Alessi Museum was opened in Crusinallo di Omegna. It was designed by Mendini and run by Francesca Appiani. At the end of the 1990s, Alessi decided to enter a new sector with the 'Comics' range of kitchen and table linen. The project was not a success due to the fact that Alessi did not thoroughly understand what was necessary to operate in a new sector and offered products that were high quality but over-priced, underestimating the production problems.

It was during this period that almost all production was moved abroad and part of it to the Far East. The decision to produce in countries like Korea, China, Vietnam and India was taken because of government incentives, low labour costs and the availability of new and technologically advanced supply firms.

The beginning of 2000 saw a new development at Alessi: joint ventures with other firms working in very different product areas. The aim was to create objects that featured a mixture of eccentricity, style, irony and elegance. In July 2007 Alessandro Bonfiglioli (external to the family) was appointed General Manager of Alessi and the top management was restructured; Michele, Alessio and Stefano Alessi now occupy exclusively executive roles, while Alberto Alessi continues to direct the strategic activities linked to the design function management. Today Alessi exports 65 per cent of its turnover – with four subsidiaries in France, Germany, England, USA. It has a network of over 5000 sales outlets in more than 60 countries. The company is planning to set up 14 own brand stores (showroom and flagship) and 175 Shop-in-shops in strategic parts of the globe.

Table 5.4 Alessi turnover and number of employees (1997–2006)

Year	Employees	Turnover (€M)
1997	418	80,00
1998	569	81,44
1999	479	90,07
2000	459	95,74
2001	472	93,68
2002	469	89,26
2003	n.a.	n.a.
2004	483	76,87
2005	466	76,19
2006	461	82,67

Source: personal elaboration on AIDA data (consolidated balance sheet)

5.4.   THE PERFORMANCES OF ALESSI

5.4.1.   The Company Growth

Table 5.4 shows the trends in turnover and number of employees at Alessi. The consolidated balance sheet is used as a reference to include all the activities (production, design and marketing) relevant to the case studied. Since 1997, the turnover has remained mainly constant around the 80 million euro mark, with some peaks in 1999–2000–2001. Similarly the structure in terms of number of employees has stayed at around 450–500 with the odd rise or fall in certain years. The period considered saw a fall in demand for household articles and in particular for metal goods. In the same period, the life cycle of all metal household goods has reached maturity (except for the segment of dietetic cooking pots, which is expanding, and aluminium articles which have been re-launched). Critical success factors in the sector have also changed. Image, product innovation and quality have taken the place of price, service, process and cost innovation (although economies of scale and supply policy remain critical factors in determining low production costs).

In this context, Alessi has continued to focus on design and quality, a policy that has been followed coherently since the 1970s, at the same time reducing the room given to mature or declining products within the catalogue (mainly metal pans), in favour of products still in the growth phase (plastic kitchenware and tableware and other kitchen utensils). Thus, despite the negative trend in the sector and the market, Alessi has succeeded in maintaining its turnover more or less constant since 1997. This levelling off – which the owners and management judge to be in line with the market situation and their management objectives – nevertheless comes after a period of almost exponential company growth.

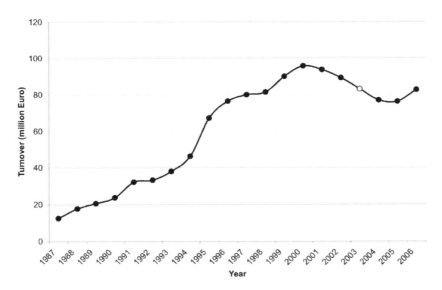

Notes: the figure for 2003 is not available and has been interpolated
Source: personal elaboration on AIDA data

Figure 5.1 Growth in Alessi's turnover over the last 20 years (1987–2006)

Looking at the trend in turnover over a 20-year period (Figure 5.1), it is immediately obvious how, in a mature and contracting sector, Alessi was able to increase its turnover from around €12 million in1987 to almost €83 million today.

Alessi's growth cannot just be evaluated in terms of turnover but above all in relation to its capacity to innovate and introduce new products, as shown in Chapter 9.

Table 5.5 Comparison between Alessi and Italian competitors in the houseware sector (financial data 1995–2002)

Company	ID[*]	Sales growth	Average ROI	Average ROE	Cash flow/sales average
Guzzini	---	n.a.	3.51%	4.85%	11.80
Inoxpran	LUM	-41.2%	1.02%	-9.62%	1.47
Mepra	LUM	-34.5%	7.52%	6.65%	6.90
Pinti Inox	LUM	-27.5%	5.13%	2.44%	5.48
Calderoni	VCO	-17.4%	0.37%	-4.97%	2.53
Metaltex Italia	---	-6.7%	5.83%	7.53%	6.30
Barazzoni	VCO	-5.8%	2.72%	0.81%	8.71
Frabosk	LUM	16.7%	0.87%	-1.87%	37.95
Abert	LUM	17.5%	3.86%	2.54%	9.51
Alessi	**VCO**	**32.8%**	**18.17**	**39.7%**	**9.78**
Lagostina	VCO	47.5%	2.28%	-8.70%	4.96
Lumenflon	LUM	65.3%	6.64%	6.68%	4.13
Bialetti[**]	VCO	359.4%	6.93%	8.85%	4.54

Notes: *   *ID indicates the industrial district where competitors are located, where applicable. VCO stands for the Verbano-Cusio-Ossola industrial district; LUM stands for the Lumezzane industrial district, near Brescia in northern Italy.*

        **   *Effect of the merger between Bialetti and Rondine (Lumezzane industrial district, Brescia), which gave rise to the multibrand group Bialetti Industrie Spa.*

Source: Databank (2002)

5.4.2.   Comparison with the Industry and the District

Unlike the main competitors in the metal houseware sector, who remained faithful to their original material, Alessi gradually introduced new production technologies such as ceramic, wood, glass and plastic, from the 1980s onwards. This allowed the designers greater liberty in terms of form, colour, functions and applications without being limited by the material. The company also looked outside the traditional product sector of household goods. The catalogue includes a high number of different product types, from trays and baskets to watches, from cutlery sets and glasses to kitchen accessories, jugs and coffee makers.

In recent years Alessi has stipulated a series of licensing agreements for the manufacture of other products: bath accessories (taps, tiles, fixtures and textiles), wrist watches, fabrics as well as an agreement with FIAT for a model of car with the Alessi signature. Thus Alessi can be said to be unique in the sector of household goods and kitchenware. No other competitor can offer such a wide product portfolio, although specific competitors can be identified in individual segments. In any case, the main rivals are still to be found in the West rather than in Asia. The main manufacturers in each segment in the top market range and thus in direct competition with Alessi are:

- stainless steel accessories (Sambonet, Lagostina, Stelton e Bodum);
- pots and pans (Sambonet, ICM, Lagostina, Barazzoni, Elettrofiamma);
- cutlery (Sambonet, Berndorf, WMF);
- aluminium (Lagostina, Bialetti, ICM, Giannini, Zani&Zani);
- plastic (Bodum, Guzzini, Kozjol);
- china (Rosenthal, Richard Ginori, Villeroy, Wedgewood).

As this overview suggests, it is difficult to compare Alessi with similar firms, given that the majority of firms in the houseware sector focus on one or at any rate a limited number of product types.

The comparison between Alessi and the main competitors in the sector in Italy (Table 5.5) shows that Alessi has greater growth capacity in the more profitable segments. The company's performance has generally (with a few exceptions) been better than that of its competitors in terms of operating profit and net profit and in terms of liquidity generated by the operational activities. Alessi's growth process can also be usefully compared to that of the district it belongs to (Table 5.6), in terms both of turnover and of number of employees.

Looking at the last ten years, Alessi has increased both the number of employees (+10,3 per cent) and (to a slightly lesser extent) turnover (+3,75 per cent). This growth took place within an industrial context (that of the Verbano-Cusio-Ossola district) in sharp decline. In the same period (1997–2006) the district lost over 66 per cent of the workforce and turnover dropped by almost 39 per cent. Alessi, with its positive growth, thus increased its contribution to the economy of the district, increasing its percentage of overall turnover from 16 to 18 per cent and percentage of the workforce from 7 per cent to 28 per cent.

Table 5.6 Alessi and the district over the 10 year period (1997–2006)

		District VCO	Alessi	Alessi/VCO
Employees	1997	6 000	418	7%
	2006	2 000	461	23%
	Var. %	-66.7%	+10.3%	-
Turnover	1997	491	80	16%
(€M)	2006	300	83	28%
	Var. %	-38,9%	+3,75%	-

Source: personal elaboration on AIDA data and Sole 24 Ore

Table 5.7 Operating income, net profit and profitability of Alessi

Year	Operating Income (euro)	Net Profit (euro)	ROA (%)	ROE (%)
1997	9 296 208	1 722 346	6.67	6.35
1998	8 626 030	1 397 836	5.68	5.22
1999	8 454 713	710 070	4.75	2.68
2000	15 620 088	3 685 334	11.88	13.64
2001	16 620 909	4 663 668	12.43	15.54
2002	20 182 072	5 952 417	17.26	19.03
2003	n.a.	n.a.	n.a.	n.a.
2004	19 636 540	7 305 873	20.01	29.17
2005	17 704 041	7 220 849	19.69	33.88
2006	19 723 091	7 310 357	23.85	36.13

Source: personal elaboration on AIDA data

5.4.3.   Financial Results

Alessi's growth process over this period has been marked by the capacity to generate good financial results both in absolute terms (see operating profit and net profit in Table 5.7) and in relation to assets (ROA) and equity (ROE). These two profitability indices in particular show a continuing growth trend for the ten-year period. ROA went up from 6.67 per cent in 1997 to 23.85 per cent in 2006 and ROE from 6.35 per cent in 1997 to 36.13 per cent in 2006.

6. Geox

S. Sciascia

This chapter presents the case study of Geox, a manufacturing company located in the area of Montebelluna that specialises in footwear. The aim of this chapter is to describe the entrepreneurial growth process of the firm, setting it within the context of the sector and the industrial district and presenting the economic-financial consequences of this growth. The chapter is thus divided into four sections: the footwear sector; the footwear manufacturing district of Montebelluna; the history of Geox; and the performances of Geox.

6.1. THE FOOTWEAR INDUSTRY

6.1.1. The Market and the Industry at European Level

The footwear industry is now a mature one in Europe. The companies working in the industry share a market, that has become very fragmented, and focus mainly on cost and differentiation strategies to achieve margins which are becoming smaller and smaller. The situation has been made worse by the advent of globalisation, which has more or less overturned the whole world economy in the last few years. The larger firms, with superior managerial and entrepreneurial skills, have managed to seize opportunities for development, such as locating production in areas of the world where labour costs are low. On the other hand, the smaller firms find it difficult to survive and many have been forced to abandon the sector. Table 6.1 compares the results in terms of production, exports and imports of footwear in Europe from 2002 to 2005. As can be seen, there was a fall in production, substantial stability in exports and an increase in imports. Times are hard for the European footwear industry; over 107 000 jobs were lost between 2000 and 2005 according to the European Confederation of Footwear Industries.

Table 6.1 Main figures for the European footwear industry (1000 pairs)

Year	Production	Exports	Imports	Consumption
2002	900 535	214 348	1 232 914	1 919 101
2003	780 811	181 276	1 455 036	2 054 571
2004	728 211	170 085	1 709 875	2 268 001
2005	641 852	225 998	1 939 813	2 355 667

Source: personal elaboration on EUROSTAT

The sector has witnessed the exponential growth of competition from China, above all at the lower end of the market. With the elimination of maximum import quotas (from 1 January 2005), the number of shoes imported from China to the EU25 rose to over 1 250 million pairs in 2005 (+250 per cent compared to 1999) and alone represents 64.5 per cent of the shoes coming into Europe. As can be seen from Table 6.2, imports from India, Brazil, Romania and Tunisia have also increased, while those from Thailand, Indonesia, Vietnam and Turkey have fallen.

Table 6.2 Imports of footwear to Europe in 2005 (1000 pairs)

Country	Number of Pairs	Percentage of Pairs	% growth 2002–2005
World	1 939 813	100%	57.3%
China	1 250 802	64.5%	171.1%
Vietnam	265 271	13.7%	-6.6%
Romania	71 467	3.7%	7.5%
India	52 629	2.7%	45.9%
Indonesia	50 772	2.6%	-18.8%
Brazil	30 978	1.6%	105.2%
Thailand	28 056	1.4%	-25.0%
Turkey	2 465	0.1%	-4.8%
Hong-Kong	22 654	1.2%	-13.1%
Tunisia	19 766	1.0%	8.4%

Source: personal elaboration on EUROSTAT

The main markets for shoes produced in Europe are USA, Switzerland and Russia. Exports are holding up due to the growth of the Swiss, Russian, Norwegian and Turkish markets; in most other countries, European shoes are losing market share, as shown by Table 6.3.

Table 6.3 Exports of footwear from Europe in 2005 (1000 pairs)

Country	Number of Pairs	Percentage of Pairs	% growth 2002–2005
World	225 998	100.0%	5.4%
Switzerland	84 616	37.4%	270.6%
USA	41 805	18.5%	-43.1%
Russia	12 190	5.4%	3.8%
Norway	8 534	3.8%	6.3%
Japan	7 125	3.2%	-18.8%
Canada	6 773	3.0%	-33.5%
Turkey	6 349	2.8%	164.6%
Ukraine	5 755	2.5%	-25.7%
Croatia	5 214	2.3%	-12.3%
UA Emirates	3 010	1.3%	-25.8%

Source: personal elaboration on EUROSTAT

6.1.2.   Trends in the Italian Footwear Industry

Italy can boast a long tradition in footwear; the value of 'Made in Italy' in this sector is recognised all over the world and the average price of Italian shoes bears witness to this. The main producing regions (Marches, Tuscany, Veneto, Lombardy, Puglia and Emilia Romagna) concentrate 96.7 per cent of national firms in the footwear industry; in these regions production is organised according to the industrial district model.

Over the last few years the country has felt the effects of the negative economic climate, which has brought about significant changes. A period of expansion from 1990 to 1995, due to the favourable exchange rate (the depreciation of the lira made national products cheaper), was followed from 1996 onwards by a period of recession, which led to a reduction in the number of firms and employees; in the last ten years approximately 2 200 shoe manufacturing firms have closed down and some 30 000 jobs have been lost. Only those firms with a 'healthier' balance sheet and more flexible strategy have overcome the recession and are going through a positive phase. Many of them have moved production and purchasing outside Italy in order to remain competitive in the global market. Turnover itself has remained at around 7 million euros, while the quantity of footwear manufactured has decreased and the average price of the shoes themselves has gone up.

Table 6.4 Main figures for the Italian footwear industry in 2005

Year	Firms	Employees	Turnover (€K)
1995	8 861	124 228	7 856
1996	8 467	122 186	8 092
1997	8 150	120 500	8 052
1998	7 900	117 300	7 910
1999	7 660	114 015	7 416
2000	7 570	113 100	8 269
2001	7 500	111 650	8 670
2002	7 380	107 008	8 171
2003	7 283	103 275	7 582
2004	7 084	100 934	7 310
2005	6 831	97 005	6 974
2006	6 657	94 143	7 074

Source: personal elaboration on ISTAT

Table 6.5 Italian international trade in footwear (1 000 000 pairs)

Year	Export	Import
1995	394.6	130.6
1996	402.6	121.7
1997	385.8	143.9
1998	357.1	149.0
1999	323.4	170.4
2000	336.4	182.4
2001	330.9	189.8
2002	303.1	208.6
2003	282.0	247.9
2004	261.4	289.9
2005	231.3	307.6
2006	228.1	340.8

Source: personal elaboration on ISTAT

Recent years have seen a decrease in exports and an increase in imports, particularly from 2001 onwards, following the introduction of the single European currency. The appreciation of the euro compared to other currencies – particularly the dollar – has made our products more expensive, thus limiting exports. From 2004, imports to Italy first reached the level of exports and then rapidly overtook them with the elimination of the quotas on imports of shoes from China, thus leading to a negative balance of trade. With 230 million pairs sold abroad in 2005, representing a turnover of €6093 million, this was over €30 million fewer than in 2004, which was already low.

6.1.3.   The Italian Footwear Industry Today

According to ANCI (Associazione Nazionale Calzaturifici Italiani), the Italian industry today is in second place in terms of exporting countries behind China and ahead of Vietnam and Belgium. In 2005 China accounted for 34.6 per cent of the market, while Italy represented 12.9 per cent.

Table 6.6 Italian footwear exports in 2005 by country

Country	Export Share
United States	14.5%
Germany	12.1%
France	10.4%
U.K.	6.5%
Switzerland	5.1%
Russian Federation	4.7%
Netherlands	2.8%
Japan	2.8%
Belgium	2.8%
Spain	2.4%
Austria	2.2%

Source: personal elaboration on ISTAT

Italy exports shoes mainly to USA, Germany, France, UK, Switzerland and Russia, as can be seen from Table 6.6. Considering the categories of product traded internationally over 2005, we can see from Table 6.7 that leather shoes remain relatively stable (-0.2 per cent in volume but +6.9 per cent in value); these are the shoes that represent the strength of the 'Made in Italy' label, accounting for over 67 per cent of foreign sales. The increase (+29 per cent) in exports of rubber-soled shoes has helped compensate for the reduction in sales of shoes made of synthetic materials (less 5.5 per cent), of fabric shoes (less 2.7 per cent) and of slippers (less 7.6 per cent), down-market products with low value added and thus inevitably more exposed to cut-throat competition from Asia.

Table 6.7 Italian international trade in footwear by material (2005)

Material of upper	Export (Volume)	Export (Value)	Import (Volume)	Import (Value)
Leather	-0.2	6.93	11.06	2.81
Synthetic	-5.54	1.18	15.58	-3.75
Slippers	-7.56	-8.04	17.39	-6.15
Rubber	29.15	18.67	-17.12	13.02
Other materials	-2.73	8.42	-0.19	5.73
Total	**-1.39**	**6.42**	**12.19**	**1.25**

Source: personal elaboration on ANCI

6.1.4.   The Main Dynamics in the Industry

The main results of the recession in the Italian footwear industry are the reduction in the workforce and in the number of production units, particularly small ones. Companies are still finding it tough in the main markets (Germany, France, USA and UK) and at the same time there is no halt to the influx of shoe imports from the Far East. There is fierce competition in all segments of the sector, above all for products in the low- and medium-priced range. For this reason Italy took on the role of 'spokesperson' for the interests of European small firms, requesting and obtaining the imposition of duties on shoes imported to Europe from China and Vietnam at the end of 2006. Moreover the joint label 'I love Italian shoes' was launched in 2003, guaranteeing that the shoes are manufactured entirely in Italy and that certain quality standards are respected. So far 100 small firms have joined the venture. Overall average export prices have risen, thanks also to the repositioning of Italian production towards the top end of the market. Cheaper goods, overtaken by the Chinese competitors, are being phased out in favour of high quality. The largest Italian footwear manufacturers now aim at enhancing Italian style, investing more in advertising and developing aggressive distribution policies. At the same time they are outsourcing production phases with low value added and are aiming at gaining a foothold in the new emerging markets such as the Indian one.

6.2.   THE MONTEBELLUNA SHOE-MAKING DISTRICT

6.2.1.   Origins and Specialisations

The Montebelluna industrial district is specialised in the manufacture of sports shoes and is one of the most typical and important of the Italian footwear manufacturing clusters. The district has adapted continuously to meet market needs, not only in terms of products but also in the organisation of production, so that now it is quite different from what it was in the 1980s (Corò, Gurisatti and Rossi, 1998).

The district developed at the beginning of the nineteenth century in the foothills north of Treviso, where there was a concentration of local workshops making mountain boots by hand. By the turn of the century there were as many as 200 firms in Montebelluna, most of which consisted of members of farming families, who turned to this activity for additional revenue at times when there was little agricultural work. Some of these workshops, however, soon grew from family-run artisan workshops to production units on an industrial scale. The establishment of important companies, such as Tecnica (1890), Dolomite (1897), Alpina e Munari (1908) and, a bit later, Pivetta e Vendramin (1919) and Nordica (1926) date from this period. The introduction of the Vibram sole in 1937 allowed companies in the sector to produce boots of a markedly superior quality. In the immediate post-war period some firms started to produce the first ski-boots; made in leather entirely by hand, these were a huge success. The technological evolution of the ski-boot was practically continuous from then on. New materials began to be used to make them safer and more rigid, from rubber for the sole to iron for the fastenings. The district went through a boom period in 1967 when Nordica experimented with the first ski-boots with the outer covering entirely in plastic. Not only did the new boots guarantee enhanced performance and safety but they were also easier to produce. The new technology was adopted by most of the firms, who were thus able to compete in world markets. Ski-boot production grew exponentially; from 180 000 pairs manufactured in 1963 to 1 million pairs in 1970 and 4 million in 1979. At the same time there was an increase in the number of firms manufacturing mountain shoes and ski-boots, reaching over 500 at the end of the 1970s and employing approximately 9 700 people. In 1970 there was a second diversification in production with the invention of the après-ski boot in plastic material; the first was the famous 'Moon boot' by Tecnica. In the early 1980s there was a third diversification with the development of specific footwear for all types of sport: football, tennis, basketball, motorcycling, cycling, dance, roller-skating and ice-skating and for leisure wear. The last diversification took place in the early 1990s with the advent of so-called 'new sports': trekking, jogging, snow-boarding and roller-blades. These last two product diversifications led to further growth in the number of companies and employees in the district.

6.2.2. Trends in Structure and Performance

Table 6.8 shows the recent trends in the structure and performance of the district. Between 1997 and 2005 the number of firms went down from 538 to

391 and the workforce shrank from 9 830 to 7 876. Thus from a structural perspective, the district followed the same evolutionary trend as the industry in general. This involved the closing down of smaller firms, particularly those sub-contracting for larger firms; the outsourcing of many production units; and the carrying out of a number of mergers and takeovers. Today 28.1 per cent of firms in the district are involved in offshoring, which represents the optimum solution to the lack of low-cost labour in Italy. Romania is the main area where operations are located.

Table 6.8 Main figures for the Montebelluna district

Year	Firms	Employees	Turnover (€M)	Exports (€M)
1997	538	9 830	1 024	627
1998	509	9 106	908	596
1999	492	8 596	943	633
2000	450	8 897	1 117	765
2001	464	8 943	1 199	788
2002	428	8 608	1 239	809
2003	430	8 031	1 297	964
2004	413	8 078	1 343	888
2005	391	7 876	1 360	923

Source: personal elaboration on OSEM

In terms of performance, however, turnover for the district continues to grow; exports have also increased as has their contribution to turnover. The 1997 turnover of approximately €1 024 million increased to €1 360 million in 2005; exports increased from €627 million to €923 million. The majority of the 391 firms making up the industrial fabric of the district are still small to medium-sized firms; 46 per cent have 2 to 9 employees, 31 per cent between 10 and 50, while only 1 per cent has more than 250 employees.

6.2.3.   The Main Dynamics in the District

Different types of firm in terms of size, organisational structure and competence co-exist within the industrial district of Montebelluna. These include not only SMEs but also some multinational companies, which entered the district as a result of mergers and acquisitions. Some firms are leaders, with well-known brands, which they have extended also to sportswear; other smaller firms are followers in terms of style and very competitive in terms of price. There are also firms that are specialised in technical components and many sub-contractors, who are highly dependent on the leading firms and characterised by a high level of risk. According to OSEM, the district observatory, the 391 firms in the area can be classified as shown in Table 6.9.

Table 6.9   Distribution of firms and employees in the Montebelluna district by type of firm in 2005

Type of firm	Number of firms	Employees
Accessories	10	84
Laminating	7	201
Assembly/mounting	29	362
Marketing & sales	12	201
Punching	4	54
Shoelace manufacture	4	29
Pattern maker	2	8
Garment production	12	439
Footwear production	104	2 979
Footwear & garment prod.	21	1 777
Machinery production	16	117
Non-productive office	2	48
Moulding	23	509
Die-sinking	11	153
Studio Design	27	112
Sole manufacture	6	197
Cutting	28	72
Uppers manufacture	51	224
Other	22	310
Total	**391**	**7 876**

Source: personal elaboration on OSEM

Over the last 20 years market globalisation has led to a gradual loss of emphasis on production with the consequent development of offshoring processes, involving above all the network of sub-contractors and sub-suppliers. This has affected the non-specialised jobs of cutting, hemming, assembly and generally all essentially manual work. The main factory now only employs specialised workers, who produce prototypes and niche products with high levels of added value. In terms of the type of product offered, as a result of the various product diversifications, the Montebelluna district has developed the distribution profile shown in Table 6.10.

Table 6.10 Distribution of production in the Montebelluna district by type of shoe in 2005

Type of shoe	Production share
Urban-wear	44%
Snow	19%
Mountain	12%
Motorcycling	7%
Safety	5%
Skates	5%
Football	3%
Cycling	2%
Tennis	1%
Running	1%

Source: personal elaboration on OSEM

During the 1990s, the biggest world group for snow products was set up by Nordica, Dolomite, Tecnica and Lowa. Nevertheless, after 1995, following a series of winters with little snow, the retirement of charismatic Italian ski champions like Alberto Tomba and growing competition, the segment downsized and now only accounts for 19 per cent of the production of the district. The top product of the 1990s was in fact the rollerblade, which proved to be a real winner for the ski boot manufacturers of the region, allowing them to use their machinery for the moulding of the plastic casing rather than leaving it underused for about half the year. Another product, which helped fill the gap left by the market contraction in the snow segment, was the trekking shoe. This was a new sports discipline, for which the district was able to revive its manufacturing skills for the old mountain boots. Today, however, just under half of the district's turnover is linked to the production of comfortable shoes for urban-wear and walking (44 per cent) – a segment which has grown incredibly since the end of the 1990s. Finally there has been the launch of a new segment – that of the safety boot, used for the prevention of accidents in the workplace and compulsory by law in many businesses.

As far as worldwide markets are concerned, the district exports mainly to Germany, France, Romania, Spain, USA and UK. In particular the last 15 years have seen a strong growth of exports to the first four countries, while there has been a drop in exports to Japan, which had previously been one of the main markets. There are four main challenges facing the Montebelluna district today. The first is the small size of the firms, given that economies of scale are a significant phenomenon in this sector. The second is under-capitalisation, given that only Geox is listed on the stock exchange; company owners are reluctant to give up total control, renouncing the financial and managerial benefits to be gained by going public. The third is the lack of managerial skills; only the leading firms can avail themselves of adequate managerial skills, while many SMEs have serious gaps in this area. The fourth is represented by a lack of market orientation; as often happens in industrial districts, the firms are more interested in the product and in technology and less in investment in communication and customer relations. The firms in the district are conscious of these limits and are trying to overcome them.

6.3. THE HISTORY OF GEOX

The name 'Geox' comes from the Greek word 'geo' meaning the earth that we all walk on and the letter 'x', symbolising technology. The origin of the name highlights the vocation and the DNA of a firm that grew out of a revolutionary idea based on comfort, well-being and health. Today Geox is one of the best-known footwear manufacturing firms in Italy and the world. It is a leader in Italy in the classic/casual sector and is a growing world presence: 59.3 per cent of the consolidated revenue at 31 December 2006 (€612.3 million) came from the main foreign markets, including Germany, France, Spain and USA. This process of entrepreneurial growth has taken place over little more than ten years.

6.3.1. 1989–1994: Developing the Business Idea

In 1989 the idea of a 'shoe that could breath' was thought up by Mario Moretti Polegato, who was at that time working in the family agricultural and wine-growing business. As often happens this innovative idea came up by chance. The business idea behind Geox did not come out of a brain-storming session or complex strategic market analysis but out of a banal foot allergy of the entrepreneur himself. In fact, Moretti Polegato was attending a wine-growers fair at Reno in Nevada and going jogging to keep himself fit. The unbearable heat and the shoes he was wearing combined to make his feet sweaty, so much so that he decided to make a hole in the sole with a knife: and this was the beginning of an ingenious idea that was to change the destiny of the entrepreneur.

The rubber sole had been introduced more than 50 years earlier and had represented a technological advance that had changed the lives of millions of people around the world. Thanks to rubber soles in fact, shoes had been made impermeable and thus able to keep the feet dry and warm, particularly in the winter months. Rubber soles, however, did not let the feet perspire – and this was a serious disadvantage if you consider that the sole of the foot has the highest concentration of sweat glands in the body. Mario Moretti Polegato thus revolutionised the role of holes in shoes; once associated with old shoes to be thrown away, the holes now became a plus. On his return to Italy, he tried to put his idea into practice by developing it in the workshop of the small shoe manufacturing company owned by the family, Pol. In this way he created the prototype of a shoe with a rubber sole and holes that allowed the foot to breathe while preventing water from getting in, leaving the foot dry and comfortable. In fact he managed to adapt a special membrane invented by NASA for spacesuits to shoe soles. The material (polytetrafluoroethylene or expanded Teflon) has approximately 1.4 billion holes per square centimetre; each hole is 20 000 times smaller than a drop of water but 700 times larger than a molecule of water steam. The membrane is thus impermeable to water but allows perspiration to escape. At this point he offered his idea to large footwear manufacturing companies, but after three years with no national or international firm willing to invest in the idea of a shoe that breathes, Moretti Polegato was so convinced of his idea's potential that he decided to go it alone. Thanks to a pool of young people coming from important firms in the district and in collaboration with ENEA, the University of Padua and the Italian National Centre of Research (CNR) in Rome, the first breathing sole was developed and patented. With no idea of the potential market and no sample of consumers on which to test the prototypes, Moretti Polegato decided to distribute shoes free to nursery schools (to approximately 5 000 children between the ages of 3 and 6 years). The choice was not a random one, given that children wear their shoes out more quickly, thus allowing the technicians to get faster feedback; after one year of tests the development of the first range of shoes for children started.

6.3.2.   1995–1999: Internationalisation

Two years after entering the children's market Geox started to develop shoes for men and women. In the trade off between comfort (waterproof rubber shoes) and hygiene (guaranteed by the leather shoe that allows the feet to perspire), Geox shoes came out winners and began to be viewed positively by the market. The production process was almost exclusively outsourced (initially mainly in the Montebelluna district) and Geox itself concentrated on the initial stages of the chain (R&D) and the final stages (Marketing, Distribution and Sales). Huge investments were made in promoting the Geox brand, buying up pages of advertising space in specialised magazines aimed initially at parents and following that, in all kinds of magazines. The outsourcing of most of the production (now 80 per cent) not only reduced start-up costs but also enabled the firm to remain flexible and invest in value-generating activities.

In 1997 the company from Montebelluna, nevertheless, built a factory in Romania and one in Slovakia in addition to the four factories in the Treviso area. Since then Geox has built up a 'mini-district for footwear manufacture' around the Romanian site (which cost over €10 million), attracting several Italian suppliers (mainly from the Veneto and Marches regions), specialising in particular phases of the production process, such as cutting or assembling. An internal training school was also set up in Timisoara, alongside the factory. The aim was to train workers, specialised technical workers and foremen in order to create the skills needed to manufacture technologically advanced products in line with the innovations developed at the Montebelluna headquarters. At this time Geox enjoyed exponential growth, helped also by the weak lira, which gave an incentive to exports.

6.3.3.   2000–2004: Developing the Offer

The research laboratory of Geox continued studying the body's perspiration and heat dynamics and in 1999 came up with a solution that allowed the warm humid air from the body to expand, rise through a hollow chamber created around the body and finally escape via a system of air vents at shoulder level. This discovery marked a turning point for the Montebelluna group, which moved from the footwear sector to that of the total look. The patent was applied to clothes such as jackets and coats. Following a series of successful tests, Geox launched a complete range of apparel on the Italian market.

In 2001 the Geox laboratory developed the leather patent. Leather is the highly favourable material for shoe soles because it is hard-wearing, flexible and workable. Geox introduced a breathing impermeable membrane into the sole to eliminate the uncomfortable sensation of dampness in wet and rainy conditions, making leather shoes finally waterproof. In 2002 the STS (Side Transpiration System) was finally patented. This was an innovation in the world of sports shoes, allowing the air to circulate more and thus the foot to breathe, thanks to the holes in the sides of the sole. At the same time as developing their product range, important structural changes took place inside the Geox organisation. Aware of the importance of training, the group's directors set up an internal training unit in 2001. Initially dedicated only to managers, it now runs courses for technical and managerial staff, top managers and new graduates. Young graduates in chemistry, engineering, mechanical engineering and economics are given the opportunity to take part in courses organised by the company. The courses, lasting from 4 to 6 months, combine in-depth theoretical study of each particular discipline with hands-on practical work to give the specific training needed by the firm; at the end of the course the graduates are given a role within the company. A specific unit for the study of design was also set up in 2001 in the Marches. The models of the new lines that will be offered to the market are hand-made by artisan craftsmen in this major traditional shoe-making district.

On the marketing side Geox began, in the same year, to set up a network of single brand stores, some directly owned and some franchised. Situated in the high streets of major cities, they represent real tools of communication. The décor is such that the technology behind Geox products is immediately evident when customers enter the shop and trained personnel are on hand to glean information that may be useful for the company.

Since 2003 a large percentage of production has been carried out in the Far East, thanks to an agreement with the second largest Chinese footwear group, Aokang of Shanghai. Some 140 shops have been opened all over China with these partners, in marketing as well as production. Using local producers in each market has the advantage, among others, of paying attention to the morphological characteristics of feet; in fact, the Chinese have much wider feet and much shorter toes than Europeans.

6.3.4.   2004 Onwards: on the Stock Exchange

On 1 December 2004, Geox was listed on the Milan Stock Exchange, placing 29 per cent of its capital on the market. Following this operation, in June 2005 an ethical code of practice was drawn up by, among others, the Vatican spokesperson for Pope Benedict XVI, Joaquin Navarro-Valls from Spain, and the number one of Microsoft in Italy, Umberto Paolucci.

In recent years Italian manufacturing has suffered from the combined effect of Chinese competition and the strong euro but this does not seem to have had any adverse effect on Geox, which has continued to develop on the international markets, offering a complete range of clothing. Today the group produces a wide range of models (classic, casual and sport) for men, women and children, earning itself the name of 'family brand'. It launches two collections a year with a retail price positioning in the mid-market range. Turnover for 2006 was over €610 million, due to the work of its approximately 3 000 employees.

The company continues to develop the range of products on offer. At the Dubai Index 2007 salon, specialised in defence technology and held in the United Arab Emirates at the end of February, the Montebelluna group presented the 'breathing' military shoe that it supplies to the Saudi military. The latest Geox project is one of its most ambitious; together with Nicholas Negroponte, well-known IT expert and founder of Medialab, it is developing a laptop, which can be better protected from water and over-heating, thanks to Geox technology.

6.4.   THE PERFORMANCES OF GEOX

6.4.1.   The Company Growth

Table 6.11 shows the trends in turnover and number of employees of the Geox group, including all sales and production units that are not based within the geographical area of the district. The figures for 1995–1999 still refer to Pol and this explains the 'jump' in terms of number of employees. In 1995 turnover was less than €20 million, 11 years later it was 30 times as much. From a workforce of 32 in 1995 it grew to over 3 200 in 2006. In terms of speed the Geox growth process is a rare example within the Italian industrial panorama.

Table 6.11 Employees and turnover of the Geox group

Year	Employees	Turnover (€K)
1995	32	19 654
1996	52	27 711
1997	90	33 178
1998	119	41 735
1999	80	55 123
2000	1 123	92 849
2001	1 543	14 577
2002	2 200	180 260
2003	2 525	254 052
2004	2 571	340 050
2005	2 876	454 963
2006	3 206	612 258

Source: personal elaboration on AIDA and company reports

6.4.2. Comparison with the Industry and the District

What is striking about the growth of Geox is the fact that it came about in a mature sector of industry, in serious difficulty particularly in the new millennium. As Table 6.12 shows, the rate of growth of turnover and employees at Geox has always been higher than the rest of the sector where the rate is often negative. The only exception is 1999, when the Geox project moved from Pol to the newly set-up Geox and many employees remained with Pol. In comparison with the district, Geox also shows a decidedly higher rate of growth of turnover and employees, even though the Montebelluna firms felt the effects of the difficulties in the Italian shoe sector less than elsewhere.

6.4.3. Financial Results

The growth of Geox is characterised by the fact that it took place in a highly profitable way. From its establishment onwards, Geox had good returns, especially in relation to the capital invested. Table 6.13 shows the company's operating profit, net profit, ROA and ROE. While the first three show a clear growth trend, the fourth is more irregular, although the values are still high and above average for the sector.

Table 6.12 Employee and turnover growth of the Geox group, the district of Montebelluna and the Italian sector

	Turnover Growth			Employee Growth		
Year	Geox	District	Sector	Geox	District	Sector
1995	n.a.	n.a.	n.a.	n.a.	n.a.	4%
1996	41%	n.a.	3%	63%	n.a.	-2%
1997	20%	n.a.	0%	73%	n.a.	-1%
1998	26%	-11%	-2%	32%	-7%	-3%
1999	32%	4%	-6%	-33%	-6%	-3%
2000	68%	18%	12%	1 304%	4%	-1%
2001	59%	7%	5%	37%	1%	-1%
2002	22%	3%	-6%	43%	-4%	-4%
2003	41%	5%	-7%	15%	-7%	-3%
2004	34%	4%	-4%	2%	1%	-2%
2005	34%	1%	-5%	12%	-3%	-4%
2006	35%	n.a.	1%	11%	n.a.	-3%

Source: personal elaboration on AIDA, company reports, ANCI and OSEM

Table 6.13 Operating income, net profit and profitability of the Geox group

Year	Operating Income (€M)	Net Profit (€M)	ROA	ROE
1995	1.2	0.4	n.a.	n.a.
1996	0.7	0.0	16.6%	2.9%
1997	1.1	0.2	13.2%	16.0%
1998	1.6	0.3	18.4%	18.1%
1999	0.8	0.5	10.6%	51.5%
2000	6.2	3.4	n.a.	n.a.
2001	11.9	7.5	25.0%	21.7%
2002	23.9	19.4	43.8%	103.7%
2003	38.7	30.7	49.6%	79.7%
2004	72.8	52.8	65.1%	76.7%
2005	102.9	75.3	78.9%	51.6%
2006	134.9	97.3	84.6%	47.7%

Source: personal elaboration on AIDA and company reports

7. Illycaffè

S. Sciascia

This chapter presents the case study of Illycaffè, a company based in the Trieste coffee district that specialises in the production of high quality coffee. The aim of this chapter is to describe the entrepreneurial growth process of the firm, setting it within the context of the sector and the industrial district and presenting the economic–financial consequences of this growth. The chapter is thus divided into four sections: the coffee sector; the coffee district; the history of Illycaffè; and the performances of Illycaffè.

7.1. THE COFFEE INDUSTRY

7.1.1. The Market and the Industry at World Level

Since the eighteenth century coffee has conquered over 90 per cent of the world adult population and is the third most widely consumed beverage in the world, after water and wine. Since the 1990s the coffee market has reached a significant size making it one of the major commodities of international trade.

There are two main types of coffee: Arabica and Robusta. The first comes originally from the Middle East and is generally considered to be the best quality; the beans have a copper-green colour and produce a coffee that has a rich aroma and full flavour. The second comes originally from the Congo, is less costly to produce and is particularly resistant to disease; for this reason it is becoming more and more widely used in preference to the first.

Coffee is in every respect a global industry; it is characterised by the presence of a few large multinational companies involved in coffee roasting and retail distribution and by numerous small local firms. Nevertheless, a progressive agglomeration of the industry is taking place. The so-called 'Big Four' – Nestlé, Phillip-Morris/Kraft, Sara Lee and Procter & Gamble – control the world coffee roasting activity and account for over 90 per cent of instant coffee production. Other smaller multinational companies, such as

Lavazza in Italy and Tchibo in Germany, operate in the main domestic markets of western Europe.

Table 7.1 World coffee production (in thousands of 60 kg bags)

Year	Supply	Variation	Year	Supply	Variation
1991	101 568	9%	1999	114 901	7%
1992	97 448	-4%	2000	116 662	2%
1993	92 015	-6%	2001	107 021	-8%
1994	93 909	2%	2002	122 068	14%
1995	86 928	-7%	2003	103 673	-15%
1996	103 186	19%	2004	115 828	12%
1997	99 942	-3%	2005	109 933	-5%
1998	107 842	8%	2006	121 157	10%

Source: personal elaboration on ICO

Almost all coffee growing is concentrated in the developing countries, where it is an important source of employment and subsistence; on the other hand nearly all the coffee produced is exported to and consumed in the western world. Coffee is cultivated in four main areas: South America (Brazil, Venezuela, Columbia, Peru and Ecuador), Central America and the Caribbean, Africa and Asia (in particular India and Indonesia). The coffee trade is of vital importance for the economy of many of the producing countries. The biggest producer is still Brazil, which, together with Columbia and Vietnam, represents almost 60 per cent of world production.

According to ICO (International Coffee Organisation), the figure of 40 million bags in 1950s consumed annually has almost trebled today, although consumption has levelled off over the last few years, with a growth rate of 1–2 per cent. Production has fluctuated more, as shown in Table 7.1, and in the increasingly frequent periods where offer exceeds demand, coffee prices collapse. In fact the world market is rather volatile and linked to climatic change, financial speculation, economic policy, the entry of new coffee producing countries and changes in consumption patterns. In some countries this has led to a fall in prices, in some cases to much lower than cost price, creating difficulties for workers and growers, particularly in Vietnam, Columbia, Central America and Africa. Brazil, however, the world's biggest producer, manages to remain competitive even in these kinds of periods due to a high level of productivity and favourable price differential.

7.1.2. Trends in the Italian Industry

The following table shows Italy's exports of roasted coffee from 1995 to 2006. It can be seen that exports rose constantly with only a slight setback in 2000.

Table 7.2 Italian exports of roasted coffee (in euro)

Year	Export
1995	180 216 409
1996	178 399 079
1997	196 199 042
1998	228 950 537
1999	237 846 422
2000	168 440 984
2001	292 867 952
2002	321 713 722
2003	330 661 542
2004	367 636 523
2005	414 450 101
2006	488 594 130

Source: personal elaboration on ISTAT

Table 7.3 Local coffee roasting units and employees in Italy

Year	Local Units	Employees
1991	82	1729
1996	52	1376
2001	108	2567

Source: personal elaboration on ISTAT

As far as the number of local units involved in coffee roasting is concerned, these went up from 82 units in 1996 to 108 in 2001, while employees increased from 1 729 to approximately 2 567. This growth was not linear, however, as Table 7.3 shows. If we look at the entire coffee production chain, there are approximately 750 firms equally spread around the country and some 7 000 employees. The majority of these are small firms, with an average of less than 10 employees, but there are also a number of large size firms with an internationally known brand and image.

7.1.3.   The Italian Coffee Industry Today

In terms of raw coffee imports Italy is in fifth position in the world behind the USA, Germany, Japan and France. According to ISTAT figures for 2005, Italy imported 6.6 million 60kg bags, coming mainly from Brazil, Vietnam and India. See Table 7.4 for further details of country of origin and type of coffee imported, provided by ECF (European Coffee Federation).

Table 7.4   Italian coffee imports according to country of origin and type (2005)

Country		Type	
Brazil	36.13%	Colombian Milds	6.90%
Vietnam	14.74%	Other Milds	19.66%
India	11.24%	Brazilian Naturals	38.47%
Others	37.89%	Robustas	34.97%
Total	100.00%	Total	100.00%

Source: personal elaboration on ECR (European Coffee Report) by ECF

The high level of per capita consumption (approximately 5.5 kg/year) makes Italy one of the main consumer markets. The DATABANK 2005 estimated the figure for roasted coffee consumption in Italy to be approximately 250 million kilos. This corresponds to a value (ex-factory) of approximately €2018 million and a production value of approximately €2 500 million, thanks to a positive export–import balance of over €480 million. The mass distribution market accounts for two thirds of purchases, HoReCa accounts for another quarter, while the remaining 8 per cent comes from vending and serving systems.

Firms operating in the retail channels have high national coverage and well-known brands thanks to huge investments in advertising. The leader on the Italian market is Lavazza with approximately 50 per cent of the market. Other firms with a smaller market share include: Segafredo Zanetti, Kraft, Café do Brasil and Illy. Communication is the fundamental lever guaranteeing success in this channel.

In HoReCa three main firms (Illy, Segafredo and Lavazza) cover approximately 15 per cent of the market, while the other 85 per cent is represented by small and medium-sized coffee roasting firms, operating mainly at regional level (De Toni and Tracogna, 2005). It is easier to survive in this kind of channel; the capacity to offer the right quality product and to guarantee a series of accessory services such as punctual delivery, technical and commercial assistance and some financial incentives are the necessary conditions to obtain the exclusive supply to a certain bar, restaurant or hotel.

The automatic distribution channel is divided into vending and serving; this is still a minor category but with high potential for growth. Lavazza is the leader in serving with 30 per cent of the market share.

In addition to the high level of consumption, the Italian coffee market is important for roasting and re-exportation activities. Italian coffee production is about 350 thousand tons a year with an industrial turnover of over €2 billion; a quarter is destined to export. Table 7.5 shows the distribution of different types of coffee exported.

Table 7.5 Italian coffee exports in 2005 (in tons)

Type	Tons
Green Coffee	4 992
Green Decaffeinated Coffee	812
Roasted Coffee	76 318
Roasted Decaffeinated Coffee	2 972
Coffee Extract	472
Preparations with Coffee	3 262
Total	88 828

Source: personal elaboration on ECR

7.1.4. The Main Dynamics in the Industry

In Italy the market is mature. Demand has reached the saturation level and stable consumption makes for intense competition between firms. It is difficult for the different firms to find room for growth in the sector. The offer is made up of many small firms, working at regional or cross-regional level, and a dozen large companies, which are big enough to be present throughout Italy and are expanding abroad.

In recent years market dynamics that can be linked to changes in society and in consumer tastes have begun to develop within the coffee sector.

It should be emphasised that the main effect of these changes is the fact that the product is no longer seen as a simple commodity but has become a distinctive sign and a powerful means of communication, as shown by the evolution taking place in the way of preparing and consuming coffee.

The trend towards organic products, fair and ethical trade is also making an appearance both in mass distribution and in HoReCa, with an impact in terms of communication and values.

As society evolves towards the so-called 'experience economy' (Pine and Gilmore, 1999), important changes have taken place in terms of where coffee is purchased and drunk. Consumers tend more and more to value the socialising aspect of the point of sale, which is no longer simply the place where they drink coffee. Thus, the environment the consumers meet must have a pleasant atmosphere and create the right ambience. A mix of sound, light, colour and comfortable surroundings add to a high quality product and service and act positively on the consumer's perception, transforming the coffee moment into a unique sensorial experience. These changes have set in motion a series of strategic responses on the part of some firms, who have seized the opportunity offered by this experiential revolution to develop means that can anticipate and satisfy new consumer demands.

7.2.   THE TRIESTE COFFEE DISTRICT

7.2.1.   Origins and Specialisations

The coffee district, officially recognised as such by the Friuli regional government, extends over an area that includes Trieste and the municipalities of San Dorligo, Monrupino, Muggia and Sgonico.

From 1719 onwards the port of Trieste and the favourable geographical position, affording an opening towards the Central European market, enabled the area to develop a unique coffee district. The passion for coffee and the presence of all the operators in the chain, except for the grower, were critical success factors.

The history of the district is 300 years old. Coffee appeared in the city of Trieste around 1700. During the period of Hapsburg domination the infrastructure and economy of Trieste grew and with it the coffee tradition. The port underwent exponential growth, which made it the heart and economic centre of the city. Many bars and shops selling coffee were opened to the public and many small coffee roasting businesses were established. The opening of the Suez Canal in 1869 led to a positive turn in the economy of Trieste by increasing trade with the east. The Trieste Coffee Association was set up in 1891, the third oldest coffee dealers' association in the world. The district's development was also helped by the presence of a strong banking and insurance system, which could handle exchange and transformation activities. When ICO was set up in Brazil in 1958, a representative of the Trieste association was included in the panel of members.

7.2.2.   Trends in Structure and Performance

Overall there has been a slight increase in the number of local units and employees in the Trieste coffee district. Following a slight drop in 1996, the number of firms grew in 2001 and reached 23 in 2005. The number of employees has grown constantly over the years from 294 in 1991 to 517 in

2005. The slight fall registered by local units and employees at national level in 1996 did not really affect the firms and employees of the Trieste district. In fact, while there was a very slight drop in the number of firms, the number of employees actually increased in that year (Table 7.6). Today the Trieste district accounts for approximately 15 per cent of the Italian coffee trade.

Table 7.6   Local units and employees involved in coffee roasting in the Trieste District

Year	Local Units	Employees
1991	17	294
1996	15	305
2001	16	393
2005	23	517

Source: personal elaboration on ISTAT and Qualicaf

As far as exports are concerned, Table 7.7 shows how exports from the district went up from approximately €6 million in 1995 to €25 million in 2006. Thus, in only 10 years exports increased fourfold. Although Italian coffee exports increased generally – almost doubled – the performance of the Trieste district had the greatest impact.

Table 7.7   Coffee exports from the province of Trieste (in euro)

Year	Exports
1995	6 095 101
1996	5 534 711
1997	7 381 394
1998	8 250 269
1999	11 401 206
2000	13 903 120
2001	12 825 620
2002	14 685 473
2003	13 745 499
2004	15 619 113
2005	21 019 992
2006	25 145 645

Source: personal elaboration on ISTAT

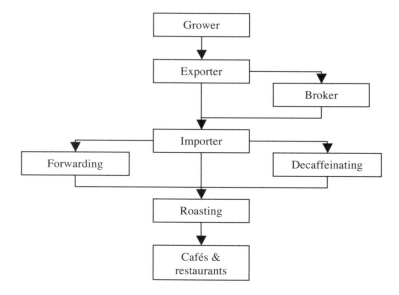

Source: Personal elaboration

Figure 7.1 The coffee chain

7.2.3. Transformation of the Supply Chain and Type of Firm

The Trieste coffee district is unique in the world in that all the various coffee processing stages are covered by the firms making up the district; only the grower is missing. The coffee chain is shown is Figure 7.1. The heart of the process is the roasting plant, which transforms the green coffee beans into roasted coffee destined for consumption. The coffee roasting phase is the most important part of the chain for Trieste. Historically Hausbrandt was the first firm to roast coffee in the city of Trieste and was one of the first coffee roasting businesses on a worldwide scale. Hausbrandt, Illy and Cremcafé are some of the household names in the Trieste coffee roasting tradition. Today, however, the golden age that the Trieste coffee roasting companies enjoyed in the post-war period is well and truly over. Present-day competition no longer allows them to exploit the advantages of the port to the full, as in the past, and demands reactions that they have been able to put into practice only in part. Figures for market share and company performance of the coffee roasting firms, apart from Illy, are some cause for concern.

Six of the 23 coffee roasting firms were founded before 1960, while the rest were established between 1960 and 1980. Seven of them have fewer than four employees and have a turnover of less than €500 000.

The decaffeinating phase, outsourced by nearly all the Italian coffee roasters, is carried out by only one firm in the Trieste area: Demus Spa, founded in 1962. It has a turnover of €2 million and employs about twenty people. There are two other similar companies in Italy.

An important role within the chain is also played by the importers. This role grew up around 1700, when large quantities of coffee transited through the port before being sorted and distributed. Over the years the Trieste importers have increased their range of activity, not only specialising in high quality coffee, due to the setting up of continuous quality controls on the goods, but also offering consultancy services to the coffee roasters.

Only one exporter operates in the Trieste area: the Z-Trading company, founded in 1996 and part of the Tristao group, the biggest Brazilian coffee exporter. The different companies in the group have the job of buying the coffee directly from the farmers and preparing it for export. The group does not operate directly in every country but uses different companies, such as Z-Trading in the case of Trieste.

The broker is an intermediary between the exporter and importer. This role is now disappearing due to the development and spread of new technologies, which allow for faster and easier communication. One of the main brokers is Alberto Hesse, one of the foremost coffee experts in the world and president of the Trieste Coffee Association for twenty years.

Last but not least is the forwarding agent. There are about ten in the Trieste district but the largest and best known is Pacorini. This firm is the world leader in the selection and cleaning of coffee, handling more than 10 per cent of the world's raw coffee. The work of the forwarding agent has in fact changed a lot over the years; today its role is to carry out a series of operations on the coffee beans, improving their condition and appearance in order to guarantee quality. The conviction is growing generally that in order to guarantee a constant high quality of coffee bean all the players in the chain must be involved.

7.2.4.   The Main Dynamics in the District

The Trieste district is an example of a production and distribution chain on a local scale projected onto a global scale; a model of area development based on the geographical concentration of the firms and the institutions connected. Almost all the operators in the chain, except for the growers, are present in the Trieste district. This important feature, together with the city's strong historical links with coffee, the continued support of local institutions and the initiatives of the Trieste scientific community have made the Trieste coffee chain a unique example of the interaction of economic, technological, social and cultural development.

The district's main limits are the small size of the area and of the firms as well as a lack of integration of logistics structures.

The chief forms of action undertaken by the local institutions have aimed to improve interaction between firms in the chain in order to develop a strong spirit of cooperation that could encourage the district's growth, to improve promotion with the start of co-marketing actions, to enhance penetration of eastern European markets, and to develop events such as the international coffee day organised by the Trieste Coffee Association, the Trieste Espresso Expo with the help of the Trieste Fair and the Trieste Coffee Assembly, the Science Café, the Schools' Competition, the Art Prize.

7.3.   THE HISTORY OF ILLYCAFFÈ

Illycaffè grew according to a clearly defined path. The growth process can be divided into four main phases; the key moments for the development of the business model in each phase are highlighted below.

7.3.1.   From 1933 to 1989: Building the Business Model and the Positioning

The Illycaffe company was founded by Francesco Illy in 1933. At first it dealt with the production and sale of coffee and cocoa but after just two years the founder decided to focus on coffee.

During the first decades the company focused on the coffee trade and on the continuous search for improvement of product quality. During the 1930s Francesco came up with some important innovations; he invented the espresso machine, the 'Illetta', and developed the technique of vacuum packing to maintain the freshness of the coffee for a longer time, thus expanding the geographical area of sales. This search for new ideas helped to turn the company into a real research laboratory in the 1950s. At that time Illy was still a medium-sized coffee roaster in competition mainly with small and medium-sized coffee roasters working at local or, in some cases, national level. Consumers considered coffee as a simple commodity good and focused their attention mainly on product quality. Against this background, Illy was already working at national level due partly to pressurised packing.

When Ernesto entered the company after World War II, they began to export in a more systematic way and affirmed the market positioning as a high quality coffee brand. Illy was the only company in the world offering a blend of nine different qualities of Arabica to satisfy the demands of an increasingly quality-aware consumer. As a graduate in Chemistry, Ernesto was interested in scientific and technological research and formed alliances with other companies, institutions and universities. In the 1980s Illy consolidated its image as a quality company and the 'Illy' signs began to appear in cities all over Italy.

7.3.2. From 1989 to 1994: Illy Comes into People's Homes

The second phase in the company development saw a significant acceleration in the process of growth and development, turning Illy into one of the big coffee companies on the international scene.

In 1989 Illy entered Italian homes via mass distribution. The basic idea was to continue to offer the best coffee, packed in pressurised cans with a strong visual impact and sold through supermarkets, to enable the consumer to enjoy at home the same quality of coffee as served in an Italian bar. The range was gradually widened to include coffee beans, espresso ground coffee, moka ground coffee and decaffeinated coffee.

In 1992 Illy further expanded its range with the launch of the Illy Collection coffee cups. In partnership with famous artists, who contributed their particular skills, the company produced a line of very individual coffee cups - not just accessories but real collectors' items. By doing this, the Illy brand image became not only synonymous with innovation and quality but also aesthetic taste. Thus with the Illy's entry into mass distribution and the launch of the Illy collection, Illy entered people's homes with products that had previously been available exclusively to bars and restaurants.

The search for even higher quality continued throughout this period and in 1992 the company received the 'Qualité France' certification and in 1996 the ISO 9001 production quality certification. Quality control was again enhanced by the creation, in 1991, and development of a complete system of selection, training and control of the supply chain, eliminating the coffee broker. The company, in fact, decided to buy directly from the grower in order to guarantee the quality of the beans. An award system, the Brazil prize, was also set up to reward the best coffee supplier with highly advantageous purchase prices.

7.3.3. From 1994 to 1999: Andrea Illy and the Development of Espresso Systems

The third phase in the Illy story is marked by the appointment of Andrea, Ernesto's son, as CEO and by the development of serving systems for espresso coffee.

Andrea's entry into the company heralded the start of a managerial approach and the elimination of obstacles to growth caused by excessive family interference in the running of the company. In fact a family agreement was stipulated in 1996, under the terms of which no family member could take on a managerial role unless he or she was suitably trained and motivated. Andrea Illy recruited a number of managers from outside the company, all of whom had significant past experience and company-strategic competences. He also introduced a training programme at different levels.

The corporate organisational model was redrawn in 1999 to give maximum autonomy and responsibility to the managerial team.

In terms of the product range, in 1996 Illy launched the 'Easy Serving Espresso' (ESE) for making espresso coffee using single serving pods. With this Illy entered the automatic distribution channel using a network of agents for the distribution of the pods. The Trieste company was the first to develop this kind of product. The system is an open one; in other words, any firm can manufacture machines with the ESE standard for use with pods. The system means that a high quality coffee can be obtained in a simple, fast and practical way. Naturally its development would not have been possible without the cooperation of coffee machine manufacturers such as Alessi, Gaggia, Saeco, De Longhi and Itaca. A consortium was formed by these firms with the aim of promoting the ESE industrial standard. The system was widely adopted not only in offices but also for domestic use and in the HoReCa trade, particularly abroad (given that Italy already has an espresso tradition and does not need a single portion system).

This period also saw the setting up of Aroma Lab, an Illy laboratory dedicated to the study of coffee aroma and quality. The third phase is a period of technology-push development, with high technological content. The next phase links this development strand to one that is less technological in content and more linked to art and culture.

7.3.4.   From 2000 to Today: Design and Culture

In recent years the company has reacted to changes taking place in society and in consumers' perceptions of coffee drinking. Coffee is no longer seen as a product but as a total experience, no longer just a drink but a moment in which different emotions are created. This is why in 2003, following some years of study, Illy launched the Espressamente Illy project, to encompass all those elements that make the coffee experience unique. Espressamente Illy consists in a network of innovative, authentically Italian cafés that are being opened up all over the world as franchises. The objective is to offer atmosphere, colour and music, to create a total coffee experience that appeals to all the senses and creates a feeling of well-being.

The format, designed by well-known Italian architects – Luca Trazzi, Claudio Silvestrin and Paola Navone – is offered to HoReCa clients all over the world, together with training and consultancy on how to manage the product and the service. The franchising contracts last for 6 years and involve payment of a franchise entrance fee and royalties. So far there are about 50 cafés in Italy and another 70 in the rest of the world.

The fourth phase in the history of Illy is marked, then, by the move from coffee selling to coffee culture. Art and creativity are two concepts that characterise the language chosen by Illy to express its values and philosophy. The coffee concept is raised to the level of a cultural moment. This notion already expressed in the Illy Collection has now become a real communication strategy based on the artistic and cultural involvement of the consumer. This philosophy is demonstrated in the launch of 'Espressamente Illy', some experimentation in contemporary communication, the promotion and development of internationally important cultural events. At the Venice Biennale, the red colour of Illycaffè indicates a place or moment to stop, admire a work of art and absorb the emotion. On leaving visitors take with them, together with pleasant memories, a special edition of the Illywords magazine. Together with the 'Festivaletturatura' of Mantua, Illycaffè has developed the 'Scritture Giovani' project: a circuit of four European literary festivals to select a new generation of writers and make them known to the public; their stories are published by Illy in four languages in the Illystories series and distributed through the bars. Illystories also publishes collections of dialogues and opinions on subjects such as the value of knowledge, the concept of the ethical firm, space, courage, dreams, multi-cultural society, awareness, chaos, nomadism of learning. The magazine is illustrated by art and design students from all over the world, who make it their personal and collective laboratory.

Galleria Illy is another example of this trend. It represents an event or happening, which can take place in big cities and where good taste, culture, art and beauty come together to provide an amazing experience for the visitor. The event includes coffee and food, all the Illy collections, the books and writers, photos and design, major contemporary artists and the young artists who illustrate Illystories and the Illywords magazine.

More generally, the company helps young artists with scholarships, Illy collection projects, money prizes, publications and exhibitions. Illy has understood that investing in culture facilitates contact with today's customers, coinciding with the development of a new sensibility, stimulating the senses and involving the emotions.

At the same time, Illy has continued to invest in technology and grow via the development of systems with a high technological content. Firstly, it has created Sensory Lab, TechLab and BioLab, three laboratories whose purpose is to study respectively the effects of coffee on the senses, the technologies to improve coffee production and different aspects of the biology of coffee. Secondly, Illy has launched two other single portion systems: I Espresso and Hyper Espresso.

The I Espresso system is the result of collaboration between Illy and Itaca, a company producing coffee machines and espresso coffee capsules for offices. The fruit of this venture is a type of capsule with a completely closed base, which opens only when the water reaches the right pressure, as well as a series of espresso coffee machines for use with these capsules.

The Hyper Espresso System has been devised for venues that want to serve a perfect espresso coffee but do not have a continuous high demand for coffee nor specialised bar personnel and so for whom the purchase of a professional espresso machine is not worthwhile. The system uses innovative capsules with a special valve in the base and which can provide a totally pure and unique quality espresso coffee. The 'retro' style machines for this system, the Francis Francis, are produced by Illy itself.

7.4.   THE PERFORMANCES OF ILLYCAFFÈ

7.4.1.   The Company Growth

Table 7.8 shows the growth in turnover and number of employees for the Illy group. This includes not only Illy SpA but also all the trading companies that are not based within the confines of the Trieste district. In 1998 turnover stood at €131 million, approximately 57 per cent of 2005 turnover; the same can be said of the number of employees, which went up from 380 to 661 over the same period. The biggest growth was in the periods 1998–2001 and 2004–5.

Table 7.8 Turnover and number of employees of Illycaffè

Year	Turnover (€M)	Employees
1998	131	380
1999	152	426
2000	176	504
2001	190	525
2002	193	527
2003	190	546
2004	205	633
2005	227	661

Source: personal elaboration on company data

7.4.2.   Financial Results

Over the last few years Illy has demonstrated its capacity not only to grow but also to be profitable, as shown in Table 7.9. Operating income and profit grew until 2000, reaching excellent levels of profitability: ROE and ROA up by 30 per cent and 20 per cent respectively. The following years saw a slowdown in operating income and profit, with a corresponding fall in profitability, which, however, remained high compared to that of the sector. 2005 saw a recovery in all figures and indices.

Table 7.9 Operating income, net profit and profitability of Illycaffè

Year	Operating Income (€)	Net Profit (€)	ROE	ROA
1998	12 187 866	4 398 663		
1999	15 972 463	8 906 299	36%	21%
2000	21 081 254	10 422 100	30%	22%
2001	19 809 664	10 091 411	21%	16%
2002	22 554 895	11 014 869	19%	19%
2003	20 356 978	10 802 474	17%	17%
2004	17 607 747	7 924 805	11%	14%
2005	22 856 287	10 603 188	14%	15%

Source: personal elaboration on company data

7.4.3.   Comparison with the Industry and the District

Illycaffè's growth process can be compared with that of the district in terms of the number of employees. Between 2001 and 2005 the growth in number of employees was greater in absolute terms than that of the employees in the district, as shown in Table 7.10. There are no up-to-date figures, however, for the number of employees in the coffee industry in Italy in general.

Table 7.10 Recent trends in the number of employees at Illycaffè and in the industrial district

Year	Illycaffè	Trieste
2001	525	393
2005	661	527
2001–2005	136	124

Source: personal elaboration on company data and ISTAT

In order to make a comparison with the whole sector, we can look at Illy's ROA compared to that of the main competitors. The data in Table 7.11 refer to 2004. It is evident that Illy's profitability is very close to that of the market leader, Lavazza, while investing much less capital, and noticeably higher than that of the other Italian firms, of whatever size.

Table 7.11 Turnover and ROA of the main Italian competitors in the coffee industry (2004)

Company	ROA	Turnover (€M)
Lavazza	14.3%	804 377
Segafredo Zanetti	8.4%	386 838
Illycaffè	14.0%	207 144
Cafè do Brasil	7.1%	107 598
Pellini	12.7%	52 398
Hausbrandt	12.2%	45 082
Vergnano	4.9%	29 125
Mauro	0.8%	15 512
Danesi	6.6%	15 081
Corsini	2.6%	8 291

Source: personal elaboration on AIDA

8.   Luxottica

C. Tripodi

This chapter presents the case study of Luxottica, a company that specialises in the manufacture and distribution of eyewear and is based in the district of Belluno. The aim of this chapter is to describe the entrepreneurial growth process of the firm, setting it within the context of the sector and the industrial district and presenting the economic–financial consequences of this growth. The chapter is thus divided into four parts: the eyewear industry; the Belluno eyewear manufacturing district; the history of Luxottica; and the performances of Luxottica.

8.1.   THE EYEWEAR INDUSTRY

8.1.1.   The Market and the Industry at World Level

The worldwide turnover for the eyewear industry is approximately €6 billion; the prescription frame sector accounts for 65 per cent of that turnover, while the remaining 35 per cent is represented by sunglasses.

Worldwide demand for glasses can be subdivided into the three main segments and retail price ranges shown in Table 8.1, bearing in mind that in USA the price range for prescription frames and sunglasses is more or less equivalent in US dollars to the European price range, whereas the retail prices in the luxury and premium segments in the Asian market are generally 20–40 per cent higher.

The aspects that differentiate between the products in one segment and another are not just the quality of the components and the materials used, but also the accuracy of the working and above all the quality of the design and the fashion content.

In particular, the glasses in the top market segment combine high quality materials and working with a fashion brand name. The middle segment pays more attention to the technical quality rather than the image, while the bottom segment is obviously characterised by greater price elasticity.

Table 8.1 Market segmentation in the eyewear sector (2006)

Market segment	Profile	Retail price range
	Luxury	> 150 €
High	Premium (high fashion)	125-150 €
	Sub-premium (fashion)	100-125 €
Middle	Casual – Sport	75-100 €
Low	Mass	< 75 €
	Discount	< 30 €

Source: personal elaboration on Bain & Company

In terms of product offer Italy is world leader in the sector with 27.6 per cent of the market. The other main players in the international market are Hong Kong with 17.6 per cent, and China with 12.9 per cent of world turnover.

The Italian manufacturers, particularly the larger ones concentrate their production on the luxury and premium segments while the bottom segment is mainly dominated by the Chinese firms.

Table 8.2 Market segmentation in the eyewear sector and position of Italian manufacturers (2006)

Market segment	World production	Italian production
High	25%	71%
Middle	25%	25%
Low	50%	4%

Source: Pambianco

Further confirmation of Italian leadership in the world market is the number of brands produced and sold under license by Italian companies; 154 out of 300 brand licenses are held by Italian manufacturers. As can be seen from Table 8.3 the first five world manufacturers in terms of brands under license are all Italian. This fact is particularly significant if we consider that from the 1980s onwards the granting of brand licenses by the main fashion houses has helped to characterise the eyewear market as a market for fashion products and accessories, thus increasing growth rate in the sector in terms both of prescription frames and sunglasses.

Table 8.3 The top 5 brands under license in the world (2006)

Company	Brands under license
Safilo (Italy)	19
Luxottica (Italy)	18
De Rigo (Italy)	16
Allison (Italy)	15
Marcolin (Italy)	12

Source: Pambianco

Table 8.4 Main figures for the Italian glasses industry

Year	Firms	Employees	Turnover (€M)
1990	700	n.a.	983
1991	700	n.a.	621
1992	970	12 000	904
1993	1 000	12 500	982
1994	1 256	16 500	1 137
1995	1 450	17 850	1 390
1996	1 510	17 850	1 457
1997	1 510	17 850	1 498
1998	1 500	17 900	1 545
1999	1 500	18 000	1 472
2000	1 410	18 900	1 694
2001	1 400	19 000	1 836
2002	1 350	19 200	1 859
2003	1 120	17 500	1 871
2004	1 180	16 980	1 908
2005	1 130	16 800	2 104

Source: personal elaboration on ANFAO

8.1.2. Trends in the Italian Industry

Figures for the number of firms operating in the eyewear sector show a more or less regular increase in the number of local units up until 1996, when they began to fall drastically (-380, or -25 per cent, between 1997 and 2005).

The number of employees in the sector, however, continued to increase until 2002, bearing witness to a process of concentration of the industry in a smaller number of larger firms. Turnover also increased steadily – except for a slight fall in 1999 – at an average annual rate of 7 per cent, as further evidence of the increase in average company size. For some time the eyewear sector has shown a strong international trend. In 1995, 63 per cent of turnover was already realised in foreign markets; within ten years this share had grown to over 82 per cent. Only in the period 2002–2004 did exports suffer a slowdown due to the negative world economic climate following the terrorist attacks of 2001, combined with the unfavourable euro–dollar exchange rate, the increasingly fierce competition from Asian countries and the growth in counterfeiting.

Table 8.5 Italian exports of glasses

Year	Export (€M)	% Export/Turnover
1995	879	63.2
1996	1 008	69.2
1997	1 042	69.6
1998	1 075	69.6
1999	1 037	70.4
2000	1 405	82.9
2001	1 532	83.4
2002	1 568	84.3
2003	1 514	80.9
2004	1 536	80.5
2005	1 734	82.4

Source: personal elaboration on ANFAO

As far as the export destinations are concerned, the main markets are other European countries and the United States, which account for 49 per cent and 28 per cent of Italian production respectively; 16 per cent goes to the Asian markets.

8.1.3.   The Italian Industry Today

On the one hand the Italian optical industry is very fragmented with a total of 1130 small firms, with an average number of 15 employees. On the other, however, the greatest part of production is concentrated in a few large industrial groups: Luxottica, Safilo, De Rigo and Marcolin, all based in the industrial district of Belluno and together accounting for 63 per cent of the market.

The optical industry therefore consists, on the one hand, of a few large vertically integrated players, who occupy a key role on the national and international scene and, on the other, a myriad of small workshops or firms, specialised in one or more phases of the production chain, and sub-contracting for larger firms. It is these small firms that have been hardest hit by the economic recession of recent years and by the large firms' policies of internalising and/or offshoring production.

The production chain is typically made up of many phases, most of which tend to involve manual work rather than automated processes. In spite of its complexity, the production process may be divided into six main stages: design, planning and development; manufacture of separate parts of the glasses, movable parts and other components; soldering; electroplating, coating and varnishing treatments; final assembly.

Table 8.6 Production, import, export and consumption of glasses in the Italian market

Quantity (mln.)	2001	2002	2003	2004	2005
Production	**82 935**	**78 850**	**76 780**	**73 050**	**75 690**
Prescription frames	40 955	36 050	36 100	31 200	30 800
Sunglasses	41 980	42 800	40 680	41 850	44 890
Exports	**73 329**	**69 240**	**67 143**	**64 165**	**68 330**
Prescription frames	36 429	33 073	32 507	28 877	29 550
Sunglasses	36 900	36 167	34 636	35 288	38 780
Imports	**17 426**	**18 160**	**16 425**	**18 620**	**20 680**
Prescription frames	6 061	7 500	6 975	8 870	10 100
Sunglasses	11 365	10 660	9 450	9 750	10 580
Conspicuous consumption	**27 032**	**27 770**	**26 062**	**27 505**	**28 040**
Prescription frames	10 587	10 477	10 568	11 193	11 350
Sunglasses	16 445	17 293	15 494	16 312	16 690

Source: personal elaboration on Databank, Istat

Over the years, not only have the sector leaders followed a strategy of internalising all or most of the phases in the production process, but most of them have expanded by means of forwards integration, entering the retail market via the acquisition of some of the main international eyewear chains. This strategy was deemed necessary because of the potentially high bargaining power of the distribution network, due to the fact that the optician in general has a lot of influence over consumer purchasing decisions, particularly in the choice of prescription frames, to which the lenses will be fitted.

8.1.4.   The Main Dynamics in the Industry

Analysing the trends in the different divisions of the sector (prescription frames and sunglasses), over the last few years a move can be noted in production mix and export towards sunglasses.

This also explains the sluggish performance of exports in the period 2002–2004. The recent general fall in consumption affected mainly luxury goods and leisure goods, which can include sunglasses. Nevertheless, 2005 marked a change in trend and it was the sunglasses division that launched the recovery with increases in production volumes and exports of 7.3 per cent and 9.9 per cent respectively compared to the previous year.

The results for 2006 and the first months of 2007 confirm the recovery. In 2006 production in the Italian eyewear sector increased 17.4 per cent in value compared to 2005; exports grew by 18.2 per cent compared to 2005 and almost 35 per cent compared to 2004, confirming Italy's leadership in the world market. In particular, exports of sunglasses increased 23 per cent compared to 2005, to stand at almost €1 354 million, while prescription frames saw a smaller but still significant increase (+10.5 per cent), finishing the year at over €675 million.

It is significant that there was also an increase in employment for the first time in several years; the number of employees in the sector in fact increased by 6.5 per cent.

The main beneficiaries of this performance have first of all been the sector leaders. Small and medium-sized firms have also managed to renew and focus on the quality of Italian products, although undeniably they find it difficult to survive in an increasingly global market, where as in other sectors, Asian competition is growing in terms of quantity, quality and range. For example, the main Chinese brands (Moulin International, Arts Optical International, Sun Hing Vision Group, Elegance International) are gradually focusing on higher quality products, acquiring brands under license and expanding into the retail market with the acquisition of retail distribution chains not only in China, but also abroad.

8.2.   THE BELLUNO EYEWEAR DISTRICT

8.2.1.   Origins and Specialisations

In Italy eyewear production is concentrated mainly in the province of Belluno and in particular in the Valle del Cadore. In fact more that 70 per cent of employees in the sector work in this area, which generates approximately 82 per cent of Italian turnover.

Table 8.7 The Belluno district compared to the sector in general (2006)

	Employees	Turnover (€M)
Belluno Province	12 000	1 800
Total Italy	16 800	2 200
%	71.4	81.8

Source: personal elaboration on Assindustria Belluno

Moreover, considering that the four leading manufacturers on a global scale – Luxottica, Safilo, De Rigo and Marcolin – are based in the district, it is reasonable to identify the Italian eyewear sector with the Veneto district. In this way we can understand the main trends in the district basing our observations on the figures for the sector as a whole and vice versa.

The first workshop producing spectacles was set up in the Province of Belluno in 1878 by Angelo Frescura, together with his brother, Leone Frescura, and Giovanni Lozza. The Calalzo workshop gradually grew, due to its technicians and collaborators, into a series a small firms in the Cadore valley, specialising in the manufacture of lenses, small metal parts, cases and frames, to become, around 1930, the company now known as Safilo.

A second glasses manufacturing area grew up in the nearby Valle dell'Agordino at the beginning of the 1960s, following the setting up of Luxottica di Del Vecchio & C. Sas (Brunetti and Camuffo, 2000).

From the early 1960s onwards, 2 manufacturing clusters could thus be clearly identified in the Province of Belluno. On the one hand the small and medium-sized businesses in the Cadore area, specialising in single phases of the production process and thus strongly interdependent; on the other, in the adjacent Agordino valley, another smaller group of companies which had grown up around Luxottica. Right from the start, Luxottica's founder, Leonardo Del Vecchio, had supported new entrepreneurial initiatives, encouraging his employees to start their own businesses, providing them with machinery on loan. Contracts signed with Luxottica guaranteed survival for these subcontractors and at the same time allowed Luxottica to maintain considerable flexibility in production.

To sum up, we can see how initially the industrial model based on a network of small firms with a high level of specialisation was the winning one in the glasses district as in other sectors, so much so that by the early 1970s the Belluno district had gained a strong competitive position at an international level, overtaking German and French competitors who had until then held the lead.

The productive set up of the area, based on specialisation and helped by the division of the production process into parts, meant that the firms in the district were able to control costs and allowed them a good level of flexibility in production right from the beginning.

8.2.2.   Trends in the Structure and Performance

Trends in numbers of local units and employees at district level confirms what we have seen at national level, as might be expected from the substantial overlap between the district and sector mentioned above.

In fact, here too, we see a reduction in the number of firms from 1996 onwards, while the number of employees continued to grow until 2002, before falling back. In terms of trends in both employment and average turnover there are evident signs of the process of concentration that over time has affected the whole glasses sector.

Table 8.8 Main figures for the Belluno district

Year	Firms	Employees	Turnover (€M)
1992	630	7 700	723
1993	650	8 100	785
1994	810	10 000	950
1995	930	11 200	1 157
1996	935	11 760	1 195
1997	920	12 700	1 291
1998	930	13 000	1 343
1999	850	13 552	1 281
2000	820	13 700	1 446
2001	780	13 800	1 470
2002	750	14 000	1 500
2003	684	12 470	1 490
2004	606	11 660	1 510
2005	560	11 540	1 585
2006	530	12 000	1 800

Source: personal elaboration on Assindustria Belluno, ANFAO

Taking a closer look at the figures for employees and turnover for the district in comparison with those of the sector as a whole, we can see that the concentration was noticeably more intense in the district. This can probably be explained by the fact that the main operators in the sector are based in the province of Belluno. Finally, the signs of recovery seen at national level from 2005 onwards were obviously given added thrust within the district, which is the fulcrum of national production in the eyewear sector.

Table 8.9   Number of employees according to company size in the district of Belluno

Number of employees per company	1996	1997	1998	1999	2001	Total variation
< 50	5 156	5 080	4 913	4 615	4 032	- 1 124
51–100	1 101	966	931	932	1 176	+ 75
101–500	2 276	2 007	1 677	1 677	1 890	- 386
501–999	-	-	579	579	667	+ 667
> 999	2 951	3 005	3 168	3 168	3 379	+ 428

Source: personal elaboration on Belluno Chamber of Commerce data

8.2.3.   The Main Dynamics in the District

From the 1980s onwards there was a change in the consumers' perception of glasses: from a medical aid they became seen as a fashion object. This opened up a whole series of previously unimaginable opportunities to the operators in the sector, who became linked to the fashion system by marketing agreements, and led to a change in the way critical success factors were determined. As the product took on symbolic and intangible value and demand shifted towards upmarket products with a higher level of sophistication and often accompanied by a famous brand name, it became fundamental for the manufacturers to constantly monitor product quality and innovation processes (new raw materials, new chemical treatments, and so on) as well as trends in consumer preferences and tastes in order to be fast and flexible in meeting demand.

In terms of offer there was a clear dichotomy between, on the one hand, the large firms, who began a process of vertical integration with the objective of both supervising all the qualitative aspects of manufacture and technological innovation and of monitoring trends in demand via a tighter control on distribution, and, on the other hand, the small firms, who remained focused on a single part of the manufacturing process, failing to develop marketing skills. In this way the small firms put their own survival at risk inasmuch as the vertically integrated larger firms started to dispense with the services of small sub-contractors as soon as the internal control of all phases of production was able to guarantee quality and cost levels that the external suppliers could not match. The slow but steady reduction in the number of employees of small firms, starting from the second half of the 1990s, is evidence of the loss of competitiveness, as shown in Table 8.9.

More recently there have again been moments of difficulty for the Belluno glasses manufacturers. From 2002 to 2004 there was a sharp fall in the number of production units, mainly due to the negative world economic climate as a result of the terrorist attacks of 2001, followed by the unfavourable euro–dollar exchange rate and then the rapid expansion of the 'world factory' that is China. The fact that China has become the number one source of Italian imports is conclusive and bears witness to the growing trend of the large eyewear manufacturers to outsource production to the huge and economical Chinese production capacity, cutting out the local suppliers. Added to this is the threat that China represents in terms of being the biggest manufacturer of counterfeit 'Made in Italy' goods.

However, 2005, 2006 and the first few months of 2007 have registered a change of trend, bringing back optimism to the sector. In order to consolidate the small firm recovery and lay the foundations for long-term growth, many initiatives have been taken at both corporate and institutional level.

For example, more and more space at Mido, the most important trade fair in the sector, held annually in Milan, is being taken up by small firms. The firms belonging to Confartigianato have created a consortium with local opticians to make their entry into the world of distribution.

A recent agreement between Banca Ifis, Assindustria Belluno and Consorzio Neafidi will give the Belluno SMEs access to financing (in particular factoring), based on an evaluation of the credit solvency/credit rating of the five leading firms who have joined the pact (Luxottica, Safilo, De Rigo, Marcolin and Allison). In return, the 'big five' will be able to rely on continuous high quality supplies from within the district and obtain payment terms of up to 180 days. This initiative shows how crucial the financial aspect is for the survival of the small and medium-sized operators in the district, who are finally coming out of the crisis of 2002–2004, and could be the basis for a new and profitable collaboration between the big players in the sector and the small firms, making links with the district again advantageous for the former.

8.3. THE HISTORY OF LUXOTTICA

The Luxottica Group is world leader in the manufacture and distribution of prescription frames and sunglasses in the premium and luxury market segments. As well as eight manufacturing plants, the company also benefits from a capillary distribution network, organised in two divisions: retail, which accounts for approximately 70 per cent of turnover, and wholesale, which represents the remaining 30 per cent. This marketing structure is one of the most widespread in the industry and enables the company to cover more than 130 countries all over the world with direct presence in 38 of the most important markets in terms of wholesale sales and direct control of 5800 outlets worldwide operating in the eyeglasses and sunglasses segments. The company's strong international profile is confirmed by the geographical breakdown of turnover, with North America accounting for approximately 65 per cent, and by the fact that the group is listed on the NYSE as well as on the Italian stock market.

The company profile is thus quite different from the typical industrial district firm and seems to have little in common with the context in which it developed. Furthermore, unlike its direct competitors, who have remained anchored in the Veneto district, Luxottica transferred its headquarters to Milan in 1999, whilst keeping most of its plants in the north-east.

The corporate growth process can be divided into four principal phases, each one corresponding to a ten year period, starting from its foundation in 1961.

8.3.1. The 1960s: the Birth of Luxottica

'Luxottica di Del Vecchio & C. S.a.s' was founded in 1961 as a limited partnership between Del Vecchio, general partner, and the two founders of Metalflex, a sunglass frame manufacturing company based in the Cadore area, sleeping partners.

The decision to set the business up in Agordo was mainly linked to the availability of land and funding from the municipality, which was trying to face the unemployment problem following the closure of the Val Imperina mines. The Agordino location was, however, favorable for Del Vecchio and partners, given the vicinity to the Cadore area, where Metalflex operated and the availability of labour, otherwise destined to emigrate. For several years production was limited to dies, moulds, small handmade accessories and frame parts for other glasses manufacturers in the Belluno area.

A few years later, Del Vecchio decided to make the first 'leap' forward, compared to the rest of the industry in the district. In 1967, when Luxottica had 54 employees, they started to manufacture complete glasses, although still with some parts of the production process contracted externally.

Meanwhile the company began to develop the technical skills that were to lay the foundations for long-term leadership. Investments were made to improve product quality and guarantee that costs were kept down. With the recruitment of well qualified staff, who were prepared to work up to 15 hours a day, Luxottica quickly built up the manufacturing know-how that larger companies had taken many years to develop.

Another important step in the company history was taken at the end of the 1960s: the launch of their own brand, Luxottica. This step, perhaps taken too early in the eyes of some, cost Del Vecchio the break-up of the partnership, when the other two associates left in disagreement with the founder's ambitious expansion plans.

At this time the company organisation was still very simple, with decision-making power held solidly in the hands of the entrepreneur, who was helped by members of his family and a small staff.

8.3.2.   The 1970s: Entering Foreign Markets

Left as the sole partner at the head of the company, Del Vecchio was able to give form to his ideas of growth. The 1970s thus saw a continuous contribution of capital and recourse to loans to feed the growth and in particular the drives towards globalisation and forwards integration.

Expansion into the international market started with the export of frames to foreign distributors immediately after the company's first participation in the Mido (Mostra Internazionale dell'Ottica) in Milan in 1971.

In 1978, together with one of those distributors, Avant Garde Optics, the company set up a plant in the USA to manufacture a private label range to be sold through the American partner's retail network. By doing this the company's market share increased considerably, above all abroad. By the end of the 1970s, 85 per cent of production was exported, while the remaining 15 per cent was destined for the domestic market.

At the same time Del Vecchio was beginning to see the importance of forwards integration for the creation of long-term competitive advantage. He often said 'the wholesaler is the death of firms because he forces them to live day by day'. Direct control of distribution, in fact, would allow the company to monitor the market and market trends without the wholesaler's 'filter'. Thus, in 1974, Luxottica acquired the Scarrone company of Turin, a distributor operating throughout Italy.

With the increase in size the business obviously had to make decisions to change the organisational set-up and in 1978 it became a limited company. In the early eighties the organisation went public, setting up a holding company Luxottica Group SpA.

8.3.3.   The 1980s: Globalization and Entry into the Fashion System

By the early 1980s Luxottica was to all intents and purposes a large company and, as such, had to continue its activity according to two orders of priority.

In the first place, it had to continue expanding production capacity, which was already quite large, and to consolidate the control of the whole production cycle. With this in mind, in 1981, Luxottica acquired the Meccanoptica Leonardo firm and its plant in Rovereto, as well as the well-known brand of Sferoflex, which takes its name from the typical flexible arm, which allows the glasses to adapt to any size of face, guaranteeing a comfortable fit. Following that, another two factories were opened: a new one at Sedico and another at Cencenighe, from the incorporation of a sub-contractor. This increase in production capacity meant that from 1988 onwards work contracted to outside suppliers accounted for only 10 per cent of manufacturing costs.

Secondly, it had to consolidate and develop the position gained in the foreign and domestic markets. To this end the setting up of a global distribution network was crucial. In fact, the use of wholesalers as intermediaries in the international markets, too, made it difficult to monitor the market directly and prevented the firm from dealing directly with the end user. The complex process of expanding Luxottica's international network was carried out by a joint strategy of opening sales branches abroad and making trading agreements and/or joint ventures with local distributors.

However, as we have said above, the 1980s also witnessed important changes in terms of demand: the transformation of glasses from an aid to remedy a sight deficiency to a fashion accessory to be displayed as a distinctive sign.

Luxottica joined the trend, putting its experience and technical expertise at the service of designers, giving them the means to create the eyewear that best interpreted the spirit of the collections and continually offering the market a range of new avant-garde models.

Luxottica confirmed its presence in this new scenario due to two winning strategies: partnerships with well-known designers and the acquisition of famous brands.

The first partnership with the world of high fashion dates from 1988, when the company signed a licensing agreement with Giorgio Armani. This was soon followed by agreements with many other internationally known big industry players.

This strategic decision, however, implied, a certain number of managerial issues. First of all the problem of managing the relationship with the designers, a problem that Luxottica had partially solved by linking Armani to the company by means of venture capital shares. Moreover, signing a licensing agreement involved considerable commitment in terms of respect of certain qualitative standards, the guarantee of a certain turnover of sample models, constant attention to innovation in materials and finishes, search for new packaging, display materials for the points of sale and sales campaigns. The company was able to meet these commitments, due to the technical and manufacturing skills developed over time, and took the opportunity to learn from the confrontation with different types of businesses.

Furthermore, the decision to position itself in the premium-luxury market segment, thanks to the agreements with fashion houses, turned out to be particularly productive in a competitive context that witnessed the progressive affirmation of Chinese competitors in the lower market segment.

8.3.4. The 1990s: Entry into the Financial Markets, the Focus on the Sun Segment and Expansion of the Retail Segment

The 1990s opened with the listing of the Luxottica group on the New York Stock Exchange (NYSE). With this decision Luxottica became the first company in the world to be listed on one of the big international stock markets before its own domestic one. This, certainly unconventional, move was not only due to the need to raise the necessary capital for further expansion but also corresponded to a coherent strategy of a now multinational group to give itself a global image.

From an organisational point of view this 'revolutionary' decision posed an even greater challenge to Del Vecchio. From now on corporate culture would have to become more managerial and corporate strategy would have to be decided by a number of stakeholders.

This decade also marks the moment in which the company decided to direct production more towards sunglasses. At the end of the 1980s in fact, 90 per cent of Luxottica's production was prescription frames, but the market trend was definitely aimed towards sunglasses, a product that followed fashion, was liable to be changed more frequently and thus more likely to open up channels for profit and growth, despite the lower unit price compared to prescription frames. The re-designing of the product mix began in 1990 with the acquisition of Vogue and continued in 1995 with the purchase of Persol, two leading Italian brands. The most important step, however, was taken in 1999 with the acquisition of the optical division of the American firm Bausch & Lomb and thus the historical brand of Ray-Ban, which was going through a period of crisis due to a distribution strategy based on quantity rather than quality. On completion of the takeover, Luxottica immediately began a strategy of integration and re-launching of the brand, exploiting its own manufacturing, marketing and distribution skills. Due to a vigorous communication campaign, the Ray-Ban brand, together with the Luxottica group, regained its prestige position as market leader.

In terms of marketing potential another important step in the growth of Luxottica must be mentioned; that is the acquisition in 1995 of the US Shoe Corporation, owner of LensCrafters and the biggest North American chain of retail optical services. The size of the operation to integrate such a large corporate structure was significant both from a financial and organisational point of view.

The last seven years of the Group history have been concerned with consolidating group strategy and at the same time keeping an eye on any new opportunities that may arise.

In December 2000 the company was also listed on the MTA in Milan, with the aim of opening up shareholder capital to European investors and increasing the liquidity of the stocks, which in September 2003 was listed in the MIB30 index.

In 2001 the takeover of Sunglass Hut Inc. – the largest sunglass chain in the world with over 1 550 sales outlets in North America and about 300 shops in the rest of the world – was completed.

This operation consolidated Luxottica's dominant position in the market (in the USA and elsewhere) and allowed the company to reinforce its competitive position in the sunglasses segment.

In terms of production, a process of rationalisation was started with the closing down of factories not in line with the corporate efficiency standard – the American Ray-Ban factories and the one in Gazzada – and the opening of two manufacturing plants in China.

Finally, 2004 marked an important turning point in terms of corporate governance; the giving up on the part of the founder of all executive roles within the corporate administration, maintaining only the institutional function of Chairman of the Board, coincided with the appointment of the new CEO, Andrea Guerra, with the aim of giving the group a more managerial set-up. This was coherent with the increased size of the company and the prospects of future growth.

8.4. THE PERFORMANCES OF LUXOTTICA

8.4.1. The Company Growth

Table 8.10 shows the trend in turnover and number of employees of the Luxottica group, including all the marketing and manufacturing subsidiaries which are not located within the geographical area of the district.

Little more than 30 years after the birth of Luxottica di Del Vecchio & C. Sas, in 1995 the Group already had 17 000 employees worldwide and this figure had almost trebled by the end of 2006.

Between 1995 and 2006 Group turnover had multiplied by four times, going from just under €1 billion to €4.6 billion. In the last 5 years turnover has increased by approximately 50 per cent. Only in 2003 was there a slight fall in sales (-11 per cent) due partly to the international economic situation, marked by a fall in consumption and by the devaluation of the dollar against the euro, but above all to the loss of sales of the Giorgio Armani and Emporio Armani brands following the breaking-off of the licensing contract with the designer.

Table 8.10 Employees and turnover of the Luxottica Group

Year	Employees	Turnover (€K)
1995	16 753	954 901
1996	17 556	1 225 528
1997	n.d.	1 430 502
1998	19 667	1 538 092
1999	23 224	1 874 137
2000	21 000	2 439 166
2001	30 053	3 105 498
2002	35 502	3 201 788
2003	34 000	2 852 194
2004	47 126	3 179 613
2005	46 401	4 134 263
2006	49 325	4 676 156

Source: personal elaboration on company reports

8.4.2. Comparison with the Industry and the District

The Luxottica Group growth trend takes on an even more important role when compared to the results of the eyewear sector and district.

As shown in Table 8.11, the rate of variation in turnover and employees of the Luxottica group are almost always superior to those in the sector and the district of Belluno, demonstrating the validity of the competitive strategies pursued over time.

Moreover, comparing the turnover in absolute terms, highlights how the Group alone overtook the district from 1996 onwards and the whole sector from 1998, following a growth path that led it further away from the average profile of the operators in the sector.

Table 8.11   Employees and turnover growth of the Luxottica Group, the district of Belluno and the Italian industry

	Turnover Growth			Employee Growth		
Year	**Luxottica**	**District**	**Sector**	**Luxottica**	**District**	**Sector**
1995	127.4%	21.8%	22.3%	n.d.	12.0%	8.2%
1996	28.3%	3.3%	4.8%	4.8%	5.0%	0.0%
1997	16.7%	8.0%	2.8%	n.d.	8.0%	0.0%
1998	7.5%	4.0%	3.1%	n.d.	2.4%	0.3%
1999	21.8%	-4.6%	-4.7%	18.1%	4.2%	0.6%
2000	30.1%	12.9%	15.1%	-9.6%	1.1%	5.0%
2001	27.3%	1.7%	8.4%	43.1%	0.7%	0.5%
2002	3.1%	2.0%	1.3%	18.1%	1.4%	1.1%
2003	-10.9%	-0.7%	0.6%	-4.2%	-10.9%	-8.9%
2004	11.5%	1.3%	2.0%	38.6%	-6.5%	-3.0%
2005	30.0%	5.0%	10.3%	-1.5%	-1.0%	-1.1%
2006	13.1%	13.6%	n.d.	6.3%	4.0%	6.5%

Source: personal elaboration on ANFAO, Assindustria Belluno company reports

8.4.3.   Financial Results

Luxottica's growth path is marked by the ability to generate positive results not only in absolute terms, but also in terms of capital invested (ROI) and net equity (ROE), as shown in Table 8.12.

Four Italian cases

Table 8.12 Profitability indicators of Luxottica Group

Year	Operating Income (€K)	Net Profit (€K)	ROI	ROE
1995	153 412	83 496	n.d.	n.d.
1996	177 707	106 241	n.d.	n.d.
1997	221 085	129 457	n.d.	n.d.
1998	226 291	133 064	n.d.	n.d.
1999	237 658	152 463	9.3%	19.4%
2000	411 921	255 277	13.9%	24.3%
2001	509 492	316 373	25.2%	23.6%
2002	601 508	372 077	31.0%	26.2%
2003	431 787	267 343	11.0%	19.4%
2004	479 499	286 874	10.5%	19.2%
2005	581 401	342 294	11.7%	17.5%
2006	755 987	424 286	15.4%	19.1%

Source: personal elaboration on company reports

PART THREE

Entrepreneurial Growth in Industrial Districts

9. Cross-case analysis

F. G. Alberti, S. Sciascia and C. Tripodi

This chapter aims at reporting the first group of results of the cross-case analysis. Such a report contains the holistic interpretation of the phenomena investigated, along the set of areas of inquiry presented in Chapter 4. We report on the different types of opportunities identified and exploited in the four companies, the sources of them, the resources possessed by the firms that allowed the identification and exploitation of the entrepreneurial opportunities and the organisational mechanisms of knowledge acquisition and exploitation employed. Tables throughout the chapter display such elements as resulting from the four cases. The chapter concludes with a discussion of the consistencies identified among cases regarding the antecedents of firm growth.

9.1. INTRODUCING CROSS-CASE ANALYSIS

Complying with the nature of our research question and the aim of the book, introduced in Chapter 1, after arriving at a case interpretation per each company (that is within-case analyses presented in Chapters 5 to 8) we interpreted the case studies in cross-sectional terms.

In this chapter, we analyse data across all of the cases in order to identify the antecedents of firm growth through the lenses of entrepreneurship.

According to Eisenhardt (1989), the overall idea of cross-case analysis is to force the researcher to go beyond the initial impressions using structured and diverse lenses on the data. As a result, the likelihood of achieving an accurate and reliable theory is improved. Three tactics are suggested: 1) select categories and look for within-group similarities coupled with inter-group differences; 2) select pairs of cases and list the similarities and differences between each pair; and 3) divide the data by data source to exploit 'unique insights possible from different types of data collection'

(Eisenhardt 1989: 540-541). Specifically, we relied mainly on the first tactic proposed by Eisenhardt (1989).

Table 9.1 Entrepreneurial opportunities

	New products	**New markets**	**New processes**
Alessi	50–100 new products in the catalogue each year making a total of over 2000 products per catalogue. Products under license (household appliances, wall paper, wrist watches, bathroom fittings, cordless phones, ceramic tile, cars, home textiles, kitchen furniture)	Export = 60% Change from working to order, to supplying hotels and then private customers. Gradual opening up to new market segments (younger, less wealthy)	Cold-moulding Mass production Use of wood, china, ceramics and plastic Purchasing internationalisation Reduction in number of wholesalers and outlets Retail design
Geox	Rubber shoes that breathe Leather military and sports shoes that breathe Apparel that breathes	Export = 59% Opening up to all footwear segments	Setting up of R&D function Geox school Geox shops Communication focused on production Production internationalisation
Illy	New Arabica coffee blend Coffee beans for moka machine and coffee filters Illy collection Espressamente Illy Individual portion system Tea and cocoa	Opening up to all distribution channels	Pressurized cans Elimination of purchasing intermediaries Quality control of raw materials
Luxottica	Own brand products Products under licence New brands	Export = 77% Opening up to all segments of eyewear trade	Production internationalisation Entry into wholesale and retail distribution

Source: personal elaboration

A cross-case report has been produced as result of the cross-sectional analysis. Such a report contains the holistic interpretation of the phenomena investigated. Cross-case analysis enables the comparison of multiple cases in many divergent ways, which would not be possible within a single case analysis. The present chapter builds on the cross-case report, offering a holistic interpretation of the phenomena investigated, along the set of areas of inquiry presented in Chapter 4. The cross-case analysis enabled the comparison of different cases against predefined categories, so as to explore if any patterns can be identified concerning the entrepreneurial growth of firms in industrial districts. We report on the different types of opportunities identified and exploited in the four companies, the sources of them, the resources possessed by the firms that allowed the identification and exploitation of the entrepreneurial opportunities and the organisational mechanisms of knowledge acquisition and exploitation employed. The method proved useful and efficient since it enabled the comparison of different cases from the chosen perspectives, which would not have been possible otherwise.

9.2. ENTREPRENEURIAL OPPORTUNITIES

The entrepreneurial growth process – the research subject of this book – consists in the continuous identification and exploitation of entrepreneurial opportunities. Many different types of opportunities, with varying degrees of innovativeness, were identified and exploited by the firms studied. A comparative analysis of the opportunities exploited by the four firms in the study is proposed; the opportunities are subdivided into product, market and process opportunities (Table 9.1).

9.2.1. New Products

In the case of Alessi, the company grew out of the identification of an opportunity mix to introduce new products in a new market and with new processes. This was the experience of the founder, Giovanni Alessi, who, like many others of his generation, left the Strona Valley to seize the opportunity to service a new market (the Cusio area) with new products (coffee pots, trays and metal accessories) by means of new processes (from turning to pressing). In many respects Alessi is unique in the household article and kitchenware industry. Its catalogue includes hundreds of products of different types, from trays to baskets and watches, from barware to articles for children, from glasses and cutlery to kitchen accessories, jugs and coffee makers. If the articles manufactured under license are then added the Alessi catalogue becomes huge.

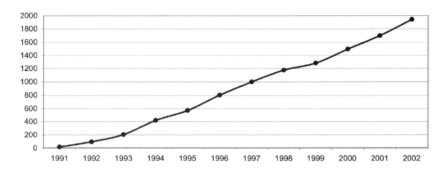

Source: personal elaboration based on company data

Figure 9.1 Cumulative growth of Alessi products (1991–2002)

The graph in Figure 9.1. shows the rate of growth of development in terms of number of products with 1 942 new products being introduced onto the market between 1991 and 2002. Every year Alesssi introduces from 50 to 100 new products and manages a catalogue that in 2006 contained over 2 000 products. The company's products can be classified into six areas: tableware (eight product categories); kitchenware (six product categories); bar and wine (two product categories); other (eight product categories); household appliances; and silver articles. The products made under license are not included in the catalogue although they are sold with the Alessi brand. The continuous product development process (renewing and introducing new products) represents the core activity at Alessi, in terms of personnel and financial resources employed. Investment is made in R&D and engineering which accounts for a constant figure of over 3 per cent of turnover on the profit and loss account, over and above what is spent on equipment and moulds. In 2001, for example, Alessi started a €2.4 million research project aimed at planning and setting up a re-engineering of some product lines and new products.

Overall the Alessi catalogue, called the 'Encyclopedia' inside the company, is so exhaustive that it is relatively difficult to come up with and develop important new product lines, even if the prospect for the creation of profitable new high-quality design products is still good due to the wide network of designers from all over the world. Alessi's innovations mainly regard form and not function. On this point Alberto Alessi comments: 'we work on the expressive language of the objects, giving the creativity that exists around us the opportunity to express itself. The problem with industry, on the other hand, is that by definition it tends to destroy creativity'.

As far as Luxottica is concerned, the first big turning point in its history came a few years after its founding, in 1967, when the company moved from producing stamps, moulds, small accessories and frame parts for other manufacturers to the production of the complete glasses, itself using a network of sub-contractors.

Shortly after this, Leonardo Del Vecchio, the firm's founder, decided to take another important leap forward in creating his own brand, Luxottica. This decision caused a split in the company ownership and the withdrawal of the other shareholders who had founded the company with him in 1961. From the early 1980s onwards Luxottica made another series of moves to broaden its offer.

The first step in 1981 was the acquisition of the Sferoflex brand from Meccanoptica Leonardo. This brand consists of a quality range of prescription frames only, aimed at consumers desiring a classic and comfortable frame with high quality. Next came the entry into the premium-luxury market segment thanks to licensing agreements with fashion houses, first of all with Giorgio Armani in 1988. Luxottica had the intuition to see that the transformation of glasses from medical aid to fashion accessory was not a transitory phenomenon and from the 1990s onwards began a strategy of developing its own brands as well as widening its portfolio of brands under license. The objective was both to direct the product mix more towards sunglasses, which at the end of the 1980s only represented 10 per cent of company production and to balance the sales of products under license. Thus we see the acquisitions of Vogue (1990), Persol (1995) and the famous American brand Ray-Ban (1999). These were followed over the next few years by the Arnette, Revo e Killer Loop brands.

Today Luxottica's brand portfolio is made up of 19 licenses and 8 wholly owned brands.

Geox was also born out of the identification of a new product opportunity that was to revolutionise the market and change the rules of competition in the shoe sector (Camuffo, Furlan, Romano and Vinelli, 2004). In 1993, Geox began production of the first rubber shoes that breathe aimed at the children's footwear market; it then progressively widened the offer to meet the needs of different market segments. The new products developed from 2000 onwards were leather shoes, sports shoes and military boots. If the breathing membrane of the first Geox rubber shoes can be called a radical innovation, the subsequent adaptations can be classified as incremental.

The final addition to the new footwear products was the line of clothing: like the shoes, Geox clothes also allow the body to perspire due to a patented air-flow system.

Finally the entrepreneurial growth path followed by Illy is linked essentially to the identification and exploitation of product development opportunities. From its foundation until the 1980s the company remained focused on the production of high quality coffee. Starting from this base product, an expanding offer was built up and enriched by a variety of innovative additions. The launch in 1980 of a blend of nine different types of Arabica coffee allowed the company to lay the foundations for highly profitable growth, due to a clearly defined positioning in the premium segment of the global market. The product was further enhanced by introducing new packaging to reinforce the image. At the end of the 1980s, Illy enriched its range, which had up to then been focused on espresso coffee, by launching ground coffee for moka machines and filters, coffee beans and decaffeinated coffee via the mass distribution channel. Different types of roasting were used for the different product types.

In 1992 the product system was enlarged with an addition of great symbolic value; the introduction of the Illycollection coffee cups, to complement the coffee range, represented the beginning of the experiential product development, which was completed in 2003 with the launch of the Espressamente Illy project. Illy succeeded in developing a product that was coherent with the experiential content of the so-called 'coffee experience', in expressing both the tangible and intangible benefits that consumers were looking for during the coffee moment.

The aim of the Espressamente Illy project, in fact, was to develop a complete experience, involving the senses and the mind, in an environment that would exalt the quality of the coffee. This idea gave Illy the impetus to develop the concept of a chain of Italian style bars, purpose-designed by leading architects (Luca Trazzi, Claudio Silvestrin and Paola Navone). There are now over 120 such bars, characterised by a distinctive style and unique atmosphere and service.

From 1996 onwards, Illy began to widen the range of products on offer with the addition of portioned systems, starting with the single portion pods, an innovation in the coffee market. The pod system aimed to make espresso coffee similar to that of a bar espresso machine available everywhere. The ESE system was followed by the I Espresso for offices and the Hyper Espresso for the HoReCa. The development of these systems then gave the company the opportunity to develop its own espresso machines.

In 2006 Illy decided to take advantage of its reputation in coffee to add two other beverages of colonial origin to its range, entering into the tea and cocoa business by buying the majority shareholdings in two firms operating in the industry.

9.2.2.   New Markets

Alessi's entrepreneurial growth is also linked to the continuous entry into new markets both in geographical terms and in terms of new segments served. At the beginning Alessi only worked to order from private customers. The second generation of the Alessi family was the first to open up to a new market, supplying the hotel trade. Later the company gradually returned to private customers, abandoning the wholesale and hotel trade. Alessi's main target market is a segment made up of well-educated high-income professionals with a propensity to consume.

Today's end users are numerous and together account for more than a million purchases per year. The traditional Alessi client is adult but the plastic articles widened the customer base to younger purchasers, opening up new market segments. Alessi products are essentially seen as 'ideal gifts' and the gift market, in fact, accounts for approximately 50 per cent of sales with 65 per cent of purchasers being female.

In 1935 Alessi was already selling in some European markets (Switzerland in particular). Following the pause caused by the Second World War, Alessi soon noticed the opportunity to increase its penetration of some key markets, such as France, the UK and the USA and began to expand rapidly towards new geographical markets.

To this end Alessi began selecting shops to display its goods in. Geographical location, type and quality of outlet, and usual customer base were fundamental elements considered in making the decision. Alessi products are generally sold through retail outlets (65 per cent of sales through some 4 500 retail outlets), a limited number of shop-in-shops mainly concentrated in Europe (25 per cent of sales via the 100 shop-in-shops at present in existence), showrooms and exclusive outlets (5 per cent each). Due to international expansion, Alessi now has approximately 5 000 outlets in 60 countries. Today 40 per cent of turnover comes from national sales. Out of some 5 000 outlets, 4 500 are located in Europe, 200 in the USA and about 40 in Asia.

The opening up to new market segments and distribution channels in recent years has led Alessi to reorganise its market positioning via three brands: 'Officina Alessi', 'Alessi' and 'A di Alessi'. The 'Officina Alessi' brand includes the most prestigious products, one-off pieces and limited series. The traditional 'Alessi' brand comprises the best of mass produced household articles, in which the distinguishing features are manufacturing quality and innovative design. Finally, the 'A di Alessi' brand offers high quality goods to as wide a market as possible.

The various licensing projects undertaken by Alessi have allowed the company to open up to new market segments outside the strictly household article industry. Examples are kitchen and bathroom furnishings as well as the creation of the Panda Alessi for FIAT.

The growth of Luxottica is also undoubtedly linked to the expansion into new markets, first of all new geographic markets.

The quality of Luxottica's products was first noted by international customers in 1971 when the company exhibited for the first time at the MIDO fair, (Mostra Internazionale dell'Ottica di Milano). This event opened the gates to globalisation with the export of frames for foreign distributors. By the end of that decade 85 per cent of production was already destined for the international market.

The management soon realised, however, that an export strategy mediated by the use of wholesale distributors was not sufficient to satisfy the company's needs for growth and efficiency in servicing the markets.

Thus, from the early 1980s onwards a series of trading partnerships were set up and the strategy of overseas expansion developed by means of opening subsidiaries and, in some cases, the setting up of joint ventures. Within ten years, then, the Luxottica Group succeeded in building up an impressive international sales network, which today includes 38 subsidiaries and 100 independent distributors serving 130 countries. Today North America accounts for 66 per cent of turnover and the Asia-Pacific region represents 11 per cent.

In the case of Geox, too, entrepreneurial growth is linked to the continuous entry into new markets. The firm began in the market of children's footwear, before moving into the men and women's footwear market, followed by the sportswear market and more recently the market for military apparel. In Italy, Geox is market leader in its segment and it is ninth in the world. The youth market (12–25 years old) is the only one not covered. This positioning across several segments makes Geox a 'family brand', which is quite unusual in the footwear market. This policy was adopted in order to fully exploit the membrane technology and was made possible by the strategic decision to be a follower in terms of style; in fact Geox concentrates investments in research and not in the design of fashion collections.

Geox has grown geographically due to a gradual entry into new markets. Today Italy accounts for 41 per cent of sales and the rest of Europe 46 per cent; 10 per cent of sales come from USA and 3 per cent from the rest of the world. Until 2000 the company aimed essentially at the Italian market, mainly in order to learn how to compete in the sector. At that point, having consolidated its own financial situation, Geox moved first into the main European markets (Germany, France and Spain) and then began to expand globally. In 2003, thanks to an agreement with one of the large Chinese shoe companies, Geox entered the rich Asian market and in the same year opened shops in Japan and Russia. The following year, with the opening of a 600sqm own brand outlet on Madison Avenue, the group reinforced its position in the US market, which it had first entered in 2001.

Finally, in the case of Illy, the company had already begun to move towards new markets, such as Germany, France and Holland, in the 1950s, thanks to the invention of vacuum packing.

During the 1980s, Ernesto Illy encouraged the penetration of these markets as well as the entry into new ones; the high-quality espresso coffee niche held numerous opportunities to be exploited. The 1990s saw the development of sales networks due to the setting up of subsidiaries in the main export markets, such as France, Germany, USA, Spain, Benelux, Canada and Portugal.

Foreign market penetration followed the same strategy as in the Italian market; that is, brand consolidation in the HoReCa channel followed by the entry into mass distribution with an already well-known brand.

If coffee can be said to have developed gradually from a national to an international business, Espressamente Illy, on the other hand, was launched with a global perspective: the coffee experience business has an international flavour.

9.2.3.   New Processes

In terms of manufacturing, Alessi gradually introduced new processes. The first innovation was in 1938, following technological changes in the sector; the firm abandoned turning of the metals in favour of cold pressing and replaced the traditional materials (silver- and chrome-plated brass) by stainless steel. A few years later, in 1945, Alessi responded to another opportunity in the export field, the supply of brass ladles to the US army, and further modified the production process, taking the first steps towards mass production. However, it was with Richard Sapper's '9090' coffee pot in 1977 that Alessi moved away from a type of production that was a kind of mechanisation of craft workshops towards the large scale manufacturing that was already being practiced by two famous firms in the houseware district: Lagostina and Bialetti. The Sapper coffee maker was Alessi's first real step towards product policy and also the firm's biggest success. Moreover, the technical complexity that a new approach to production meant led Alessi to look for creative designers with technological awareness.

In 1989, with the takeover of 'Piazza Battista' (which was to become 'Twergi' brand in the Alessi's portfolio), Alessi introduced the first wooden household articles into its catalogue. At the same time another innovation in the technological process led Alessi to start production of household articles in china and ceramics (under the 'Tendentse' brand). In 1993, Alessi took another step towards new technologies and processes. The external designers, with whom the company was working more and more, came up with creative ideas that were difficult to produce in stainless steel. These technical limitations led to the search for new materials and the production of plastic articles began; this material was easy to handle and had limited costs.

This radical process (for a metal household article manufacturer based in the VCO district) innovation allowed Alessi to innovate more in terms of design. In fact, instead of focusing on creativity and then having to suffer the technological limitations imposed by external suppliers, this innovative use of materials allowed Alessi to oblige its suppliers to adapt their manufacturing technology to the product features imposed by the design.

Alessi was also able to exploit opportunities in terms of supplies and supplier network management. Starting with a small network of district suppliers, managed by a head of supplies, innovations introduced in the purchasing process from 1986 onwards, helped Alessi to take advantage of opportunities for product development. Several buyers were appointed and, coordinated by a purchasing director; they looked towards setting up a mainly European supply network. The purchasing processes were revised and some guiding principles introduced together with different types of supplier relationship (normal, integrated or partner), contractual agreements and parameters of evaluation. Purchase marketing thus became a central competence for Alessi. A third innovation in the purchasing process came with the opening up to the Far East: first via Hong Kong trading companies and then with direct presence in Korea, Indonesia, China, Vietnam and, in the near future, India.

Other innovative processes developed by the company regard sales and distribution. Originally the relationship between the company and the points of sale were managed by houseware wholesalers or foreign importers. The distribution chain included own brand shops, traditional multibrand outlets, space in mass distribution stores, and airport corners. In order to maintain (or further improve) the competitive position reached and consolidate brand value, Alessi decided to rely less on wholesalers. The strategy thus was to pay more attention to the reorganisation of the distribution network.

In the early 1980s, Alessi began reorganising its international product distribution in order to invest in geographical areas held to be strategic, by means of setting up subsidiaries or using exclusive agents, and to reduce the number of outlets throughout the world. The opportunity taken in this process of reorganisation of distribution was that of creating a more selective and effective distribution system, which was coherent with the market positioning and the reputation Alessi now had.

A specific project, started in 1999, led to the setting up of 14 flagship stores and 140 shop-in-shops, designed by Alessandro Mendini, in order to pay maximum attention to the way Alessi products were displayed in shops, bearing in mind the complexity of the product range in terms of catalogue items and related meta-projects, which must not be displayed in such a way as to cause confusion. For this reason the company decided on a project for the existing outlets (with new display models and graphic elements) and for the new shops. The objective of this retail design exercise, which is totally in keeping with the new distribution processes, is to immerse the visitor emotionally in the world of Alessi, emphasising the visual energy of the products.

Luxottica's growth also came about thanks to innovative strategic decisions in terms both of production and marketing.

The pursuit of production efficiency led over time to the almost total insourcing of production. The thinking behind this was that relying on sub-contractors on the one hand discourages experimentation with new modes of production and, on the other, makes it more difficult to maintain constant quality in the manufacture of the products.

In this way, a virtuous circle is created; that is the total control of production allows improvements to be made to the production system, facilitates research into new operational modes, stimulates technological development and raises quality. These factors in turn lead to increased efficiency, thus creating more resources to invest in research, innovation and staff training. Over the years vertical integration in production was accompanied by forwards expansion with the entry into the wholesale and retail distribution world. Here again, the process was based on Leonardo Del Vecchio's underlying conviction that for a company to be a leader it was not enough to be an excellent manufacturer but that it also had to be in contact with the market in order to read it and anticipate future trends.

This was followed in 1974 by the first acquisition of a distribution company, 'Scarrone' based in Turin; on the international markets too, in line with the philosophy outlined above, Luxottica pursued a policy of expansion.

In 1995, Luxottica entered the retail market with the acquisition of the 'US Shoe Corporation', owners of 'LensCrafters' and the biggest retail optical service chain in North America. In 2001 it took over 'Sunglass Hut Inc.', the world's biggest chain of sunglass shops, with over 1 550 retail outlets in North America and approximately 300 shops in the rest of the world. Today the group controls some 5 800 shops mainly in USA, Canada, Australia, New Zealand, Hong Kong, China and the Gulf countries. On the European market, on the other hand, it is present mainly in the UK with approximately 100 'Sunglass Hut' outlets.

The direct management of so many retail outlets has meant that Luxottica has been able to develop a level of competence and understanding of the eyewear market that is unique in the industry.

What is remarkable in the case of Geox is the fact that the continuous development of new products is backed by the adoption of innovative processes for the footwear market.

Firstly, no other footwear company had previously developed such an efficient technological research system; firms usually invest, if at all, in shoe design and style but not in the scientific study of the movement of body heat. A sophisticated research centre was set up in Montebelluna with some of the most advanced purpose-built and patented machinery in Europe. Every year, 3 per cent of turnover is reinvested in research (Bettiol and Bosa, 2004).

Another process that distinguishes Geox from its competitors is training; the company has created an internal training centre, the Geox School, which operates at four levels (technicians, new graduates, managers and top managers).

Another innovation is the opening of Geox shops. Here the innovation lies not so much in the fact that the company has set up exclusive outlets for its products but in the way the shops have been designed and the particular mode of product display, known as the 'sail'. This slightly curved structure with special metal hooks and removable shoe supports was designed specifically for Geox shops. The display allows the consumer to appreciate at a glance the look and the material of the uppers as well as the technical features of the sole with micro-holes. The shops' décor is minimalist and airy, reinforcing the idea of the 'shoe that breathes'. The environment is light and clean, like a research laboratory, to underline the aspect that differentiates Geox from its competitors.

 Geox is innovative also in its communication. It is the Italian footwear top spender in advertising, with an absolutely new type of communication focused on the product itself and not on the product context in certain situations of the consumer's life. The campaigns have never used famous people to advertise the product but just the model of the shoe itself with the air coming out of the holes in the sole. This is in sharp contrast to the traditional type of communication for a fashion product such as shoes.

Lastly, Geox has exploited the opportunities offered by moving production abroad. With manufacturing units in 68 different countries, Geox is now the third largest company in the world in comfort shoe production, behind Clarks and ECCO.

Finally, Illy's entrepreneurial growth again came about due to the ability to exploit three opportunities for the development of new processes: the packing of coffee under pressure, the elimination of intermediaries in the purchasing process and the quality control of the raw material. These innovations were combined in a single objective: to guarantee the highest possible quality of the coffee blend.

The pressurised can process, invented and patented by Francesco Illy a few years after the company's foundation, involves the introduction of inert gas into the can containing the coffee, so that the aroma and flavour are conserved intact for a long time. This process innovation allowed Illycaffè to expand the geographical confines of its sales.

The innovation in the coffee purchasing process was started in the 1990s. Up until then, Illycaffè had bought the raw coffee from intermediaries (importers or traders), who bought the coffee from the producers and resold it to roasters like Illy. The company decided instead to buy the coffee directly from the Brazilian producers in order to personally control the quality. The producers were given incentives to keep the quality standards high: the 'Premio Brasile' award and particularly generous purchasing prices. Due to this, Illy won the first edition of the 'Ethic Award', a prize for social and environmental responsibility promoted by the GDO Week magazine in collaboration with KPMG Consulting.

Another of the process innovations was the electronic selecting of the coffee beans. This was set up in the 1980s in collaboration with the British company, 'Sortex Ltd'. The machine can select the beans with great precision, eliminating those, not suitable to be transformed into the highest quality blend. The beans are sorted with absolute precision at very high speed (1 200 beans per second).

9.3. SOURCES OF ENTREPRENEURIAL OPPORTUNITIES

Like the opportunities themselves, the sources of entrepreneurial opportunity were of quite diverse origin in the firms analysed. Over time the entrepreneurial growth processes in the four firms were fed both by internal sources of opportunity (within the firm or the sector) – such as, for example, incongruence in economic variables or unexpected events coming out of the process and change at sector level – and by external sources of opportunity (in the macro-environment) – such as demographic change, new socio-cultural perceptions and needs and new scientific knowledge. A comparative review of the sources of opportunity the four companies had referred to during their entrepreneurial growth process is outlined next (Table 9.2).

Table 9.2 Sources of entrepreneurial opportunities

	Internal sources	**External sources**
Alessi	Need to: - remove inconsistency between offer and demand - satisfy designers' creative needs - produce limited edition articles - produce complex articles on a large scale	Change in consumer perception (objects are enriched with a symbolic-aesthetic significance) Demographic changes (need to optimise use of space and time dedicated to household care)
Geox	Need to: - control production costs - differentiate the offer in terms of technological content	Availability of expanded Teflon Social and cultural changes (greater wealth, greater attention to body care) Change in consumer perception (emphasis on comfort rather than look)
Illy	Need to: - guarantee top quality - maintain product quality over time - offer everybody the opportunity to make top quality coffee	Demographic changes (less free time) Change in consumer perception (need for multi-sensory experience)
Luxottica	Need to: - produce high quality goods - reduce dependence on distributors - have a direct relationship with the market	Change in consumer perception (spectacles are seen as a fashion accessory)

Source: personal elaboration

9.3.1.   Sources inside the Firm and the Industry

The initial opportunity from which Alessi was born was the result of an incongruence between (high) demand and (low) offer for metal household articles, not only in the Cusio area (where the district system of offer gradually grew up) but more in general in the Italian market in the early decades of the twentieth century.

A few years later, new technologies and working techniques within the metal-working industry drove some firms (including Alessi) to innovate their production processes, changing the process from turning to cold moulding of the metal. In the immediate post-war period the household article sector underwent other transformations in terms of production; on the one hand mass production began (set off by the need to produce for the war) and on the other the advent of the modern stainless steel made it possible to substitute materials such as brass and nickel silver. All this opened up a series of new opportunities for firms in the household article sector and Alessi was one of the first to seize them.

The new product development process was given impetus by the creative work of Alessi's network of designers; at the same time the need arose for a material that was more ductile and fungible than metal. This growing need in the new product creation and development process led Alessi to move on to plastics in order to create objects that were not feasible in metal.

In the same way the outsourcing to the Far East of some phases of production on the part of other world players in the household article industry gave Alessi the idea of new production opportunities (and not just in terms of cost) to back up the creative process of its designers even more. The low labour costs, the technological level of the production plants and the know-how of firms in the Far East facilitated on the one hand the production of limited series (for example the hand-decorated corkscrews) and on the other large-scale production of complex articles (for example, the fruit basket designed by Fratelli Campana and made up of 120 metal sticks, each one with a different length and inclination).

Right from the start Luxottica was able to exploit the opportunities deriving from its location in the Agordino area, near the Cadore industrial district. The decision to start producing the end product, rather than to do contract work producing components for other glasses manufacturers in that area, led the company along a different route to that of the other firms in the district. This was possible due to the availability of sub-contractors in the district, who were able to supply materials that matched the quality standards required.

Nevertheless, in the Luxottica case the strategic decisions taken in terms of the market, products and processes that marked the most significant steps in the company's growth path represented a real break from normal practice within the district.

The processes of vertical integration both backwards and forwards that led Luxottica Group to become world leader in the design, production and distribution of premium prescription frames and sunglasses are undoubtedly the result of internal impulses within the company and in particular come from two process needs. In fact, Leonardo Del Vecchio maintained that 'outsourcing has the advantage of always giving you a regular piece ... yet, while it simplifies corporate life, it does not improve it (in that) the contract worker is not stimulated to improve the quality of the pieces or look for innovation; whereas on the inside we have to improve'.

In the same way, changes in distribution stem essentially from the desire not to be over-dependent on independent wholesalers, who, as such, are not willing to be bound to a single producer. Secondly, given the importance of the end user, a closer relationship with the market enables the company to develop its collections from year to year on the basis of experience and sales data.

It is clear, moreover, that these processes of vertical integration proved to be winning moves for the growth of Luxottica, inasmuch as the company succeeded in transforming every step taken in the direction of forwards and backwards expansion into an opportunity for continuous learning and consolidation of the production and marketing skills so far built up.

The opportunities for product, process and market development identified by Geox derive from customer needs, from the availability of technological knowledge coming not just from outside the district but from outside the whole industry, from strategic corporate needs and from the great changes taking place within the sector. None of the opportunity sources were found within the district. Geox's localisation within a district did, however, favour the exploitation of some opportunities via the resources available, as will be shown later in the chapter.

The sources of opportunity for process development that Geox succeeded in exploiting are, however, typical of the sector. The changes taking place in the footwear sector induced the firm to move production outside Italy. Footwear is a mature sector influenced by globalisation: the development of ICT has cut down distances and barriers between countries, increasing market size and intensifying competition. Geox saw this situation, considered only as a threat by many Italian firms, as a source of opportunity and succeeded in exploiting it. Many production units were localised in countries with low labour costs and much of the production was outsourced to other firms in those countries. The need to contain production costs of the end product in order to make it competitive in the face of Asian rivalry led the group to localise low value added activities in Eastern European countries.

The differentiation strategy regarding the technological product content led the company to make changes in its mode of communication and sales. In order to communicate to the customer that the Geox product was different due to its exclusive technology rather than the style, communication was focused on the product itself and its innovative practicality. The shops were designed like show windows, which allowed the customer to fully appreciate the technological content of the firm's products.

Finally, the Geox strategy, centred on a technologically different product, led the company to dedicate an organisational unit to research, in order to continue to develop the breathing membrane technology for further applications.

The source of the opportunities for entrepreneurial growth identified and exploited by Illycaffè cannot be found within the district. The opportunities for product, process and market development derive, in fact, from the needs of customers, the firm or the catering trade. Illycaffè's location in an industrial district favoured the exploitation of certain opportunities, as will be shown later in the chapter.

Further, even process opportunities are exclusively within the firm itself. The opportunity to adopt the pressurisation technique, for example, derived from the need to keep the coffee's organoleptic properties intact during transport because this was essential for its success on the market. The previous packaging techniques did not allow the company to sell its product and guarantee the best quality outside the local area.

The opportunity to adopt a machine to accurately sort the coffee beans comes from a process need; wanting to guarantee the highest possible quality of blend, Illy decided to collaborate with Sortex in the development of an electronic machine to sort the beans, making it possible to rapidly identify the poor quality lots with a level of accuracy that was previously unobtainable. The decision to obtain the raw coffee directly from the supplier and to give incentives for attention to quality by means of awards and high purchasing prices comes from the same process need: to guarantee the highest possible quality product system.

The introduction of the Hyper system is a product opportunity but it comes from an internal source: a process need. By means of this system, in fact, the Trieste firm aimed to provide bar and restaurant owners who could not purchase professional machines (for economic reasons or size of clients) with the ability to produce high quality Illy coffee.

9.3.2. External Sources

The external sources of opportunity, deriving from the macro-environment, are also particularly significant in the context of the entrepreneurial growth experience of the four cases studied.

The opportunities for new product and new market development pursued by Alessi derive essentially from sources that are external to the firm and the industry.

These can all be defined as the social and cultural changes that had taken place over time in the countries of the developed world, as well as the changes in the perception of the symbolic–aesthetic component in everyday objects used in the home. In the words of Alberto Alessi:

> I observed society and it seemed to me that, at that time, people themselves were rapidly beginning to change the way in which they wanted, used and benefited from the articles .... A few years later, from the second half of the seventies, I was lucky enough to start meeting a lot of good people, who were destined to have a great influence on me personally and on the overall Alessi concept: they were the architects and designers I worked with and who became real models for me.

The socio-cultural changes were monitored by Alessi and the network of designers and incorporated into what became called 'meta-projects', in other words new product and/or market opportunity slots.

Demographic changes taking place in Italian society – and in Western society in general – during the 1970s and 1980s were equally important for Alessi's product development. The emergence of a new working class, living in smaller spaces and needing to optimise the time dedicated to housework, meant that household articles needed to be more functional and efficient as well as taking up as little domestic space as possible. This radical change in the external environment (which was also perceived by other firms in the household furnishing sector, such as Flou with its textile and container beds) was the source of a series of opportunities for Alessi to develop new product concepts. Initially this was in the form of the so-called 'Programma 8', consisting of a series of square-shaped modular household articles in stainless steel, which was instrumental to the development of Alessi.

Similarly, in the case of Luxottica, the opportunity to place the offer in the medium-high market band, where a product has to have both quality and image to be competitive, came from outside the company.

Firstly, the market was paying more and more attention to the look of the objects in daily use, including a product such as prescription glasses, which until the late 1970s had somewhat of a negative connotation. Secondly, designers perceived the change in the market and started to get interested in the possibility of developing glasses as accessories in their collections. This gave rise to the opportunities to collaborate with the world of fashion, which gave Luxottica increasing visibility and the possibility of access to the top market band, thus escaping the growing competition from Chinese manufacturers who were more focused on the lower market band.

Moreover, partnerships with fashion houses allowed the company to sharpen its skills in anticipating fashion trends and put this to good use in its own brand collections.

Also in the case of Geox, some sources of opportunity, particularly those relating to product and market development, came from outside the firm and the industry.

Firstly, the opportunity to start manufacturing a shoe that could breathe was made possible by the advance in external technological know-how: if NASA had not used polytetrafluoroethylene (expanded Teflon) to make spacesuits, the Geox researchers would not have been able to develop the first patented micro-perforated membrane nor the following innovations. Secondly, the opportunity to develop both footwear and clothing that could breathe and to extend the sale on different markets derived from changes that took place in purchasers' perceptions. Over 50 years ago, when they were introduced, rubber-soled shoes were accessible to the few. In a short time they became accessible to everyone and the footwear offer began to be distinguished between higher and lower band products according to the design offered. For women, above all, the purchase of a pair of shoes was linked more to the emotional sphere, to satisfy an aesthetic need rather than a physical one. Nevertheless, since early 1990s, the needs of many purchasers have moved from the 'look' to 'comfort'. Much more attention is now paid to a healthy lifestyle and good habits as a result of the raising of the level of education and the growth in per capita wealth also in the emerging countries. We take more care of ourselves and bodily well-being has taken on a primary importance. Footwear purchasers are more aware of the benefits offered in terms of hygiene and perspiration and this gave rise to the opportunity to introduce shoes such as Geox.

Finally the main opportunities identified and exploited by Illy were generated by sources outside the firm. It can be said that Illy's development and success were founded, right from the start, on the ability to exploit the different changes taking place in the market in the best way possible.

Right from the beginning of its activity, when coffee was still considered a simple commodity, Illy was able to anticipate the market, focusing on the high quality coffee niche.

The opportunity to develop the I Espresso and ESE single portion system was also the result of demographic changes in a market where the better-off sections of the population are often worse off in terms of free time. The most demanding consumers are often those with less time to go to the bar for a good coffee; these systems enable them to prepare a good quality coffee quickly and easily at home or in the office.

The launch of the Espressamente Illy bars was another opportunity, which arose as a result of demographic and lifestyle changes. Consumer needs have moved away from the idea of coffee as a simple commodity in favour of a coffee concept or experience involving all the senses. The atmosphere, the point of sale, the visual and auditory components of the service are all elements which the consumer now considers essential to ensure that the experience is unique.

Table 9.3 Resources and competencies

	Tangible capital	**Human capital**	**Intellectual capital**
Alessi	2 plants (1 in Italy) Equipment and moulds Alessi Museum Living catalogue	Alessi family (from Giovanni to Alberto) Designers and architects	New product development Stimulate new product design Manage flow of proposals
Geox	6 plants (4 in Italy) Specific machinery Self-financing ability Stock market listing	Mario Moretti Polegato Management team R&D engineers	Research & development Purchasing-production-sales network coordination
Illy	Port of Trieste Specific machinery Self-financing ability	Illy family (from Ernesto to Andrea) Management team	Production Purchasing & supply Design
Luxottica	8 plants (6 in Italy) Self-financing ability Stock market listing	Leonardo Del Vecchio Management team	Integrated production Distribution Marketing

Source: personal elaboration

9.4.   RESOURCES AND COMPETENCIES

The opportunities for entrepreneurial growth are identified and exploited on the basis of whether or not certain resources and competencies are present. The firms in the study were analysed in terms of the resources and competencies they had available and which allowed for the identification and exploitation of the opportunities for entrepreneurial growth (Table 9.3). The critical resources that the four firms could count on in terms of human resources (at individual level) and physical and intellectual capital (at organisational level) were not the same. Here, too, there was a disparity between the firms analyzed in terms of the amount of resources and competencies, even if a common feature was the fact that all four had assessed the level of resources and competencies available in their respective district at the start of the entrepreneurial growth process.

9.4.1. Tangible Capital

In terms of tangible capital, Alessi has an internal production plant for the manufacture of steel household articles at the headquarters in Crusinallo. This is where the cutting, moulding, shearing, assembly and quality control phases are carried out. Until 1998, the company also had a manufacturing plant in Brazil for cutlery production. Today approximately 70 per cent of products sold are purchased from sub-contractors or foreign partners.

From the financial point of view the recent agreement made between Alessi and the outlets has had a noticeable impact on capital invested in goods in stock. In return for greater shelf space in household goods outlets, Alessi in fact undertook to maintain stocks in its warehouse and to supply the shop within 24 hours.

The product development process represents the core of the firm's business in terms of people employed and commitment of financial resources. The profit and loss accounts over the last few years show a constant investment of approximately 3 per cent of turnover in research, development and engineering over and above what is capitalised in terms of equipment, moulds, above all in terms of the engineering and further developing of some product lines that were launched in 2001. Not only do equipment and moulds have considerable significance in terms of investment of tangible capital, but they also play an important role inasmuch as that they are artefacts of the corporate memory. To this effect, the Alessi museum was set up and opened in 1998, with the main purpose of strengthening activities linked to the meta-projects and to new product development. The museum is used as a work-space in which all the intangible aspects related to a new product design are made visible. Almost all the meetings relating to new product development take place around a table in the museum. Over the years the museum has accumulated a vast collection of prototypes, historical Alessi products and numerous objects coming from all parts of the world, as well as drawings, pictures and all kinds of documents relating to the history of Alessi and the sector of household goods in general. For Alessi this is therefore an important tangible asset, which plays an even greater role in providing a store of historical competencies, which contribute daily to Alessi's product development.

Another important role is played by the so-called 'living catalogue' – a permanent and constantly updated display in the firm of all the objects in the Alessi catalogue in the various versions. The area in the Crusinallo headquarters is also a space for thought, comparison and stimulus for the Alessi employees, for the designers, visitors and for the sales network.

In short, the Alessi catalogue, the Alessi museum and more generally the vast heritage of archived and abandoned projects – the so-called 'frozen projects' – are a continual source of internal inspiration.

The decision to set up 'Luxottica di Del Vecchio & C. S.a.s' at Agordo is a result of the opportunity to exploit the funds that the local administration made available to support an area that at that time had no entrepreneurial infrastructure. Only with time did the surrounding industrial context take form and develop, due mainly to the stimulus coming from the firm itself and in particular from its founder. Luxottica's location in the Belluno district allowed the firm to exploit the availability of certain resources, which in turn enabled it to seize the opportunity for entrepreneurial growth. First of all the Agordino area is near the Cadore valley, where a number of firms specialised in the manufacture of lenses, small metal parts, cases and frames had grown up from the end of the 19th century onwards. Del Vecchio's partners were owners of one of the firms in the area, 'Metalflex'.

Today the Luxottica Group has 8 manufacturing plants: 6 are located in Italy, mainly in the North-East and 2 are in the People's Republic of China.

Although the headquarters were transferred to Milan in 1999, all the manufacturing plants are part of the Belluno district production system and 80 per cent of the Group's total production comes from here. This is the result of a strategic choice to offer the market a product with high qualitative standards and the features of the best of 'Made in Italy' production, using all the know-how of the district.

Thus, practically all of Luxottica's production in concentrated in Italy and each plant concentrates on a specific production technology in order to improve the quality of the manufacturing, the efficiency and thus the overall profitability of the Group.

The decision to keep most of the production activity in Italy represents a strategic choice to create top quality glasses that can be distinguished by the 'Made in Italy' style, an important success factor in the eyewear market.

The more labour-intensive production, mainly destined for the US market, is carried out in China. For this kind of manufacturing also, the company has preferred not to sub-contract but to set up its own plants, taking advantage of the low labour costs in China.

In the light of what has been said above, we may conclude that the manufacturing plants are an important asset for corporate success. The group can also count on considerable financial resources, deriving above all from the ability to self-finance; for example in 2006 the cash-flow of operations was approximately €600 million. In fact the decision to enter the financial markets, first the NYSE (1990) and then the MTA in Milan (2000) was more a question of image than one of the need to raise capital for growth. With time however it became clear that the move was a winning one above all for the constant rigor and focus on value that the stock market imposes on management.

Geox's situation in the district of Montebelluna enabled the company to exploit resources which in turn gave rise to opportunities for entrepreneurial growth. For example, at the beginning, Moretti Polegato was able to take advantage of the organisational structure of the 'Pol' shoe factory and a network of workshops throughout the Montebelluna area to study manufacturing possibilities of his shoe and launch the product on the market. The financial resources of the Pol and the Polegato family helped to start up the Geox project, as did the local banks, which were willing to invest in typical local manufacturing.

Today, Geox owns four plants in the district, one in Romania and one in Slovakia. Approximately 80 per cent of production is outsourced to various parts of the world. The plants cannot therefore be considered to represent an important asset for corporate success.

Some of the machinery was designed and built specifically to test the capacity of the prototypes. Examples are the 'Walker', a machine that can simulate 100 000 paces in three days on wet ground, a machine to measure the level of perspiration of the foot and a machine that can evaluate the ability of the product to breathe.

The financial resources available to the firm are significant in that they facilitate not only the everyday running of the firm but also permit Geox to invest in research, a crucial activity for building success and moving along the path of entrepreneurial growth. On one hand, the Geox business generates huge cash flow – €56 million in 2006; on the other, due to the listing on the Milan stock exchange, Geox has adequate financial resources available to support its development projects.

Finally, in the case of Illycaffè, the fact that it was located in a district enabled the company to exploit resources which in turn gave rise to opportunities for entrepreneurial growth.

First of all, the Trieste area is strongly marked by the presence of the harbour; this favoured the early development of the firm when it was just a small coffee roaster. The presence of an easily accessible natural harbour and the customs regime that was favourable to the raw coffee trade certainly helped Illycaffè to take advantage of the opportunity to develop the markets. The harbour of Trieste is, however, gradually losing importance, compared to the Northern European ones, such as Rotterdam and Bremen, and can no longer guarantee Illycaffè the back-up offered in the past. Nevertheless, the harbour's logistical infrastructure undoubtedly helped Illycaffè to grow and develop. It still uses the logistic services for the product stock management and distribution all over the world.

If, on the one hand, it can be said that the geographical situation of Illy favoured its growth due to the harbour, it is also true that Trieste is a small city, less well linked to the world's big capitals; the location in the Trieste district can thus, on the other hand, be said to have hindered in some ways the exploitation of the opportunities identified.

As far as machinery is concerned, it should be emphasised that despite not having significant physical resources, Illycaffè owns technologically advanced machinery, due to the firm's continued research and collaboration with other companies. In an interview Andrea Illy termed the machinery 'Illy specific'.

In terms of financial resources, Illycaffè favours self-financing. The firm has the capacity to generate a high level of liquidity and reinvests practically all profits in the company in order to finance the investment necessary to sustain growth. Due to this policy the company has excellent negotiating power with banks. Indebtedness is, nevertheless, necessary but within the limits of financial equilibrium: on average debt–equity ratio is round 50 per cent.

So far the company has been reluctant to open up to the financial markets to finance growth. Perhaps in the distant future more radical growth plans might convince the family to turn to the stock exchange to obtain funds and give greater visibility to the decision but for the time being the historic brand remains firmly in family hands.

9.4.2.   Human Capital

In tracing the entrepreneurial growth of the four firms studied, the role played by human capital must be taken into account.

As far as Alessi is concerned, the imprinting of quality and innovation transmitted by the founder, Giovanni Alessi, was fundamental. The prior knowledge of the founder and his collaborators – coming from the VCO district – represented the real human capital on which the company founded its success. In this sense the role played by the family in terms of continuity and history has certainly been central. The second generation, Carlo and Ettore, strengthened the firm's human capital (based on craftsmanship) with technical and design skills. But it is really with the third generation, Alberto Alessi in particular, that the company's human capital took the form that it has today. Alberto played the role of 'art director' within the firm, due to his talent for design, his position at the centre of an international network of architects and designers and his open-mindedness towards the most innovative and avant-garde design concepts.

Over and above the central role of some key figures inside and outside the company, Alessi is made up of an extraordinary mix of people and professional profiles, with different but complementary attitudes, competencies and visions.

Compared to the past when Alessi production was based mainly on metal household good, the profile of today's employees leans more towards administration rather than production. Out of some 450 employees, 250 work in administration and approximately 200 in production.

It must not be forgotten that from the mid-seventies onwards all new Alessi products have been designed by external architects. Starting from the first experiments in the 1950s with Masseri and Mazzoli, Alessi gradually reduced the number of products developed internally, relying on an increasing number of external designers and architects to initiate projects. This further reinforced the human capital available to the company both numerically and qualitatively. The awareness on the part of the direction of the importance of human resources for the continuing entrepreneurial development of the company is shown to be the extreme attention the management has always paid to learning from partners and suppliers as well as from the many relations with universities, polytechnics and design institutes at international level.

Looking at the history of Luxottica, it is impossible to ignore the driving force behind the company's development: the founder. Without his experience, pragmatism and intuition, the company would not have achieved the success it has enjoyed for the last 40 years.

Born in Milan, Leonardo Del Vecchio transferred to his firm the technical know-how he had built up from his personal experience as a craftsman and from his natural inclination for manual work. Following his day's work as an employee in a printing works, he would spend the evening making moulds and small metal objects in a garage-workshop, working as a sub-contractor for other firms. He soon noticed, however, that working for the glasses industry he would have had fewer competitors and he abandoned small metal objects in favour of making first the moulds for glasses and then the pieces themselves. Since the distance from clients located in the Cadore region implied logistical problems, Del Vecchio accepted the proposal of one of them to move to the Belluno area and in 1961 he formed a partnership with his main client, 'Metalflex', founding 'Luxottica di Del Vecchio & C. S.a.s' in Agordo.

The distinct character that the entrepreneur gave to the company was a determining factor in its development and cannot be underestimated as key to understanding its success.

Del Vecchio modelled his 'creature' along two main lines: firstly his character of 'homo faber' gave the company commitment to action, to productivity and to tangible results; secondly, the fact that he came from outside the district allowed him to see beyond its confines, never being constrained but always seeking to grow in terms of a continuous and systematic opening up to new opportunities.

Right from the start, Del Vecchio's sound judgement was fundamental in building the team of people to work with and led him to build a close relationship with his employees. It guided him in recruitment and still today whenever a top manager is to be employed, the final interview is with Del Vecchio himself. At the beginning he spent a good deal of time inside the factory learning the Veneto dialect in order to be able to communicate better with employees and understand the culture of the district.

The district certainly gave Luxottica the opportunity to recruit skilled personnel, given that at the beginning the area around Agordo (that is, Agordino) did not have available labour specialised in the work that Luxottica was doing.

However, the Agordino did provide, in the words of Del Vecchio himself, 'very good human resources'. The local inhabitants showed from the start a willingness to adapt and the capacity to learn fast, as well as that constancy which is typical of mountain folk and which made them loyal to the factory once they had accepted this new job, thus reducing the problem of staff turnover.

Today the moment of generational change is approaching and with it the problem of the firm's continuity. Since 2004 Leonardo Del Vecchio has only been present as Chairman of the Board of Directors. His son has taken a different career path. The role of CEO has been covered by Andrea Guerra, in the knowledge that building up a strong team of managers to consolidate and strengthen the pool of competencies built up over the years is necessary for the future of the company.

Similarly, in the case of Geox it can be said that the founder M. Moretti Polegato represents the foundation of the firm's entrepreneurial growth.

In terms of prior knowledge, Moretti Polegato already had a good knowledge of the footwear industry, given that he was born in Crocetta del Montello in the heart of the district and that his family owned a shoe factory. However, he was more interested in working in the family's vineyard, Villa Sandi, and the identification of the entrepreneurial opportunity that Geox was founded on came from one of his hobbies. It was during a walk in Nevada (USA), where he had gone to take part in a fair to promote the family wines, that he suffered discomfort from sweaty feet and instinctively made a hole in the rubber soles of the shoes he was wearing – thus identifying the opportunity to develop a shoe that could breathe. It was certainly Moretti Polegato's intuition that represented the real human capital that the company founded it success on; in interviews he claims to be an inventor rather than an entrepreneur. Before launching Geox he had already patented an agricultural machine that can carry out 5 operations on the earth at the same time, as well as a bottle with a double layer of glass to keep wine cool, eliminating the ice bucket.

Alongside the human capital in the person of the founder, we find that of the four partners who shared his entrepreneurial project and undertook the start-up and early development of Geox. Today these people occupy key positions in the company: CEO, Chief of R&D, Chief of Production and Administrative Director. Their specific functional capacities complemented the founder's cognitive skills. He has always placed total trust in them, giving them complete autonomy and motivating a great team spirit.

The human resources initially employed at Geox all came from the district. Apart from Moretti Polegato all the partners had acquired their experience within the district. We believe that the particular cognitive competencies that came out of being rooted in the district led to the birth and growth of Geox, independently of the specific functional skills and the more general knowledge of the footwear sector. There was, in fact, a widespread conviction throughout the district that only by means of renewal, as had already happened several times in the past, could the survival of the district and its firms be guaranteed. This conviction inspired Moretti Polegato and his partners, both at the beginning of their venture and in the years that followed. Like the district itself, Geox has shown that it is possible to grow and achieve success only by means of a continuous redefinition of the business model.

The awareness on the part of the top management of the importance of human capital in entrepreneurial development meant that the level of attention paid by the management to this topic has always been very high. Approximately 70 per cent of Geox employees are graduates. Geox managers have acquired wide functional competencies, while the engineers working on research have developed skills in chemistry and physics due to training and cooperation with universities and private research institutes. With the Geox school, new resources are adequately trained at all levels.

In the case of Illy human capital was fundamental for the firm's success and in guaranteeing continuing competitive advantage. Andrea Illy introduced greater autonomy and freedom of action for managers, focusing on knowledge and skills. Once the management team's competencies and capacity had been assessed, appointments were made to complete the missing knowledge and skills. Andrea Illy's recruitment policy had the objective of creating a managerial team with a range of complementary high level competencies to guarantee the competitiveness the company needed. The new head of external relations had previously worked for a big telecommunications company; the new head of human resources management had been personnel manager in a pharmaceutical company and a motorcycle manufacturing company; and the product manager had been a consultant and technical director of a large mechanical engineering firm. Moreover, it should be underlined that Andrea Illy is also building up a team of junior managers who will be able to grow professionally and take over the important knowledge and competencies from the managerial team.

The entrepreneurial capacity rests mainly with the members of the Illy family who have led and still lead the company. They have in their character a clear ability to understand the market and its dynamics, customer needs and the best way to serve them. Both Ernesto and Andrea Illy are chemistry graduates. According to Andrea this technical preparation is a source of competitive advantage for a top manager. A number of chemical reactions take place before you get a good cup of coffee and you need to know this to guarantee a good result.

9.4.3.   Intellectual Capital

In all the cases studied, intellectual capital – understood as competencies, know-how and organisational routines – plays a key role in the entrepreneurial growth process of the firms.

Alessi's competencies are rooted in the artisan craftsman's skills and know-how, which characterise the local production of the VCO household goods district.

Yet Alessi's entrepreneurial adventure, marked by experimentation and innovation, started here in this profoundly traditional industrial production district. From the 'workshop for working brass and silver nickel sheet metal, with metal casting' (as the sign on the Alessi stand at the first Milan trade fairs in the 1920s stated) Alessi became the 'factory of Italian design'. The passage from metal engineering workshop to research lab in the field of applied arts was progressive and required several decades of acquisition of resources and skills from outside the district.

Finally, for Alessi the district does not just represent a source of resources and competencies linked to the firm's historical core business (that is, metal-working) but it is also a source of specialist knowledge which over time has strengthened Alessi's competencies and enriched its range of products. For example, in 1988, Alessi took over a district firm – Piazza Battista - specialised since the beginning of the century in the hydraulic turning of wood. This firm brought Alessi the skills necessary to introduce wooden accessories for the house and table under the new brand 'Twergi'.

Alessi was able to develop new design philosophies thanks to the organisation's cultural background and its key players. The most important corporate competency relates to new product development. This competency has gradually changed over the years; in fact, compared to what it was in the 1970s or, even more so, at the beginning of the firm's activity, the way Alessi develops new products today is significantly different.

With Giovanni Alessi, at the beginning, the craftsman's skill was widespread throughout the managerial staff and the workers, all profoundly rooted in the district's intellectual capital.

With Carlo Alessi and the objects designed between the 1930s and the mid-1940s, the first design skills (or rather industrial product design skills) were introduced and the Alessi style was given an imprinting which is still recognisable today even in objects designed by external designers. It was Ettore Alessi, who first opened the company's doors to external designers and began to mingle the district's competencies with those of the world of architecture and design.

With Alberto Alessi the firm's intellectual capital changed radically, above all in terms of its key competency: new product development. The technical office, which had developed all the successful products before the design era, became simply a back up to the development of objects designed by external collaborators. The creative function was thus outsourced and new competencies became central within the company: the ability to stimulate new product design on the part of external architects; and the ability to manage the flow of new product proposals coming from outside.

Alessi gradually took on the role of orchestrating the skills coming from the network of external designers. Organisational mechanisms for the acquisition of resources and competencies coming from outside thus became part of the firm's intellectual capital.

An important role in Alessi's intellectual capital is what is defined as 'Success formula', in other words a formal new product assessment mechanism used by members of the evaluation panel. The formula incorporates Alessi's competencies in measuring new product potential. Developed in the early 1990s, the formula's objective is to capture the particular features of Alessi production. Each member of the panel gives a score to the product prototype according to four categories: SMI (senses, memory, imagination); CL (communication; language); F (function); and P (price). The score is based on a 1 to 5 scale, which describes each evaluation category in detail. The formula allows for the calculation of an overall average score. Over the years Alessi has seen that its successful products attain a score of from 13 to 18 – the so-called 'Alessi area'. The four categories of the formula have become common language among the members of the new product development committee, Alessi employees in general and even the external designers.

The need and importance of developing a common language – a set of planning and production competencies that are common to all staff involved in new product development – has been expressed by Alessi in other areas. For example with the advent of plastic, Alessi learned to use colour in the projects, organising a series of lessons on colour with the help of external experts from the main suppliers, rather than creating a box of samples of the colours normally used. On this subject Mendini wrote (1996: 4–5), 'the idea of colour as language, as an alphabet: colour itself becomes a system of signs and one of the three ingredients in the composition of the object'. More generally, as Salvato (2006) has underlined, the competencies developed by the directors around certain corporate routines are the supporting columns of Alessi's intellectual capital. These are routines that have grown up over the years either deliberately or randomly: a) the use of workshops with external designers for product development; b) a formal system of colour cataloguing and colour development; c) the development of new versions of successful products already in the catalogue; d) activities aimed at increasing cooperation with and involvement of promising designers; e) the involvement of external consultants in the new product development process; f) the definition of a calculation procedure for target costing; and g) the definition of a deductive process of product development.

Thus, what is perceived externally as Alessi's 'secret' has, in fact, been built up over decades of dedication to design, innovation and routine carried out by the various corporate functions as well as by the external designers. This continuously repeated routine has, in fact, become (intellectual) capital available to the company.

The competencies that allow Luxottica to occupy a position of leadership within the eyewear sector are of a dual nature: productive on one hand and commercial on the other.

With reference to the first, if it cannot be denied that the firm would initially have had difficulty in starting production of finished frames without the presence of the district manufacturers, it is also true to say that with time, by internalising almost all the production process, Luxottica gradually broke free of the district by developing its own technical and production skills, together with the capacity for innovation. It was, in fact, the profound conviction that recourse to sub-contractors would limit the opportunities for product and process innovation that led the company to intensify the process of vertical integration.

Today Luxottica is a leader within the district, from both a strategic and a technological point of view; the acquisition of knowledge from firms and institutions within the district has gradually made space for the development and consolidation of competencies within the firm.

Nevertheless, Luxottica has kept up the relationship with 'Certottica', a training institution based in the district and which has collaborated with Luxottica for many years.

As far as commercial awareness is concerned, Luxottica was the first company in the sector to understand the importance of controlling distribution and to develop a business model that has since been imitated by other big competitors. Thus, it can undoubtedly be said that the district did not provide the firm with any relevant contribution in terms of commercial knowledge.

Over the years, then, the Luxottica Group has developed clear competencies both of a technical-productive and commercial nature. On the first front the company has made quality a key value and for this reason has progressively internalised almost all phases of the production process. The quality control staff regularly carry out inspections during all the production phases: during the design stage to verify the feasibility of the prototype; during working to guarantee a uniform qualitative standard for all products; and on the finished frames to verify fit, durability and optical properties according to the various conditions of use. Furthermore, controls are also carried out to verify the conformity of the production processes of the main suppliers.

Mention should also be made here of the Group's continuous investment in research and development in terms both of materials and processes, also in collaboration with important Italian universities.

On the commercial side, Luxottica can offer the market an excellent level of pre- and post-sales service, as well as a capillary distribution network.

The distribution system is totally integrated at international level; the trend in world sales and stock levels are checked daily, so that production resources can be programmed and warehouse stock reallocated according to specific market demand.

This integrated system can count on one of the most efficient logistic systems in the sector. All this means perfect coordination between demand and production, which reduces the stock of raw materials and puts Luxottica in a position to satisfy customer requests immediately in terms both of type and quantity of product.

The core competence of Geox lies definitely in technological research; it is on this capability that the company's sustained growth is based. This is an atypical phenomenon for a footwear manufacturing firm, given that it is rare to find a firm in the sector with 15 engineers on its staff and partnerships with some of the most advanced universities in the area of scientific studies. More than a shoe factory, Geox focuses on research, design, innovation and the nurturing of young talent. Constant investment is made to guarantee that the bank of technological knowledge is continuously updated. The protection of these assets is guaranteed in legal terms by the registration of numerous product and process patents. Geox has a portfolio of some 35 patents relating not only to new products but also to particular types of sewing, machinery, and so on.

Another central competence is the capacity to coordinate the purchase–production–sales network. The firm has developed a vast and complex network, coordination of which is critical to meet time-to-market deadlines.

Considering Geox's two central competencies, research into the dynamics of body heat and the coordination of business activities, it cannot be said that the district provided the firm with a crucial contribution in terms of knowledge. Nevertheless, at least as far as research is concerned, some firms in the district gave Geox the idea, giving an example of how investing in research can lead to business success, even in the footwear sector. Research led to innovations such as the 'Vibram' sole, applied to mountain boots, in 1937, and the introduction of plastic for the manufacture of ski boots, in 1967.

On the other hand, if we consider the non-distinguishing competencies, such as the technical and productive competencies, it cannot be denied that in the start-up phase, without the know-how of the shoe manufacturers in the district, the firm would have had to look outside the district, slowing down the product launch process. Still now the prototypes are made in the district of Montebelluna or in the footwear manufacturing area of the Marche.

Illy enjoys an enviable baggage of skills spread throughout the organisation. The distinguishing competencies that Illy has developed over the years and which represent a precious asset in that they are difficult to copy on the part of competitors relate to production, purchasing and design.

The district has provided a base of technical knowledge in the coffee trade and preparation, which has been built up over time. We would suggest it was not mere chance that led to the establishment here of the company making the best coffee blend in existence. The coffee culture and passion for coffee in the Trieste area were the lifeblood that fed the spirit and business activity of Illy from 1933 onwards. All the members of the entrepreneurial team have always expressed their passion for coffee and its aesthetic dimension.

In terms of production, for example, Illy is the only roaster that can blend nine different qualities of Arabica coffee; this is partly because, unlike its competitors, it performs the blending before the roasting phase. Again, unlike the competitors, the company cools the coffee beans by air and not by water. It uses four tasters to control look, aroma, taste and body of the coffee. The product is packed in pressurised containers, so that the characteristics of the coffee are preserved for three years. Illy has been able to guarantee that it is supplied with the best quality raw materials by obtaining supplies directly from the producers and setting up the 'Premio Brasile' award for the best coffee producers. This operation has been helped by the presence in Sao Paulo (Brazil) of an Illycaffè laboratory, which has the task of controlling the characteristics of the raw material in a more accurate way than the competition. Andrea Illy has underlined the importance of design and aesthetics in the company. This aspect is looked after as much as possible in the furnishings, architecture and in the places where coffee is drunk. The Illy product system also involves an aesthetic component, expressed via the brand, the Illy collection coffee cups and the environment created in the Espressamente Illy bars, to which the customers are strongly attached.

9.5.   ORGANISATIONAL MECHANISMS FOR THE ACQUISITION OF RESOURCES AND COMPETENCIES

The firms studied are all notable in that they adopted various mechanisms for acquiring the resources and competencies necessary for bringing about the process of entrepreneurial growth. In particular, as this section will show, they paid attention to staff training, recruited trained personnel, built up significant inter-organisational relations and set up roles and functions to manage key external relations.

9.5.1.   Recruitment and Training of Human Resources

Although Alessi's mission is the design and manufacture of innovative articles for the home, it has no designers on its staff and no intention of recruiting any. The company makes good use of the creative skills of external designers, but does no training or recruitment in this area, except for appointing staff who will interface with the external designers – as will be shown next. On the purely managerial front, Alessi has always been known for its strong family presence in the top corporate roles. Only recently a general manager from outside the family has been appointed: Alessandro Bonfiglioli. He has significant managerial experience in the international context, in particular with the 'American Haworth' group (furnishings for office and public spaces). Recently some restructuring has also taken place at the top; Michele, Alessio and Stefano Alessi now concentrate solely on their roles as members of the Board, while Alberto Alessi continues to manage the strategic activities more closely linked with the design function. The new manager of purchasing and new product development is Mauro Bonfanti, who built up his entire career in Alessi in the purchasing and supply function.

   In the case of Luxottica, while the technical and production skills are developed internally, the managerial competencies are acquired from outside; this has become particularly relevant in recent years, now that the question of the continuation of the business is becoming important.

Table 9.4 Organisational mechanisms for the acquisition of resources and competencies

	HR Recruitment and training	Inter-organisational relations	Gate-keepers and boundary spanners
Alessi	Designers not salaried employees Other key HR figures are family members New external appointment of CEO with wide experience	Specialised firms in the district Designers Large companies in other sectors	Ettore and Alberto Alessi Architects and Designers CSA Workshops Design Assistancy
Geox	Training at all levels (Geox School) Training of Geox shop personnel Recruitment in cooperation with universities Recruitment of technical staff from within district	Universities Outside contractors	Montebelluna research laboratory CRM system Geox Shop Geox School
Illy	Renewal of management team Training at all levels	Direct relationship with coffee producers Universities and research centres Coffee machine manufacturers Artists and architects	Ernesto Illy Total quality and continuous improvement function Andrea Illy
Luxottica	Meticulous recruitment and training procedure for managerial staff	Universities Firms in the fashion system Specialised firms in the district	Distribution system Stock and order control system Liaison with fashion houses

Source: personal elaboration

Experience in the eyewear sector is not important as far as recruitment is concerned, because there are few firms in the sector big enough to have developed strong managerial competencies. Moreover, the group's activity is difficult to categorise, being situated somewhere between mass consumption, the luxury goods market and the world of fashion.

Consequently, the management's approach to the market must be, at the same time, the very structured one typical of the mass market and a more flexible one, enabling it to move according to the logic of the fashion system and the luxury goods market.

Leonardo Del Vecchio himself, when asked about the management characteristics that can guarantee continuity to the group, replied 'you just have to choose someone who has the basic skills, a huge capacity to communicate with colleagues, employees and interlocutors; a person who has the essential cultural background, who knows languages, and with these characteristics it does not matter which sector they come from'.

In the case of Geox, by setting up the Geox School in 2001, the firm decided not only to invest significantly in training but also to take charge of it directly. The top management believed in the need to transfer the so-called 'DNA Geox' to the new recruits, in other words the overall corporate philosophy, over and above any specific functional content (Azzariti and Mazzon, 2005). At the beginning the training concerned only the cadres, with a series of seminars aimed at the different business areas (production, product development, marketing, and so on). The training aims to provide the skills to take on operational responsibility within each particular functional area and is technical and practical in nature, combining classroom teaching and hands-on experience in the firm. Each participant, assisted by a tutor, works on specific work projects, based on indications given by their line managers. There is also an internal motivator and visits to strategic suppliers are planned. The teaching staff is mostly (80 per cent) made up of managers and top managers from inside the firm and they are supported by external research and training institutes, with lessons by experts and scholars, including directors of large companies, university lecturers, and sports personalities. Since 2003, the Geox school has provided training courses at four levels: for new graduates, technicians, managers and top managers. As well as the Geox School, there is a system of personalised training at external institutions, in collaboration with training consultants, universities, and training institutes (such as the 'Politecnico calzaturiero della Riviera del Brenta').

Particular attention is paid to the training of the Geox Shop sales staff, as they represent the interface between Geox and the customer and thus play a crucial role in perceiving signals from the market. The training takes place via periodic meetings organised in the firm for staff of the new shops and at the point of sale for the staff already working there. Although this type of training does not directly provide skills and knowledge to be used in the firm, it has a strong influence on Geox's capacity to acquire information about purchasers via the sales staff.

As far as recruiting trained staff is concerned, it should be underlined that a growing firm like Geox has a relatively high rate of recruitment. Engineers, chemists and physicists taken on by the R&D function play a crucial role in developing new knowledge about the dynamics of body heat.

Between 1998 and 2002, during the period when the company moved towards a managerial type of organisation, good people from well-known firms in the textile-clothing and footwear sectors were appointed to positions of responsibility. More recently an agreement has been made with Cà Foscari University, Venice, to provide scholarships for research doctorates, training placements and internships in order to guarantee a supply of the best graduates to Geox.

The managers responsible for creating the prototypes are recruited by firms located in the Montebelluna and in the Ascoli Piceno (Marche) footwear districts, where there is a long tradition of this type of work.

Since Andrea Illy has been at the head, the Illy company has been well aware of the importance of training and the recruitment of adequately trained human resources.

Andrea, in fact, renewed the management team, bringing in some strong people from other sectors and this has contributed significantly to the firm's entrepreneurial growth. In 1992, Sergio Vallini, previously technical manager and production consultant for a mechanical engineering firm, was taken on with the mission of product supervision in terms of production, purchasing, logistics and programming. In 1998 the decision was made to recruit Anna Adriani; coming from Omnitel, she became head of Public Relations. The following year Sergio Silvestrin became art director of Illy. A few years later, in 2002, Daniele Manara was appointed as HR manager, a role that he had occupied in Aprilia, Glaxo and SEA. Manara was responsible for the integration of different functions, which will be discussed later, and for encouraging the recruitment and training of excellent middle managers. It is significant that in that year the number of top managers reached 29, whereas a few years earlier in 1997 there had only been 17. Finally in 2006 another important appointment was made; after successfully building up the network of Ferragamo shops in Asia, Raymond De Malherbe was appointed as director of Espressamente Illy.

Illy also has a strong training programme at all levels. Many training schemes for second tier managers have been started since 2003; in fact Illy is building up a second tier with the objective of making them completely autonomous. According to the HR manager this is a fundamental step for the future of the company, given that many of the present managers will soon be reaching retirement age. There are also a number of training activities at top management level, organised by business schools and consulting firms.

9.5.2. Inter-organisational Relations

Until the end of the 1980s, Alessi was deeply rooted in the VCO district. Alessi uses only local suppliers belonging to the VCO household goods district, with whom it has had informal working relationships for a long time. Stainless steel production that is not worked in the Crusinallo plant due to lack of capacity is contracted out in the district. This work includes finishing, casting, polishing and varnishing as well as mechanical working and highly specialised manual craftsmanship. There is a codified relationship model, which is applied only to local outside firms, showing the preference for this type of arrangement.

In Alessi's case, the continuous development of new products means developing and maintaining inter-organisational relations with outside designers.

The product catalogue development is maintained by the growth of Alessi's external architect and designer network (Figure 9.2). Today Alessi manages a network of over 200 designers and receives about 1 000 proposals for new articles every year. Since the 1970s Alessi has worked with over 3 000 different designers in total. This clearly allows the firm to make constant use of a vast channel for the acquisition of external resources and skills.

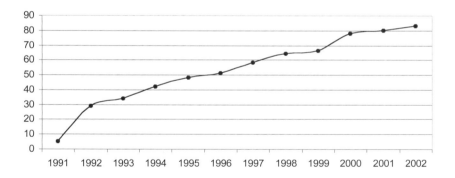

Source: company data

Figure 9.2 The growth of Alessi's designer network (1991–2002)

Interaction with suppliers is also a source of learning for Alessi, particularly with partner suppliers with whom it shares design projects, product development and investment. Alessi in fact buys 85 per cent of supplies from just 37 suppliers. In total, Alessi has a network of 190 suppliers, specialised in 70 different technological-production areas (representing €25 million in purchases).

Partnerships set up with other large groups coming from different sectors in the context of the diversification strategy also proved to be an important source of acquisition of resources and competencies. In 1994 Alessi formed a partnership with Philips; the aim was to create four household appliances, which would build on Alessi's competence in style and design on one hand and the technological competence of Philip's experience in electronic consumer goods on the other. Unfortunately the project ended in failure, like the production of the 'Comics' range of household linens a few years later. However, both these projects enabled Alessi to attempt collaboration with partners in different sectors of production in order to acquire new specialised competencies.

In this way Alessi embarked on a long period of licensing agreements, which led it to experiment in applying its skills in different areas, acquiring new knowledge and new marketing and technological skills. Projects include 'Alessi Wallpaper' (with the German Tapentenfabrik Gebr. Rasch), 'Alessi Watches' (with the Japanese Seiko-Fossil), bathroom fittings (with the Swiss Laufen, the Finnish Oras and the Italian Inda), the cordless telephone (with the German Siemens), ceramic tiles 'Alessi Tiles' (with the German Steuler Fliesen), cars 'Panda Alessi' (with FIAT), household linens 'Alessi Textile' (with the Belgian Lyntex), up to the latest models of 'La cucina Alessi' (with the Italian kitchen manufacturers Foster and Valcucine and the Finnish Oras).

In the case of Luxottica, given that product quality is a fundamental element in the top market range, where Luxottica operates, meeting high quality standards does not only mean checking every single phase of the production process, including those carried out by third parties, but implies also constant attention to product and process innovation. The relationship between Luxottica and external partners is very important here. Recently, for example, some research was carried out with suppliers and Venice University into a new type of homogenous colouring for sunglass lenses by means of a particular lacquer that can be coloured and the use of advanced injection compression moulding.

The relationships set up with the world of fashion have been and continue to be very important for the Group's growth. As already said, producing under license for the big fashion brands has in fact enabled the firm to enter the premium-luxury market segment, to acquire a growing visibility within the sector as well as refine its competencies in terms of design and innovation capacity in order to keep up with the continuing evolution of fashion and changing consumer demands.

Finally, due to the use of sub-contract work carried out by craftsman firms in the district, specialised in certain phases of the production process,

Luxottica was able, only a few years after its founding, to start production of the end product, under its own brand name, making a leap in quality.

Geox cooperates with various public and private research bodies in Italy and abroad. The company itself would never have been founded without the collaboration of ENEA and the Italian National Centre Research (CNR) in Rome, which helped Moretti Polegato's group to adapt expanded Teflon to footwear.

As far as research is concerned the most significant relationships are those set up with the University of Padua, Ca' Foscari University, Venice, the CRM in Milan and the University of Trontime (Oslo, Norway). The latter is one of the most advanced research centres in the field of the study of body heat; it is with researchers here that the Geox laboratory experimented the technology regarding fabric for clothing that breathes.

It should be emphasised that over time the original research partnerships have become less important (also because the firm's capacity for autonomous research has increased), while research partnerships relating to the application of the technology to new materials, as well as to providing training courses, has grown.

The most recent research partnership is with Venice University; the availability of trained personnel and advanced technological equipment at the science of materials laboratories allows testing and development of new lines of research to be carried out.

Geox's relationships are not limited to research but also involve production. The company could not achieve the necessary volume of production without the network of reliable sub-contractors built up over the years. This network does not give direct access to new competencies, but probably has an indirect effect on the process.

Finally, in the case of Illy, the exploitation of development opportunities has been helped by institutions, such as the Associazione Caffè Trieste, the Laboratorio Merceologico, the Qualicaf, the Università del Caffè, the AREA Science Park and the Tropical Greenhouse. These institutions have in fact helped to develop new knowledge and new skills, keeping this heritage within the Trieste area and involving several different firms.

While relationships with other firms in the district have not led Illy to acquire useful skills for entrepreneurial growth, the relationship with other types of district institutions has allowed the company to acquire new knowledge to combine with prior knowledge in order to identify and exploit opportunities for entrepreneurial growth.

The Qualicaf consortium, for example, was set up to promote coffee quality and culture within the district. It enabled Illy and other member companies to develop an integrated safety system and it has financed, together with Trieste University, the setting up of the Tropical Greenhouse.

Opened in 2001, the greenhouse was built to cultivate coffee for genetic studies and carries out research that is useful in developing technical knowledge about coffee.

Secondly the Trieste Industry Laboratory, owned by the Chamber of Commerce, carries out research into coffee as an industrial, food and environmental product. It is the only laboratory in Italy that is recognised as being able to totally classify coffee and the results of the analyses can be used by the firms in the district, including Illy.

Every year Trieste University organises a unique research doctorate in the science, technology and economics of the coffee industry to train people who can then use their knowledge in the main companies in the district.

Finally, important roles are played by the AREA Science Park, a cross-sector scientific and technological park, which carries out research, development and innovation activities, and Aroma Lab, which has been set up by Illy itself within the park, to carry out specific research into the aroma and taste of coffee. In this way Illy has gained a great deal of specific knowledge, which has been useful in the entrepreneurial growth process.

Illy has built up a strong network of relations with other bodies in order to acquire different critical functional resources and skills and to reach different objectives, all of which converge towards entrepreneurial growth.

In order to purchase the best raw materials, the company, unlike its competitors, began to set up direct relations with the coffee producers in 1990. In this way Illy receives first hand information about the raw material and the coffee bean market putting it in an excellent position to be able to deal with it.

Research has been an essential function in Illy's process of entrepreneurial growth. Over the years, the company has formed close links with the academic world and research centres. One of the most important is that with Sortex Ltd, the British company, which developed the electronic machine for sorting the coffee beans. The institutions with which Illy has collaborated in research include: ECMI (European Consortium for Mathematics and Industry), Florence University, Budapest University, Milan University, Manchester University and Udine University. Recently Illy has also worked with the Economics Faculty of San Paolo University, setting up the Universidade Illy do Cafè, an academic institution entirely dedicated to the scientific study of coffee.

Illy has also worked with some of the most important espresso coffee machine manufacturing companies: Gaggia, De Longhi, Saeco, Faema e Cimbali. Following the development of the ESE system, Illy opted for the free granting of patents to these firms in order to avoid the problem of the compatibility between pods and machines and to accelerate the development of the market for coffee pods. Due to these agreements with the main machine manufacturing firms, the company now aims to develop the market for espresso coffee in pods and capsules. Last but not least, the strategic partnership with Bialetti has led to the development of a new moka coffee pot that can make coffee of a much higher quality.

Finally, Illy has set up relationships with individuals and organisations in the world of design: art and creativity have become the language by means of which the company philosophy is expressed and a real coffee culture promoted. Since 1992, the year when the 'Illy Collection' cups were launched, there have been about three collections a year signed by famous masters or by young talent. The new logo was developed in 1996 thanks to the collaboration with pop-art master James Rosenquist. The launch of the 'Espressamente Illy' project in 2003 gave rise to other important partnerships; the concept bars were designed by three world-famous Italian architects: Luca Trazzi, Claudio Silvestrin and Paola Navone. Their avant-garde projects made Illy bars unique in terms of atmosphere and ambience. The same architects, together with other important artists and designers, including Matteo Thun, Danese, Marina Abramovic, Michael Beutler and Michael Lin, also designed a series of accessories: glasses, spoons, cups, sugar bowls, serviette holders. These partnerships have certainly added much to Illy's aesthetic and artistic wealth giving more and more weight to the intangible cultural aspect of the company's offer.

Illy's attention to the arts is also underlined by the relationships developed with the Ministry for Foreign Affairs and the young artists' circuit, by means of which the company promotes scholarships. Moreover, Illy maintains direct relations with contemporary artists and experimental contemporary art schools, supports the 'Young Writers project' of the 'Mantua Festivaletteratura', sponsors national and international contemporary art exhibitions and is a partner of the Venice 'Biennale'.

The numerous inter-organisational relations outlined above show how Illy's growth and development have come about due also to external sources of resources and competencies (Lipparini, Cazzola and Pistarelli, 1998).

9.5.3. Gatekeepers and Boundary Spanners

Different organisational mechanisms are available to firms to interface with the external environment in order to acquire resources and competencies. The theoretical outline presented in Chapter 5 refers to these mechanisms by means of the concepts of gatekeeping and boundary spanning.

In 1955 Ettore Alessi was the first member of the Alessi family and firm to play the role of boundary spanner. He was the first one, in fact, to open the firm up to external designers, who in turn, thanks to the articles proposed, opened up to a new market: the hotel trade.

When Alberto Alessi joined the company in 1970, he not only reinforced the role played years earlier by his uncle Ettore, collaborating with external designers and architects, but also enabled the company to open up to new ideas coming above all from the art world. The 'Alessi d'après' project was the first evidence of this and opened up the mass market to art objects. The partnerships with certain designers and architects allowed Alessi to extend its interface with the world outside; that is, Ettore Sottsass, who was already working with Alessi, introduced other colleagues, including Richard Sapper, who designed the famous '9090' coffee pot for Alessi. The gatekeeper role was played in an even more decisive way by another architect, Alessandro Mendini. He became design consultant to the Alessi family in 1979 and from then on was a leading figure in promoting skill and professionalism in matters of planning, art and design within the company, acting as a bridge to the world outside.

From the 1980s onwards, the Workshops represent – still in a rather elementary and sketchy form – the means by which Alessi interfaces with new designers to explore potential partnerships and acquire new ideas and skills. The first seminar or workshop on themes linked to production was held in Berlin in 1981 and called 'Cibi e Riti' (Food and Rites). Following this, Alessi set up collaborations with Achille Castiglioni and with Philippe Starck; similar seminars and research workshops were subsequently held, although not in a systematic way. Notable examples are the workshops on pans and kitchen equipment 'Cintura di Orione' (1987–1988), 'Dolce Stil Novo (della casa)' (1991), research by Dalisi on the subject of the Neapolitan coffee pot (1987–1991), research by Mendini on ceramic articles (1992) and by Mari on manufacturing objects in recycled plastic (1995). Over time the open seminars aimed at developing cultural and intellectual stimulus changed format becoming real workshops for the invention of products for the Alessi catalogue. This took place with the setting up of the Centro Studi Alessi (CSA): the workshop became a structured organisational mechanism for opening up to the skills of external designers not yet involved in the Alessi network. From that point on an average of 10 workshops a year were organised on a residential basis and lasted five days. The best-known workshops because of their impact on the Alessi catalogue were 'Family Follows Fiction' (1991) and 'Memory Containers' (1993).

The creation of the CSA stemmed from the need to give a formal framework to the gatekeeping function carried out by different figures in the company vis à vis the world of external designers. The CSA, coordinated by Laura Polinoro, is thus dedicated to the creation of a constant interface with external designers (mainly young ones) and other professional figures (sociologists, anthropologists, semiologists and opinion leaders) from whom new ideas and skills can be gained to constantly innovate the Alessi product catalogue. Last but not least, the Design Assistancy – the company function dedicated to new product development headed by Alberto Alessi – has the duty of maintaining contact with the external designers the company is developing new products with.

To sum up, Alessi today has four active interfaces with the outside world, which represent real channels of acquisition of resources and competencies from outside the company.

- New designers introduced by partners who are already part of the architect and designer network.
- Workshops organised by the CSA with well-known or unknown designers.
- Designers who are unknown to the firm (typically young designers or design students from all over the world) who contact the Design Assistancy.
- Designers already working with Alessi (with spontaneous product proposals or in response to invitations from the directors).

Luxottica has three gatekeepers. The first is undoubtedly represented by the distribution system, which is one of the most extensive in the eyewear sector. Due to its direct control of the wholesale and retail distribution chain, the company is present in all the most important world markets and can observe first hand the development of those with most growth potential, ready to intervene to consolidate its presence where necessary. Direct distribution in the main markets affords an important competitive advantage, enabling Luxottica to maintain close contact with customers, maximising the image and visibility of the brand portfolio. The second gatekeeper is represented by the centralised stock control and order system. The constant processing of sales data allows the company to make projections about demand, thus programming production and related activities in advance to better and more rapidly satisfy market needs. The final important figures who may be called gatekeepers are those who liaise with the fashion houses Luxottica produces for under license. Their role is to absorb into the company an in-depth knowledge about the image each single brand wishes to communicate in order to correctly interpret the identity in the collection development phase.

Four gatekeepers can be identified in Geox. The first is represented by the Montebelluna research laboratory, which acts as an interface with external university and other research centres, from which the company can draw scientific and technological knowledge. The second is represented by the Datamarket platform, the CRM system which allows for the real time acquisition of information about actual and potential clients in order to study their tastes and plan adequate purchasing and loyalty-promoting strategies.

Likewise, the third gatekeeper, the Geox Shop network, serves to acquire knowledge about the market. The Geox Shop personnel are trained to monitor Geox clientele, studying their tastes, habits, professions, age, and so on. The Geox Shops grew out of the need to communicate directly with consumers to better understand their needs and behaviour. The adoption of a loyalty card system, the 'Geox Card' can be interpreted in the light of this same need.   Finally, the fourth gatekeeper, the Geox School, is mainly represented by the need to acquire managerial knowledge. By means of the school, the company can enable its managers at all levels as well as new recruits to absorb the specific functional skills needed to work in Geox from external professionals.

We may identify three figures in Illy who act as gatekeepers within the company. The first is Ernesto Illy, who represents an interface with the outside world for the transfer and enhancement of technological knowledge. Ernesto is at the centre of a partnership network with several universities and research centres that Illy has set up over the years with the objective of increasing its technological and scientific knowledge about coffee and guaranteeing the total and constant quality of its product. At the same time Ernesto Illy has been responsible for the setting up and maintaining of the long-term relationships with Brazilian coffee producers. The second gatekeeper is represented by the 'Total quality and continuous improvement' function, which is at the heart of many relationships with espresso coffee machine manufacturers. This implies an interface with important mechanical engineering firms in order to create an integrated offer that is strongly influenced by the concept of quality. The third gatekeeper is Andrea Illy, who is at the centre of the relations needed to acquire skills and resources linked to the company's cultural and artistic aspect. The launch of the Illy collection cups and the development of 'Espressamente Illy' would not have been possible without the interface with world-famous contemporary artists, architects and designers. These people have contributed to the growth of corporate knowledge in the artistic field, transferring much knowledge inside Illy. The person who acted as interface with these artists and enabled the transfer and enhancement of this type of knowledge is Illy's CEO.

9.6.   ORGANISATIONAL MECHANISMS FOR THE COMBINATION OF RESOURCES AND COMPETENCIES

The firms analysed were able to bring about the processes of entrepreneurial growth due to the adoption of organisational mechanisms aimed at combining resources and competencies both at strategic and functional level.

There is a certain similarity between the firms in terms of the features of the strategic processes, whereas at a functional level they adopted quite different mechanisms. In all cases, however, the firms studied make use of mechanisms to recombine resources and competencies in order to support entrepreneurial growth.

Table 9.5 Organisational mechanisms for the combination of resources and competencies

	Strategic processes	**Integration mechanisms at functional level**
Alessi	Decentralisation: Yes Participation: Yes Flexibility: Yes Informalisation: Yes	New Product Committee Design Assistancy RUDE
Geox	Decentralisation: Yes Participation: Yes Flexibility: No (following stock market listing) Informalisation: No (following stock market listing)	Concentration of functions within same space IT system Training (as an opportunity for meeting) Teamworking
Illy	Decentralisation: Yes (following entry of Andrea) Participation: Yes (following entry of Andrea) Flexibility: Yes (following entry of Andrea) Informalisation: Yes (following entry of Andrea)	IT system
Luxottica	Decentralisation: Yes Participation: Yes Flexibility: No (following Stock Market listing) Informalisation: No (following Stock Market listing)	IT system Training (as an opportunity for meeting)

Source: personal elaboration

9.6.1. Strategic Processes

At a strategic level the most important organisational mechanism for the combination of resources and competencies is the new product development process, which involves Alessi's top management, the functional area and external designers. A new product develops out of ideas put forward by independent designers, spontaneously or on the basis of company input. The spontaneous ideas may also come from designers, who have never worked with Alessi before and are as yet unfamiliar with company needs. So, this is initially a highly decentralised strategic process, which is then channelled within the firm with a very high degree of informal participation and flexibility.

Traces of this process or part of it, can be seen in the relations between Alessi and the designers Massoni and Mazzeri as far back as the Programma 4 project in the mid fifties but it was only with Alberto Alessi at the beginning of the 1970s that the process became institutionalised. Nevertheless, it would be inaccurate to describe the process, which is based on creativity and long lasting interpersonal relations with designers, as formally structured and always repeated according to the same formal steps. Rather, it is a flexible procedure, which is difficult to define, even for the protagonists themselves, based on a 'nucleus' of routines and procedures, which have become part of the firm's intellectual capital. This 'nucleus' is made up of some fundamental phases described by Salvato (2003) as Alessi's key micro-strategies: meta-project; brief; evaluation; desiderata; engineering.

Alberto Alessi – head of design management – is responsible for preparing the brief for the external designers. This phase is based on 'meta-projects' (in which people from different cultural backgrounds take part), which define the social and cultural scenario within which the designers will operate. Often the ideas in the brief originate from the workshops organised by the 'Centro Studi Alessi'. The brief may refer to a new product type or a reworking of an already existing type. Sometimes a new product introduction is decided to revitalise a 'best seller' line.

Following project selection, Alberto Alessi draws up an 'outline of desiderata'; this includes the framework programme for the project and a description with the first hypotheses regarding times and cost.

On the basis of this document the Design Assistancy (DA) carries out a technical and production feasibility assessment. As well as the difficulty involved, this phase estimates the investment in terms of time and money involved in the new project. The DA's task is to select projects before making costly investment in machinery and moulds. On average, ten out of one hundred projects for which outlines of desiderata are drawn up reach the production stage.

Following this phase, which does not last longer than one month, the DA requests a prototype to test with area managers, who are called on to give an evaluation according to the 'success formula' devised by Alberto Alessi.

The test is carried out more than once for each product and can lead to the approval or 'freezing' of a project. If approved, a document of definitive 'desiderata' is drawn up and this usually includes 70 per cent of the original outline. The 'desiderata' is a presentation to the technical office, which includes a description of all the elements of the marketing mix (price, distribution channel, materials and communication).

The following phase regards the project engineering in which the production details are defined and the work is assigned for making the models and the drawing, and so on; contacts are made with suppliers, asking them to express an overall opinion of the project, also because they often act as general contractors for a network of specialised firms; and the economic aspects of the project regarding, for example, the checking of investment in moulds and equipment.

This stage lasts for at least two or three months and is followed by the official commitment to the project with the preparation of a document (detailing time, costs and performance features) to be presented to the monthly meeting of the New Product Committee (NPC). During this engineering stage one person is responsible for monitoring the project costs according to a 'job order' accounting system. At the same time the Design Assistancy continues to follow the project and look after contacts with designers.

At this point a list of requirements is drawn up, marking the line between project and production and indicating the final decision to go into production. The specifications include the Alberto Alessi's final approval, functionality tests, the SMI (sense, memory and imagination) index of the 'success formula' and the commitments made by the area managers and the sales and marketing manager. Before production begins the moulds are prepared (plastic outside, metal inside) which officially legitimates the investment in the project realisation.

The DA, marketing area head and Alberto Alessi meet weekly to check the project's progress. It takes an average of two years from project to product launch.

Strategic processes at Luxottica were originally largely centralised at top management level; all decisions were made by the founder and two other directors.

With time and following the Stock Exchange listing and the necessary confrontation with the interests of the financial markets, Del Vecchio realised that in this way, the firm was undermining its success and running the risk of being unprepared to face an increasingly complex competitive contest.

Little by little new managerial figures were introduced to the company and more precise responsibilities were given in production, distribution and marketing. In the words of Leonardo Del Vecchio himself: 'It's certainly difficult to find another person to be like the founder but a group of people who can do better is possible'.

Another clear step towards a more managerial leadership was taken with the appointment of Andrea Guerra as CEO. It is on his strategic leadership that the prospects for the Group's business development in terms of the identification of new market opportunities, acquisition of new chains of stores, signing of new agreements to produce under license to the fashion world, and so on, now depend.

Geox strategic processes have always been marked by participation and decentralisation. Moretti Polegato formulated the corporate mission and his task has always been to be its guarantor; however the Geox project was born and continues to function as a choral project, in which strategic plans are shared. This is why in interviews the founder always emphasises that the firm belongs to the managers who work there everyday with great enthusiasm.

Strategic management is decentralised. Geox managers enjoy freedom and trust in the running of their corporate functions. This is the result of a conscious choice on the part of Moretti Polegato; right from the start he discarded the traditional management model of the small Italian firm in favour of a model of delegating responsibility, so that the power was not concentrated in his hands.

Initially, and up until the time when the company went public, the processes and plans were typically informal and flexible, in keeping with the innovative character of the Geox business idea and the young age of the firm. The stock exchange listing imposed a change in the two dimensions of the strategic processes to enable investors to operate, but did not affect the participation and decentralisation of the decision-making, due to the express wish of the top executives.

In the case of Illy, the appointment of Andrea Illy as CEO led to significant changes in the firm's strategic processes.

In the preceding years an excessive interference on the part of the family in the running of the company limited the room for decision-making on the part of the management. With the adoption of two family pacts, Andrea set up a process of reorganisation aimed essentially at emphasising the role of management and formalising roles. In 1996 the first family pact formalised responsibilities in order to avoid a family 'shadow' organigram being set up. In 1999 greater autonomy and responsibility in strategic processes was given to the managerial team. Previously the family interference in management had led to obvious inefficiencies due to the difficulty in coordinating individual objectives.

Andrea introduced the Strategic Committee, a unit made up of the CEO and all the frontline managers; its task was to make the most important decisions and formalise them in strategic plans. The Board was thus left with the role of control and validation of these decisions.

There was thus a clear decrease in the level of flexibility and informality that had characterised the firm before Andrea Illy took over. On the other hand the introduction of the two family pacts and the setting up of a real managerial process led to an increase in manager participation in the running and consequently a greater decentralisation of executive power, which was now no longer in the hands of the Illy family but exercised by a strategic committee. As a result of the changes introduced by Andrea, the company became much more entrepreneurial and knowledge- and innovation-oriented. The high level of participation prevented knowledge being lost rather then re-used within the firm, thus exploiting its innovative potential.

9.6.2. Integration Mechanisms at Functional Level

With its partners Alessi sets up relationships that go beyond simple working cooperation, making them part of the family, and part of the great innovation- and design-generating team. Alessi's most important artistic partner, Mendini, has said: 'People are curious to know how relationships work ... The answer is that Alessi does't make us feel as if we work for Alessi. Rather, we feel as if Alessi is working for us' (Moon, Dessan and Sjoman, 2004: 3). Richard Sapper and Michael Graves also underline the positive climate of belonging to the organisation. According to the designer Michael Graves, in Alessi 'the concept of tradition is extended to the idea of family. Each designer is treated as a member of the family, there is a very close relationship between manufacturer and designer. This is what makes Alessi special, the relationship and the family atmosphere which stimulate innovation and creativity' (Alessi, 2002: 61).

Alongside this informal family set up there are organisational mechanisms and corporate functions, such as the monthly meetings of the New Product Committee (NPC), made up of the executive board (Alberto Alessi first of all), the heads of sales, purchasing, production, product development (the so-called Design Assistancy), Alberto Alessi's assistant (the Metaproject Coordinator) and Laura Polinoro, coordinator of the 'Centro Studi Alessi'.

An important linking role is also carried out by the Design Assistancy function, which follows the project throughout the various stages and looks after contacts with the external designers. The Design Assistancy, the head of marketing and Alberto Alessi have weekly meetings to check progress on the project.

Another opportunity for exchange and coordination between the various corporate functions is the RUDE (Riunione di Ufficializzazione del Desiderata) meeting, where the product features, outlined in the 'desiderata', are formally approved and the product moves into the production stage.

The product prototypes are presented to a panel of people who verify the market potential. This panel is usually made up of 10–15 Alessi employees, who, being very much in touch with the corporate philosophy, have the experience, sensibility and capacity to understand the new product potential.

For special projects, the panel is sometimes extended to 30 members, including Alessi area managers and thus encouraging further integration between functions, above all regarding core processes.

In the case of Luxottica, the different corporate 'souls' are geographically distant; the headquarters moved to Milan in 1999, the six Italian production plants are concentrated in the glasses manufacturing district, two other plants are located in the People's Republic of China and the wholesale distribution network is spread out internationally.

Despite this, the Luxottica business model features a very strong integration between planning, production and distribution. It is this business model, which is practically unique in the sector, that has led Luxottica to competitive success right from the start.

Integration between production and distribution means that the Group can have a production programme based on sales and not on distributors' orders.

From the strategic point of view, this means full control of both production and the distribution chain. In fact, only an efficient and flexible production structure can respond in a timely way to market demand and this demand can only be met by production if it also has effective control of the distribution.

From an organisational point of view, this is made possible by the complex IT system linking the logistic and sales centres with the production plants in Italy and China. This network permits the day-by-day control of world level sell-in and sell-out and remaining stock levels and allows production plans to be made according to the trend in demand.

Moreover, it is not unusual in Luxottica for employees to take part in sessions of training and information-sharing. For example, employees frequently participate in training organised by 'Certottica' (the Italian institute for the certification of optical products, professional instruments, hard hats and helmets, jewellery and other personal protection articles) to update personnel in the sector on new production technologies, planning, quality, safety, and so on.

Meetings are arranged with the fashion houses Luxottica has licensing agreements with, involving all people dealing with the brand (brand manager, key account manager, agents) in order to define guidelines for the new collections and sales objectives.

The short history of Geox has meant that the entrepreneurial growth process has taken place while the firm still has a high level of integration between corporate functions. The company has thus aimed at maintaining a structure that will continue to guarantee a high level of integration between the different functional areas.

From a strictly physical point of view, all the company functions are located in a single building, that is, on the ground floor fifty people work on prototypes; the laboratory technicians work on the first floor with the designers; and marketing people and administration are on the second floor. The company started up due to the efforts of people with complementary professional skills and has continued to grow along the lines indicated by the founder, maintaining the logic of cross-functional integration. This is why a strategic committee has been set up to bring together the heads of function, creating an arena for integration and communication.

ICT – used right from the start given that Geox was born at the beginning of the ICT age – has also contributed to the integration of the corporate functions. An intranet is used by function heads to communicate important information, while integration between head office, sales offices and production facilities, which are geographically far apart is achieved due to satellite and fibre optic links. An internal EDP service looks after the IT system, which is customised but based on standard technologies. In Geox, integration within the individual functions is achieved not only via the IT systems but also by means of training; the Geox school provides training to personnel via a process of exchanges and meetings, also using company managers as tutors.

Furthermore, each function is deliberately organised on the team-working principle. As the company itself was founded on this principle, so every function is required to work in the same way. The need to let information flow freely from top down and bottom up in order to be shared as much as possible is explicitly recognised.

In the case of Illy, a system called Illy Knowledge Management (IKM), supported by a technological infrastructure called Knowledge Management Architecture (KMA), was introduced in February 2003 in order to integrate corporate functions better by developing communication.

In order to do this, the available knowledge and its sources were mapped and classified in a knowledge tree made up of folders and sub-folders. This was studied to make it available to the top management, to teachers at the 'Università del caffè' (Coffee University) and to all internal users. The rules of access to the system were defined in order to guarantee security and functionality. Then the modes of rapid, personalised and exhaustive information retrieval via search agents were defined.

The IKM system can retrieve information from various sources (websites, file systems, and so on) and allows for Virtual Team-working; that is, by means of message boards and forums, corporate communities are set up within individual functions and across the different functions. The whole project involves a number of operators (to manage the technological infrastructure) and a committee made up of the project sponsor and the heads of the 'IT systems & process organisation' and 'Human Resources Management' functions. The committee coordinates the whole project, evaluates the results and manages the relations with the different functions, so that its potential is fully realised.

The IKM system allows for the combination of explicit knowledge, while tacit knowledge is shared by means of a policy of rotation of new recruits to different positions, formal mentoring programmes, where the transfer of knowledge is one of the tasks of the senior, more experienced managers and one on which they are also assessed.

9.7.   IN SEARCH FOR CONSISTENCIES AMONG CASES

In this chapter we conducted a cross-case analysis of all four cases, in order to search for similarities and differences in the antecedents of firm growth. Complying with the methodological approach introduced in Chapter 1 (Eisenhardt, 1989), we applied the theoretical lenses derived from the literature on firm-level entrepreneurship presented in Chapter 4 to our empirical data. This allowed us to cluster empirical data into five categories: (1) types of entrepreneurial opportunities identified and exploited; (2) sources of entrepreneurial opportunities; (3) resources and competencies used in the entrepreneurial process; (4) organisational mechanisms of resources and competencies acquisition; and (5) organisational mechanisms of resources and competencies recombination.

Cross-case analysis reveals a strong consistency among data. All four cases show similarities on the antecedents of their entrepreneurial growth, whilst differences may appear if we explore single antecedents in details.

First of all, all four cases have sustained their growth over time through continuous entrepreneurship, that is, adding new economic activities to existing ones. Thus, as stated in Chapter 1, entrepreneurship is growth, given that new economic activities add to the size of an established organisation (Davidsson et al., 2002). The entrepreneurial growth of Alessi, Geox, Illycaffè and Luxottica is grounded in the continuous and relentless identification and exploitation of entrepreneurial opportunities. To this regard, our analysis reveals some heterogeneity only at a more detailed level of analysis, which does not affect our reflections on the fact that the four cases have sustained their growth over time due to the intensity and variety of well-spotted opportunities. Nevertheless, if we categorise opportunities into product, market or process opportunities some differences among cases appear. For instance, Luxottica primarily focuses on new market opportunities, Alessi is much more concerned with identifying and exploiting product opportunities, while Geox seems to be much more on the process side, and Illy on both product and process opportunities. If we focus on single opportunities the level of heterogeneity among cases is even more stressed.

Second, we focused on the sources of entrepreneurial opportunities our four cases relied on. Over time the entrepreneurial growth of Alessi, Geox, Illycaffè and Luxottica has been fed both by internal sources of opportunity (within the firm, the industrial district or the sector) and by external ones (in the macro-environment). A comparative review reveals a wide variety of sources of opportunity that the four companies relied on, even if we can find strong consistency in the fact that all four cases mix internal sources with external ones. These four district firms have been able to continuously look inside their organisations as well as in their respective industrial districts and sectors in search for new opportunities. Furthermore, all four cases also exhibit the capability to rely on sources of opportunities that are external to their district and industry. Such a wise mix of internal and external sources of opportunities maintained over time contrasts with the inward looking attitude that seems to characterise industrial district firms.

Third, according to our framework of analysis, the opportunities for entrepreneurial growth are identified and exploited on the basis of resources and competencies possessed by firms. Thus, we compared cases even in terms of the resources and competencies they had available and which allowed for the identification and exploitation of the opportunities for entrepreneurial growth. Again, we noticed differences among cases in terms of the nature and amount of resources and competencies available. Tangible capital, human capital and intellectual capital were different in all four cases, even when common features were revealed as well. All four cases had benefited from resources and competencies available in their respective districts at the start of their entrepreneurial growth: tangible capital (proximity to similar plants and facilities) as well as intellectual capital (competencies, expertise and know-how). Further, in terms of human capital we noticed that – despite different managerial and governance approaches – in all four cases the entrepreneurial and managerial teams played a crucial role in the entrepreneurial growth. On one side we refer to the role of entrepreneurial families (Alessi and Illy) and individual entrepreneurs (Mario Moretti Polegato and Leonardo Del Vecchio). On the other, all cases exhibit the capability of entrepreneurial teams to form managerial teams who could extend their entrepreneurial orientation at a firm-level.

Fourth, all four cases show the presence of various mechanisms for acquiring the resources and competencies needed to discover and pursue entrepreneurial opportunities. Again we notice a variety of organisational mechanisms for the acquisition of external resources and competencies, but the four cases disclose similarities in the way they paid attention to train personnel, recruit skilled collaborators, weave significant inter-organisational ties and set up roles and functions expressly dedicated to manage key external relations.

Finally, all four cases converge on the adoption of organisational mechanisms aimed at combining resources and competencies both in terms of strategic processes and integration mechanisms at the functional level. More specifically, there is a certain similarity between the firms in terms of the features of their strategic processes. All firms show high degrees of decentralisation and participation in strategic processes, whilst the flexibility of such processes and their degree of informalisation vary over time. At a functional level the four firms adopted several mechanisms for integrating resources and competencies: IT systems, shared procedures, training activities, and so on. In summary all cases make use of mechanisms to recombine resources and competencies in order to support their entrepreneurial growth.

In conclusion, all four cases converge on a specific pattern of entrepreneurial growth. They are characterised by a relentless identification and exploitation of different kinds of entrepreneurial opportunities, which originate both from within the firm and the local industrial district and from the outer context. Further, the entrepreneurial growth of all four cases is linked to the organisational capability to capture external resources, including tangible resources such as capital, suppliers, and intangible resources such as information and competencies. We know from literature that this is a function of entrepreneurial accessibility and appropriability (Liao and Welsch, 2003). Accessibility is referred to as the ability of a firm to reach those organisations which may possess the resources and competencies needed for spotting and pursuing entrepreneurial opportunities. The accessibility of external resources is largely determined by the extensiveness and the firm's position in social and inter-organisational networks. In this regard, being embedded in an industrial district in a leadership position sustained the initial stages of the entrepreneurial growth of all four cases. Appropriability is the ability to capture those resources and competencies and transfer them inside the company. To this regard our analysis exhibits how all four cases have set up organisational mechanisms explicitly designed to acquire external resources and competencies – not only from their respective industrial districts but also from other industries and contexts – crucial for their entrepreneurial growth. The accumulation of knowledge, information, and other resources continuously opens new entrepreneurial opportunities and constitutes a driving force in the growth of the four firms. All cases have combined their own firm-specific resources and competencies – mainly derived from the resource endowment of the industrial district – with that of external partners, setting up specific organisational mechanisms.

In the last and conclusive chapter of this book we discuss our empirical results, in order to build theory on the basis of the chain of evidence resulting from individual case studies and cross-case analysis.

10. Discussion and conclusion

F. G. Alberti

In this chapter we discuss within-case and cross-case analyses results and we build theory on the basis of the chain of evidence resulting from such analyses. This chapter proceeds as follows. First we discuss the antecedents of entrepreneurial growth within industrial districts, identified in the four case studies. On the basis of that, we proceed to elaborate a model of entrepreneurial growth of firms within industrial districts. Then we suggest some consequences of firm-growth in industrial districts, building on the evidence from case study analyses. Next, we derive implications for practitioners in managerial and policy terms. The concluding section of this chapter summarises and discusses the main contributions of the study and examines limitations and future research paths.

10.1. INTRODUCTION

The relevant issue addressed in this book concerns the phenomenon of firm growth within industrial districts. We know from mainstream industrial district literature, discussed in Chapter 2, that district firms are treated as being one and the same, overlooking the fact that firms widely differ in terms of size, performance, structure and strategy (Boschma and Lambooy, 2002; Boschma and Ter Wal, 2007). Broadly speaking, district firms were represented as homogeneous agents, characterised as small and medium-sized and with equal access to local resources and competencies being 'in the air'. However, there is growing evidence – most strongly expressed by the literature on Italian industrial districts – of the emergence of powerful leading firms (see for example, Visconti, 1996; Lazerson and Lorenzoni, 1999; Rabellotti and Schmidtz, 1999). Often, leading firms control the supply chain through their market power and coordinate activities of suppliers and subcontractors in the district as well in the world economy, becoming global players. In some cases, leading firms have grown through local mergers/acquisitions and/or direct investments/takeovers by foreign corporations (see for example, Dei Ottati, 1996; Boari and Lipparini, Whitford, 2001; Cainelli et al., 2006), that is, acquisition growth as opposed to organic growth (Penrose, 1959).

However, despite the recent interest in literature on the role played by leading firms in industrial districts, little is known on firm growth within industrial districts. In other words, what brings some firms to detach from the industrial district cliché of being small, local and homogeneous and grow as global players? This brought us to our research question, as formulated in Chapter 1: 'what are the antecedents of firm growth within industrial districts?'

In order to answer this question we conducted empirical research on four cases (namely, Alessi, Geox, Illycaffè and Luxottica) of firm growth within industrial districts. To be able to make meaningful sense of data generated by empirical research we relied on a theoretical framework derived from the literature on entrepreneurship. Firm growth has become a major theme in the rapidly expanding field of entrepreneurship research. As discussed in Chapter 1, many researchers associate 'growth' with 'entrepreneurship' and vice versa (Gartner, 1990; Livesay, 1995; Delmar, 1997; Wiklund, 1998). In particular, Davidsson et al. (2002) state that an organisation grows as a result of recognising and exploiting opportunities for new economic activities, therefore growth is a reflection of the firm's entrepreneurship. Thus, we used the lenses of firm-level entrepreneurship as a framework for analysing, comparing and generalising the empirical results of the four cases of firm growth. As discussed in Chapter 4 we relied on a resource- and knowledge-based view of firm-level entrepreneurship, according to which resources and competencies play a key role in the process of opportunity recognition and exploitation.

In this chapter, building on the within-case and cross-case analyses presented earlier in the book, we seek to provide further insight into issues concerning the antecedents of firm growth within an industrial district by (analytically) generalising case studies results.

Studying multiple cases allowed us to build a logical chain of evidence (Yin, 1989; Miles and Huberman, 1994) for understanding the antecedents of district firms' growth on the basis of the theoretical framework we applied. Next, according to Eisenhardt (1989) who argues that the cross-case analysis should preferably be used for searching patterns, we conducted further analysis of consistencies identified across the cases (Miles and Huberman, 1994) in search for patterns, as characterised according to the theoretical lenses introduced in Chapter 4. Comparing the data for each growth pattern helped us in answering our research question on the antecedents of district firms' growth, proposing a model. We consequently developed our model into a theory that becomes the vehicle for generalisation to other cases that have not been studied (Yin, 1989). The cases that have not been studied, of course, must belong to the scope of the theory, that is they must be district firms. There is indeed no generalisation from a statistical representative sample to a population, but there is generalisation from one case to other cases that belong to the scope of the theory involved. This generalisation to a theory is an analytical generalisation (Yin, 1989), what Seale (1999) defines as 'theoretical generalisation'. Our findings allow us to also sketch some clues on the possible consequences of firm-growth in industrial districts. On the basis of our discussion on the role played by local and non-local resources and competencies, together with firm capabilities of acquisition and recombination, in the continuous process of opportunity recognition and exploitation, that is, growth; we derive implications for district practitioners at the managerial and policy level. The chapter concludes with an appraisal of the main contributions of this study as well as its limitations and a suggestion for future research paths.

10.2. ANTECEDENTS (AND CONSEQUENCES) OF FIRM GROWTH IN INDUSTRIAL DISTRICTS

Our cross-case analysis converges on a specific pattern of entrepreneurial growth. All four cases give evidence to a process of incessant identification and exploitation of different kinds of entrepreneurial opportunities (product, market or process opportunities), which originate both from within the firm and the local industrial district as well as from the outer context. Additionally, the entrepreneurial growth of all four cases is due to their organisational capability to absorb external resources (tangible and intangible) and competencies and to combine them with firm- and district-specific resources and competencies.

At first, the geographical proximity guaranteed by the industrial district of origin facilitates knowledge sharing and, thus, interactive learning and innovation. This means that knowledge does not spill over large distances: district firms can benefit from knowledge externalities that are 'in the air', but that are not available to firms located outside the district. However, simple co-location does not suffice; knowledge circulates and flows through networks. Thus, the accessibility to district resources and competencies is largely determined by the extensiveness of a firm's network and its position in the district network. In all four cases, being embedded in an industrial district in a favourable network position has sustained the initial stages of the entrepreneurial growth of firms, which have been able to capture district-specific resources and competencies and transfer them inside their organisation. This was made possible due to the setting up of organisational mechanisms of absorptive capacity. However, there is a growing awareness in literature that too much reliance on absorbing only local resources and competencies may be harmful for knowledge sharing and entrepreneurship. '[W]hen district firms become too much inward looking, their learning ability may be weakened to such an extent that they lose their innovative capacity and are unable to respond to new developments' (Boschma and Ter Wal, 2007: 181). Our findings confirm that openness (that is, being connected to extra-district knowledge networks) is a precondition for district firms' survival and development, since local and non-local relationships are important sources of resources and competencies. To this regard our analysis exhibits how all four cases have set up organisational mechanisms meant to absorb external resources and competencies – not only from their respective industrial districts but also from other industries and contexts – crucial for their entrepreneurial growth. This has brought them to stronger knowledge bases, which allow them an even higher absorptive capacity. Participation to local networks soon becomes participation to wider networks; this brings to the accumulation of new knowledge, information, and resources that incessantly open up to new entrepreneurial opportunities and constitute a driving force in the growth of the four firms. Additionally, all cases have been able to continuously combine their own firm-specific resources and competencies – mainly derived from the resource endowment of the industrial district – with that of external partners operating in different markets, industries and geographical setting. To do so, all four cases developed specific organisational mechanisms, designed for resources and competencies recombination.

Our findings even suggest some clues on the possible consequences of such growth. As a matter of fact, district firms that experienced entrepreneurial growth, like Alessi, Geox, Illycaffè and Luxottica, have affected their respective industrial districts, suggesting innovations, signalling new opportunities, detecting emerging challenges, hybridising district-specific knowledge and extending the boundaries of the district.

In the case of Alessi, since its start-up the family became well recognised and appreciated within the district, mainly due to its ability to transfer innovation, creativity, quality and technological advance. Alessi introduced in its district and in the entire houseware industry the concepts of 'author', 'project' and 'design', renovating industry recipes, norms and cognitions. In fact, Alessi was the first to adopt a design-based approach within the district (and within the industry). Furthermore, Alessi innovated with the idea of realising household articles in limited editions and by means of materials that were extraneous to the tradition of the district – such as plastic. At the beginning many competitors saw Alessi's decisions with scepticism, but as time went by they changed their views and took the same choices, replicating Alessi's strategies. For instance, in 1989 even Lagostina began to cooperate with designers and also Bialetti, traditionally focused on the production of the classical octagonal coffee maker invested in aesthetic innovations. In 1993, Piazza created a product line of multi-function boxes and professional pans in cooperation with Original Designers 6R5 Network of Milan. Several products of Alessi caused a revolution of the rules in an environment characterised by the attention paid to technological and functional aspects and by competition based on price. It introduced a new competitive variable, aesthetic, to increase the value perceived by customers. Alessi has always been a strongly proactive player, and its contribution goes beyond the district boundaries. Alessi actively contributed to the definition of industry standards mainly in terms of design-orientation. The new product lines of Alessi often became benchmarks and examples for its competitors. Besides that, Alessi was the first to experiment technological innovation in the use of materials, in particular stainless steel and plastic. To this regard, Danilo Alliata (Design Assistancy Department of Alessi) stated: '[e]very time that Alessi enters a new environment, something innovative happens. I mean, we produce radical changes and introduce new technological, methodological and mental approaches' (Salvato, 2006: 157). Alessi's proactivity was recognised by many observers and design experts, who saw that the company played a central role in the introduction of post-modern design within mass production of household articles. 'Alessi was associated with post-modern design more than any other company in the world' (Collins, 1999: 14–15). Alessi's cultural and intellectual guiding role obtained large market recognition in Italy and, in recent years, also abroad.

Even the Belluno industrial district was surely influenced by the growth process of Luxottica. At the beginning, in fact, the entrepreneurial context of the Agordino area developed due to Luxottica itself, which fostered the creation of micro and small firms in order to benefit from a network of subcontractors, which could ensure production flexibility. When Luxottica decided to in-source a large number of production phases, thus abandoning its subcontractors, the Agordino area experienced a decrease in the number of firms despite an increase in the number of workers. This brought a process of natural selection within the district that fortified the business models of those who survived. It is also worth noting that the decision of Luxottica in 1999 to keep the production in the district and move the headquarters to Milan – in order to better connect with the fashion industry and the financial market – motivated even other district firms (see for example, Safilo, De Rigo and Marcolin) to redesign their business model in search for new critical success factors.

The entrepreneurial growth of Geox had two important consequences on its district. On one side, Geox outsourced part of the production to some subcontractors in the district, to complement internal production capacity. On the other side, the strategic behaviour of Geox has been an example for the other district firms. Some firms understood how investments in research, communication and relocation of production could be critical success factors in facing current competition. Others went even further, trying to imitate Geox products (comfortable shoes that breathe) and strategies. Stonefly, for instance, is a firm located in the same industrial district of Geox, which is trying to follow a similar path to the one of Geox. Due to external laboratories (at the start-up) and internal laboratories (afterwards), Stonefly developed a breathing system similar to the one of Geox. Moreover, Stonefly even imitated the communication strategy of Geox, provoking its legal reaction. Last, we can state that the entrepreneurial growth of Geox had some influence also on other districts. In particular, the industrial relocation of Geox facilities in Timisoara (Hungary) has induced the start-up of an entire industrial district specialised in shoe-making. In other words, Geox set up in another geographical context the necessary conditions to support its entrepreneurial growth process.

Finally, in the case of Illycaffè, the area around Trieste surely benefited from the entrepreneurial growth of Illy, above all in terms of a strong brand image in global markets and also in terms of consolidation of the coffee culture. Over the years, the image built by Illy has positively affected its territory and allowed consumers to discover the Italian 300 year-old coffee tradition of Trieste. We therefore believe that small coffee producers, when able to exploit such country-of-origin effect, have indirectly benefited from the entrepreneurial growth of Illycaffè.

Hence, firms like Alessi, Geox, Illycaffè and Luxottica might become fundamental benchmarks for the rest of the district: first, because they inspire new product, new market or new process opportunities, through processes of imitation; and second, because their presence assures the introduction into the district of unfamiliar resources and competencies that can hybridise district profiles. This means that even those district firms that did not experience growth through entrepreneurial processes and did not become global players active in several contexts other than their original district may benefit from fresh ideas and new resources and competencies. In other terms, district firms like the ones we studied may act as pollinators to their own districts, producing knowledge spillovers (Breschi and Lissoni, 2001). Recently the literature has focused on the role of leading firms as gatekeepers of resources and competencies and as crucial detectors of emerging challenges to district survival (Zucchella, 2006). They search for and absorb non-local resources and competencies, and transmit them into the district (Morrison, 2004;

Owen-Smith and Powell, 2004). In this case leading firms act as 'bridging enterprises', potentially able to link the district to the outside world through the creation of in–out flows of knowledge transfer from the district to the global environment (Biggiero, 2002). As for our four cases, leading firms have well-established relations crossing the border of their own district. Boschma and Ter Wal (2007) suggest also that firms operating as district gatekeepers are able to process and decode the non-local external competencies for local district firms, favouring the resources dissemination in the district (Morrison, 2004). Lorenzoni and Baden-Fuller (1995) would have defined these district firms as 'strategic centres', that can assure the survival and the development of the entire district thanks to their superior coordination skills and ability to helm other firms to innovation and new growth opportunities. Firms like Alessi, Geox, Illycaffè and Luxottica act as focal firms in the local innovation network, often sharing and exchanging resources and competencies with only a few selected district partners. This means that knowledge will not spread widely among all district firms, because some of them will lack the competencies for effective resources and competencies transfer and use. For this to occur, local district firms should engage in inter-organisational learning processes (Giuliani and Bell, 2005) and rely on a sufficient amount of absorptive capacity (Boschma and Ter Wal, 2007).

10.3.   ENTREPRENEURIAL GROWTH IN INDUSTRIAL DISTRICTS: A MODEL

Our empirical findings suggest specific combinations of local and non-local resources and competencies, together with acquisition and recombination capabilities to be the determinants of the entrepreneurial growth of industrial district firms. The methodological approach adopted in this study allows us to theoretically generalise our finding to a conceptual model reported in Figure 10.1.

The interpretation of data with the lenses of firm-level entrepreneurship produced some theoretical insights that have been abstracted in the model presented in Figure 10.1. Hence, the model – building on the most recent literature on firm-level entrepreneurship, with a knowledge-based perspective (see Chapter 4) – theorises on the process of firm-level entrepreneurship, summarising the discussion so far.

We suggest that firm-growth is a consequence of the relentless process of opportunity recognition and exploitation, which is sustained and enhanced by the internal set of resources and competencies. These are supposed to signal new opportunities in the process of recognition and to support new opportunities in the process of exploitation.

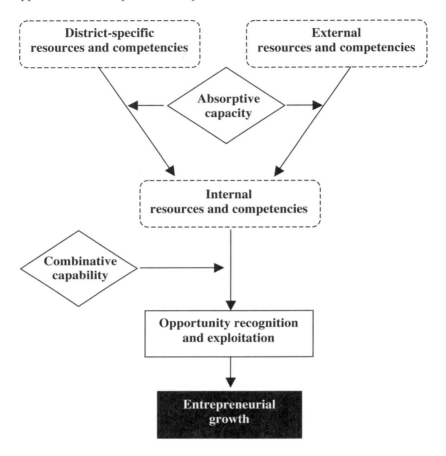

Source: personal elaboration

Figure 10.1 Entrepreneurial growth in industrial districts: a model

The relation between the incessant process of opportunity recognition and exploitation and the internal resources and competencies is mediated by the firm's capability to combine them in innovative manners. Additionally, new resources and competencies drawn from the local district environment and also from the external environment constantly feed the internal set of resources and competencies. The incessant strengthening and refreshing of a firm's resources and competencies with external ones is mediated by a firm's absorptive capacity.

Finally, we argue whether varying the weight of the antecedents proposed in our model may lead to different growth configurations. For this reason, we therefore assume possible variations in the proposed model. It is interesting to notice whether district firms: a) rely only on district-specific resources and competencies or even on external ones; b) develop only acquisition capabilities or even recombination ones. Concerning the first possible variation, we know from industrial districts' literature that embedded firms typically rely only on district-specific resources and competencies due to external economies of agglomeration (Cooke, 1999), that facilitate grasping the knowledge being 'in the air', and due to thick district boundaries (infrastructural, cognitive and cultural), that preclude firms from exploring new contexts (see for example, Alberti, 2003). Our theory suggests that the sole absorption of district-specific resources and competencies is insufficient when firm growth is expected. Rather, the sole referring to the local context in terms of resources and competencies absorption is likely to flatten a firm's business model to the industrial district stereotype. Concerning the second possible variation in our model, we know from entrepreneurship literature that absorptive capacity consists in storing, retrieving and applying externally accessed knowledge. As Malipiero et al. (2005) suggest, this guarantees superior resources and competencies base (as compared to other district firms), thus making such firms better equipped to identify new opportunities (Shane, 2000) and incorporate new resources and competencies external to the district. Empirical findings of this book confirm that bridging the district with the outer context is contributive in terms of recognising and exploiting new opportunities. However, our theory-informed empirically-driven model suggests that the sole absorptive capacity of district firms is insufficient when firm growth is expected. The relentless pursuit of entrepreneurial opportunities, which lay at the basis of firm growth, grounds also in combining resources in novel ways that allow extending a firm's activities beyond the current district domain.

The quality of our model can be judged in terms of reliability and validity of the present research (Yin, 1989). Reliability refers to the guarantee that the operation of this study can be repeated with the same results. It has been guaranteed on the one hand by the use of common protocols for data collection and analysis, and on the other hand by the development of case studies' databases, as shown in Chapter 1. Validity instead refers to the guarantee that results are correct. It can be judged with reference to measures, to cases interpretation (internal validity) and to generalisation (external validity). The validity of measures has been guaranteed by the use of multiple sources of evidence and by the establishment of chains of evidence. Internal validity has been guaranteed by data triangulation, by the use of common protocols of analysis and by the research of counter-examples and alternative interpretations. External validity has been reached through: (a) the adoption of the replication logic described in Chapter 1, according to which the results of each case are compared to the results of the previous ones; (b) the search for some kind of variety among case studies, in terms of industry, size, age and ownership.

10.4.   MAIN IMPLICATIONS

Thorough research has a potential to make a contribution to any audience in the form of trustworthy, thought-evoking suggestions. These suggestions, for instance in the form of concepts and models – as in the case of this book – become devices by which reality can be interpreted and actions can be taken. This might deliver a slightly more simplified view of the complex reality of entrepreneurial firm-growth in industrial districts, but – we believe – more understandable and manageable. To this regard, Pettigrew et al. (2002: 480) suggest: '[t]he primary role of both deductive and inductive approaches is not laying down laws, but helping practitioners to think more creatively about the complex shifting world in which they operate'.

Hopefully, this book will help practitioners operating in industrial districts – at both managerial and policy levels – to acknowledge the antecedents of entrepreneurial firm growth.

10.4.1.   Managerial implications

In general terms, this book dismantles the long-lasting idea that district firms are unavoidably the result of path-dependent agglomerations processes that cause them to be organisationally homogeneous and identical, with similar functions and tasks. If it is true that in most of the cases district firms are characterised as small and medium-sized organisations, our four case studies show how they could engage in processes of growth through the relentless recognition and exploitation of entrepreneurial opportunities. Thus a first important managerial implication of the present study is that – as in the cases of Alessi, Geox, Illycaffè and Luxottica – district firms can guide their process of entrepreneurial growth and we suggest that pattern to follow.

Further, recent studies (Boschma and Ter Wal, 2007) have shown that even if industrial district firms have potential equal access to local resources and competencies being 'in the air', they do not share similar levels of absorptive capacity. Firms are heterogeneous in their resources and competencies bases (Nelson and Winter, 1982) and, with relation to the extent of resources and competencies they have acquired in the past, they have different capabilities to absorb external resources and competencies (Cohen and Levinthal, 1990), needed to recognise and exploit new opportunities (Shane, 2000). This implies that the management can intervene in setting all the organisational conditions suitable to reinforce the absorptive capacity of their firms. We refer to organisational mechanisms such as training policies, recruitment of highly-skilled technical staff, renewal of the management team, inter-organisational relations, dedicated departments and functions, organisation of arenas for knowledge exchange and so on. If this occurs, absorbing district-specific resources and competencies becomes insufficient for sustaining growth. The implication is that managers and entrepreneurs are called to overcome district boundaries, setting up inter-organisational networks with players coming from different industrial contexts. This might guarantee the possibility to grasp new resources and competencies. However, extending the most recent literature on the centrality of absorptive capacity for leading firms (Boschma and Ter Wal, 2007; Malipiero et al., 2005; Morrison, 2004), we suggest that the sole absorption (even of ever fresh knowledge coming from outside the district) is insufficient and that the management of district firms is called to invest also on a combinative capability, in order to sustain entrepreneurial growth. We refer to the definition of highly participative, informal and decentralised strategic processes – such as the one devoted to new product development or new markets exploration – the extensive use of team-working and inter-functional teams or even the definition of organisational roles specifically designed to integrate different departments.

Thus, a third implication pertains the management of the processes of acquisition and recombination of resources and competencies, which is core according to our study. In this book we offer a comparative analysis of how our four cases have organised and managed these two processes. The heterogeneity of approaches, mechanisms and solutions reported in the in-depth analysis of Alessi, Geox, Illycaffè and Luxottica offers an invaluable set of indications on how to organise for strengthening a firm's absorptive capacity and combinative capability.

To complete this picture, the different roles of top and middle management in guiding the entrepreneurial growth have to be clarified. Our findings show that both top managers and lower-level employees have been actively involved for decades in the entrepreneurial growth of the firm. Often middle managers, collaborators and even shop-floor workers have played a crucial role in the process of opportunity recognition and exploitation, due to organisational mechanisms supporting decentralisation, participation, flexibility and informalisation. However, executives demonstrated the additional capability of being able to design and manage these organisational mechanisms.

10.4.2. Policy implications

Our study suggests that there are several possible interventions for policy makers at the district level, that is, the so-called district meta-managers (Visconti, 2002). As said, leading firms like the four we studied may pollinate their industrial districts with new opportunities and fresh resources and competencies, engendering replication or imitation processes. This means that district meta-managers on one side, should favour pollination and dissemination processes from leading firms; and on the other, should facilitate the decoding of non-local external competencies by local district firms. This could be accomplished through setting up institutional arenas for knowledge exchange and inter-organisational learning, where traditional district-specific knowledge could be hybridised with external resources and competencies brought in by leading firms.

Further, we noticed that in order to grasp new resources and competencies, all four cases we studied have developed wide inter-organisational networks with players around the world, moving away from their district origins. This poses to policy makers another important issue: how to keep these grown district firms tied to their district origins? Which are the benefits for district firms like Alessi, Geox, Illycaffè and Luxottica of remaining based in their respective industrial districts? Our findings suggest that when the local population of district firms is not keen to engage in inter-organisational learning processes or is not able to grasp new opportunities or absorb new resources and competencies then the risk of detachment from district origins becomes concrete and needs intervention. This means that policy makers should engage in preserving the competitiveness of the local business system so as to keep leading firms tied to the district.

Policy makers should also prevent the hollowing out of the local business environment, with dramatic consequences for the survival of the district itself, as an extreme drawback of the growth of a few firms. This implies interventions aimed at preserving and sustaining local specialisations through district-specific education and research.

Finally, policy makers do play an important role even in sustaining the legitimisation of leading firms that might often – when growth processes are noteworthy, as in our four cases – be perceived by the rest of the district as extraneous, thus not to be considered as benchmarks neither meriting imitation.

10.5. CONCLUSIONS

In this book we built on longitudinal data to shed light on the antecedents of the entrepreneurial growth of industrial district firms and, through the comparison of four case studies and the lenses of knowledge-based entrepreneurship, we proposed a model for interpreting this phenomenon that so far has attracted only anecdotal evidence. This allowed us also to sketch the main implications for practitioners, addressing both the managerial and entrepreneurial teams of district firms with strategic and organisational suggestions and policy makers with possible interventions.

Our study shows that firm-growth is not incompatible with industrial districts. Rather, on one side industrial districts – through their specific resources and competencies – may constitute a crucial means for initiating and sustaining growth while on the other, industrial districts may benefit from firm-growth, when leading firms pollinate the district with new resources and competencies and the local population of firms is receptive and able to absorb.

10.5.1. Main contributions

As shown in Chapter 1, the field of industrial districts' research has increasingly paid attention to district firms, and especially to those so-called leading firms, which experienced growth. Nevertheless, nothing but anecdotic evidence on district firm growth has appeared so far in literature. Our study aimed at filling such a research gap. The lenses of firm-level entrepreneurship together with a resource- and knowledge-based approach allowed us to dig into the phenomenon of district firms' growth in search for its antecedents. We analytically generalised our findings into the model illustrated above, offering a theory of firm-growth in industrial districts.

We believe our study answers the recent call – as published in *Industry and Innovation* (Boschma and Ter Wal, 2007) and debated in recent editions of the *DRUID (Danish Research Unit for Industrial Dynamics) Conference* – on researching the dynamics of industrial districts through a focus on district firms with a resource- and knowledge-based approach. Further we confide our study has the potential to open up a new wave of studies in this area, bringing in the categories and principles of entrepreneurship theory.

To our knowledge, this is also the first study on firm-level entrepreneurship entirely dedicated to firms operating in industrial districts. Thus, this book contributes to entrepreneurship literature applying existing concepts and approaches to a specific context. Results are not obvious and we believe they add some value to current knowledge. First, firm-level entrepreneurship is needed in industrial districts, where socio-cultural embeddedness may take the form of over-embeddedness (Grabher, 1993) and engender path dependent business models, unable to generate innovations or deviations from shared strategic recipes (Alberti, 2006). To this regard, our model has the potential to explain why some industrial districts do succeed in renewing themselves through firms' entrepreneurial processes, whilst some others do not. Second, firm-level entrepreneurship is needed in industrial districts, which are called to overcome current important challenges. Industrial districts' competitiveness, which used to be strong and long lasting, is under remarkable change. As suggested by Biggiero (2006), globalisation and ICT diffusion are dramatically challenging industrial districts' structure and competitive advantages. These challenges are amplified in some cases – like in 'Made in Italy' industrial districts – by mature industry conditions, where high growth and positive performances are even more dependent from entrepreneurial behaviours and strategies (Cassia, Fattore and Paleari, 2006).

Moreover, our conceptual model answers to the call for research published in *Journal of Management* by a large panel of scholars (Dess et al., 2003), which have identified the four main issues that need a deeper understanding in the study of firm-level entrepreneurship. The first one is simply the relationships between knowledge, learning and firm-level entrepreneurship, given the multi-dimensionality of all these three concepts; the scholars suggest to apply a knowledge-based approach to the study of the phenomenon, as well as it has been done in this book.

In conclusion, at a conceptual level, this book has tried to contribute to an enrichment of the variety of approaches to the study of industrial districts. This enabled us to reinforce the idea that the heterogeneity of district firms has to be taken into serious consideration to understand industrial districts' transformation and that firm growth is a core feature. Second, we refreshed the two main conceptual underpinnings of industrial districts, that is, competition and cooperation (Dei Ottati, 1994), with the idea that: competition becomes fiercer and more selective, thus requiring larger company size and richer sets of resources and competencies sustained by the relentless recognition and exploitation of entrepreneurial opportunities; cooperation occurs on more sophisticated issues than the past, that is, market and technological knowledge sharing and exchanges of tangible, human and intellectual capital.

10.5.2.   Limitations

All results and conclusions presented in this chapter and throughout the whole book may have some limitations, resulting from specific traits of both the empirical setting, and the adopted methodology.

Comparative case studies were designed with a replication approach in order to guarantee some kind of variety among cases. Hence, we selected four cases of profitable entrepreneurial growth where industry, size, age and ownership were different. Nevertheless, all firms are Italian firms and they all operate in northern-Italy industrial districts in the so-called 'Made in Italy' sectors (that is, fashion, furniture and food), which suggest similar industrial dynamics (for example, maturity, globalisation, hyper-competition, and so on) and comparable business models. The choice of our four empirical settings might represent a limitation to our findings.

Given the purpose of our research we targeted four cases to be studied in depth and longitudinally in order to develop insights through a comparative logic. This brought us to deal with large amounts of qualitative data on firms that prevented us from collecting inasmuch data even on each respective industrial district. Thus, we read the evolution of the four empirical settings through primary data collected around each case study and secondary archival data. Thus our main unit of analysis was the district firm and several levels of analysis have been accounted just inside the firm and not outside. This might be interpreted as a methodological limitation of our study.

Despite these limitations, our data illuminate several aspects of firm-growth in industrial districts, opening up to firm-level entrepreneurship as a valid interpretative framework for industrial districts' dynamics.

10.5.3. Future research paths

We believe that the aforementioned limitations may trigger several lines of further research on the topic, which we discuss hereafter.

First, analogous studies should be conducted in other countries apart from Italy and in other industries, in order to increase the external validity of our results. Different country and industry settings may have a strong impact on the sources and the nature of entrepreneurial opportunities, as well as on the knowledge-based organisational mechanisms of acquisition and recombination, which are highly dependent on socio-cultural dimensions.

Further, future studies may focus on level of analysis other than district firms, in order to confirm and strengthen our model. In particular, we believe our model would benefit from an in-depth and longitudinal account of industrial districts' dynamics in broad terms, in order to better understand the mutual interaction between the entrepreneurial growth of firms and the evolution of industrial districts. Our findings suggest that the entrepreneurial growth of our four cases had an impact on the four respective industrial districts, prompting new opportunities, freeing up new resources and competencies and suggesting new strategies. This implies two possible lines or further research. First, the entrepreneurial growth of district firms affects district institutions. Thus, future studies may rely on the growing literature on institutional entrepreneurship (see for example, Garud et al., 2007) to deeply understand how district institutions (norms, values, cognitions, recipes, practices and routines) are modified by the entrepreneurial agency of growing firms. Second, even if our study was aimed at investigating the antecedents of entrepreneurial growth in industrial districts, we have proposed some tentative clues also on the consequences of such growth. Further studies may rely on the literature on knowledge transfer in industrial districts (Biggiero, 2002; Malipiero et al., 2005; Boschma and Ter Wal, 2007) to shed some light on how other district firms may benefit from the entrepreneurial growth of a few; which organisational mechanisms and arrangements suit best for the transfer of resources and competencies; how knowledge pollination takes place within the industrial districts and under what conditions the presence of entrepreneurially-grown leading firms is beneficial to the district and when it is not.

Additionally, theory advances would benefit from an in-depth account of the role played by relational, cultural and cognitive embeddedness in the process of entrepreneurial growth within industrial districts. Literature (Grabher, 1993) suggests that the embeddedness of district firms affects both the recognition and the exploitation of new entrepreneurial opportunities and may result in path-dependent business models, characterised by homogeneous structures and strategies. Further research is needed to explain how district firms may overcome their embeddedness and move towards path-breaking business models, characterised by continuous innovation. In relational terms, this would mean exploring longitudinally the evolution of an industrial district, applying the lenses of network analysis, to understand how district firms gain centrality and boundary-spanning positions. In cognitive terms, the managerial and organisational cognition approach might help in understanding how district firms could avoid the trap of shared cognitions and schemes (Alberti, 2003), introducing new 'ways-of-thinking' (Hellgren and Melin, 1993: 87) and new cognitive capabilities (Shane, 2000) needed to recognise and exploit entrepreneurial opportunities. Finally, in cultural terms advances might come from an appreciation of how district firms could escape district macro-cultures (Abrahamson and Fombrun, 1994) that tend to flatten organisational variety and, hence, prevent entrepreneurial growth.

References

Abernathy, W.F. and K. Clark (1985), 'Innovation: Mapping the winds of creative destruction', *Research Policy*, **14** (1), 3–22.

Abrahamson, E. and C.J. Fombrun (1994), 'Macrocultures: Determinants and consequences', *Academy of Management Review*, **19** (4), 728–55.

Acs, Z.J. (1992), 'Small business economics: A global perspective', *Challenge*, **35** (6), 38–44.

Acs, Z.J. and D.B. Audretsch (1990), 'The determinants of small-firms growth in US manufacturing', *Applied Economics*, **22** (2), 143–53.

Adler, P.S. and S. Kwon (2002), 'Social capital: Prospects for a new concept', *Academy of Management Review*, **27**, 17–40.

Agrawal, A. and I.M. Cockburn (2002), 'University research, industrial R&D and the anchor tenant hypothesis', *NBER Working Paper*, 9219, Cambridge, MA.

Alberti, F.G. (2006), 'The decline of the industrial district of Como: Recession, relocation or reconversion?', *Entrepreneurship and Regional Development*, **18** (6): 473–501.

Alberti, F.G., S. Sciascia and A. Poli (2005), 'The domain of entrepreneurship education: Key issues', *International Journal of Entrepreneurship Education*, **2** (4), 453–82.

Alberti, F.G. (2003), *What makes it an industrial district? A cognitive constructionist approach*, JIBS Research Reports Series No 2003-1, Jonkoping, Sweden: Jonkoping International Business School.

Alberti, F.G., V. Tomasetto and A. Sinatra (2001), 'Thinking and acting in industrial districts', in B. Collin, I. King and P. Raimond (eds), *Proceedings of the 8th International Workshop on Management and Organization Cognition 'Thinking and Acting in/on Organizations', 2001, May 30th – June 1st*, Paris: Editions EIASM / ESCP-EAP.

Albino, V., A.C. Garavelli and G. Schiuma (1999), 'Knowledge transfer and inter-firm relationship: The role of the leader firm', *Technovation*, **19** (1), 53–63.

Alessi, A. (2002), *La fabbrica dei sogni. Alessi dal 1921*, Milano: Electa.

Allen, T.J. (1977), *Managing the flow of technology*, Cambridge (MA): MIT Press.

Alvarez, S.A. and J.B. Barney (2002), 'Resource-based theory and the entrepreneurial firm', in A.M. Hitt, D.R. Ireland, M.S. Camp and D.L. Sexton (eds), *Strategic entrepreneurship: Creating a new mindset*, Oxford: Blackwell, 89–105.

Amabile, T.M. (1988), 'A model of creativity and innovations in organizations', in B.M. Staw and L.L. Cummings (eds), *Research in organizational behaviour*, Greenwich (CT): JAI Press, 123–67.

Amatori, F. and A. Colli (2001), *Comunità di imprese. Sistemi locali in Italia tra Ottocento e Novecento*, Bologna: il Mulino.

Amin, A. and K. Robins (1991), 'These are not marshallian times', in R. Camagni (ed), *Innovation networks: Spatial perspectives*, London: Bellhaven Press, 105–18.

Amit, R. (1995), 'Comment to: Challenges in predicting new venture performance by A.C. Cooper', in I. Bull, H. Thomas and G. Willard (eds), *Entrepreneurship: Perspectives on theory building*, London: Elsevier Science.

Amit, R. and J.H. Schoemaker (1993), 'Strategic assets and organizational rent', *Strategic Management Journal*, **14**, 33–46.

Antonelli, C., R. Capellin, G. Garofoli and R. Jannaccone Pazzi (1988), *Le politiche di sviluppo locale. Nuove imprese, innovazione e servizi alla produzione per uno sviluppo endogeno*, Milano: Franco Angeli.

Appleyard, M.M. (1996), 'How does knowledge flow? Interfirm patterns in the semiconductor industry', *Strategic Management Journal*, **17**, 137–54.

Ardichvili, A., R. Cardozo and S. Ray (2003), 'A theory of entrepreneurial opportunity identification and development', *Journal of Business Venturing*, **18**, 105–23.

Argote, L. (1999), *Organizational learning: Creating, retaining, and transferring knowledge*, London: Kluwer.

Arrighetti, A. and G. Seravalli (eds) (1999), *Istituzioni intermedie e sviluppo locale*, Roma: Donzelli.

Asheim, B.T. (1996), 'Industrial districts as 'learning regions': a condition of prosperity', *European Planning Studies*, **4** (4), 379–400.

Azzariti, F. and P. Mazzon (2005), *Il valore della conoscenza. Teoria e pratica del knowledge management prossimo e venturo*, Milano: Etas.

Bagnasco, A. (1977), *Tre Italie. La problematica territoriale dello sviluppo italiano*, Bologna: il Mulino.

Bagnasco, A. (1988), *La costruzione sociale del mercato. Studi sullo sviluppo di piccola impresa in Italia*, Bologna: il Mulino.

Bailey, K.D. (1982), 'Methods of social research', New York: Free Press.

Barney, J.B. (1986), 'Strategic factors markets: Expectations, luck and business strategy', *Management science*, **32** (10), 1231–41.

Baron, R. (2000), 'Counterfactual thinking and venture formation: The potential effects of thinking about 'what might have been'', *Journal of Business Venturing*, **15** (1), 79–91.

Barringer, B.R. and A.C. Bluedorn (1999), 'The relationship between corporate entrepreneurship and strategic management', *Strategic Management Journal*, **20**, 421–44.

Barron, F.A. and D.M. Harrington (1981), 'Creativity, intelligence and personality', *Annual Review of Psychology*, **32**, 439–467.

Basadur, M.S., G.B. Graen and M. Wakabayashi (1990), 'Identifying differences in creative problem solving style', *Journal of Creative Behavior*, **24** (2), 111–31.

Baumol, W.J (1993), 'Formal entrepreneurship theory in economics: Existence and bounds', *Journal of Business Venturing*, **8**, 197–210.

Becattini, G. (1979), *Scienza economica e trasformazioni sociali*, Firenze: La Nuova Italia.

Becattini, G. (1987), *Mercato e forze locali: Il distretto industriale*, Bologna: il Mulino.

Becattini, G. (1989a), 'Riflessioni sul distretto industriale marshalliano come concetto socio-economico', *Stato e Mercato*, **25**, 111–28.

Becattini, G. (1989b), 'Considerazioni sul concetto di distretto industriale', *Impresa e Stato*, **4**, 48–53.

Becattini, G. (1990), 'The marshallian industrial district as a socio-economic notion', in F. Pyke, G. Becattini and W. Sengenberger (eds), *Industrial districts and inter-firm cooperation in Italy*, Geneva International Institute for Labor Studies, 37–51.

Becattini, G. (1991), 'The industrial district as a creative milieu', in G. Benko and M. Dunford (eds), *Industrial change and regional development*, London: Belhaven Press, 102–14.

Becattini, G. (1997), 'Totalità e cambiamento: Il paradigma dei distretti industriali', *Sviluppo Locale*, **4** (6), 75–94.

Becattini, G. (1998), *Distretti industriali e Made in Italy*, Torino: Bollati Boringhieri.

Becattini, G. (2002), 'Industrial sectors and industrial districts: Tools for industrial analysis', *European Planning Studies*, **10** (4), 483–93.

Becattini, G. and E. Rullani (1993), 'Sistema locale e mercato globale', *Economia e Politica Industriale*, **20** (80), 25–48.

Becker, G. and K. Murphy (1992), 'The division of labor, coordination costs and knowledge', *Quarterly Journal of Economics*, **107**, 1137–60.

Bellandi, M. (1982), 'Il distretto industriale in A. Marshall', *L'Industria*, **3**, 355–75.

Bellandi, M. (1989), 'The industrial district in Marshall', in E. Goodman and J. Bamford (eds), *Small firms and industrial districts in Italy*, London: Routledge, 136–52.

Bellandi, M. (1992), 'The incentive to decentralized industrial creativity in local systems of small firms', *Revue d'Economie Industrielle*, **59**, 99–110.

Bellandi, M. and F. Sforzi (2001), 'La molteplicità dei sentieri di sviluppo locale', in G. Becattini, M. Bellandi, G. Dei Ottati and F. Sforzi (eds), *Il caleidoscopio dello sviluppo locale. Trasformazioni economiche nell'Italia contemporanea*, Torino: Rosenberg and Sellier, 41–63.

Belussi, F. and L. Pilotti (2002), 'Knowledge creation and collective learning in the Italian local production systems', *Discussion paper, Dipartimento di Scienze Economiche 'Marco Fanno'*, University of Padua.

Benko, G. and M. Dunford (eds) (1991), *Industrial change and regional development*, London: Belhaven Press.

Benton, L. (1992), 'The emergence of the industrial district in Spain', in F. Pyke and W. Sengenberger (eds), *Industrial Districts and local economic regeneration*, Geneva: International Institute for Labor Studies, 48–86.

Best, M. (1990), *The New Competition: Institutions of industrial restructuring*, Cambridge (MA): Harvard University Press.

Bettiol, M. and M. Bosa (2004), 'Percorsi innovativi nel distretto della calzatura di Montebelluna: Il caso Geox', *Economia e Società Regionale*, **1**, 65–85.

Bettis, R.A. and M.A. Hitt (1995), 'The new competitive landscape', *Strategic Management Journal*, **16**, 7–19.

Biggiero, L. (1999), 'Markets, hierarchies, districts: A cybernetic approach', *Human System Management*, **18** (2), 71–86.

Biggiero, L. (2002), 'The location of multinationals in industrial districts: Knowledge transfer in biomedicals', *Journal of Technology Transfer*, **27** (1), 111–22.

Biggiero, L. (2006), 'Industrial and knowledge relocation strategies under the challenges of globalization and digitalization: The move of small and medium enterprises among territorial systems'. *Entrepreneurship & Regional Development*, **14** (4): 317–35.

Blyler, M. and R.W. Coff (2003), 'Dynamic capabilities, social capital, and rent appropriation: Ties that split pies', *Strategic Management Journal*, **24**, 677–86.

Boari, C. (2001), 'Industrial clusters: Focal firms, and economic dynamism – A perspective from Italy', *World Bank Institute Working Paper*, The International Bank for Reconstruction and Development/The World Bank.

Boari, C. and A. Lipparini (1999), 'Networks within industrial districts: Organizing knowledge creation and transfer by means of moderate hierarchies', *Journal of Management and Governance*, **3** (4), 339–60.

Boschma, R.A and A.L.J. Ter Wal (2007), 'Knowledge networks and innovative performance in an industrial district: The case of a footwear district in the south of Italy', *Industry and Innovation*, **14** (2), 177–99.

Boschma, R.A. and J.G. Lambooy (2002), 'Knowledge, market structure and economic coordination: Dynamics of industrial districts', *Growth and Change*, **33** (3), 291–311.

Bramanti, A. and L. Senn (1991), 'Innovation, firm and milieu: A dynamic and cyclic approach', in R. Camagni, *Innovation networks. Spatial perspectives*, London: Belhaven Press, 105–20.

Brock, W.A. and D.S. Evans (1989), 'Small business economics', *Small Business Economics*, **1** (1), 7–20.

Brockhaus, R.H. and P.S. Horwitz (1986), 'The psychology of the entrepreneur', in D.L. Sexton and R.W. Smilor (eds), *The art and science of entrepreneurship*, Cambridge (MA): Ballinger Publishing, 39–51.

Breschi, S. and F. Lissoni (2001), 'Knowledge spillovers and local innovation systems: A critical survey', *Industrial and Corporate Change*, **10** (4), 975–1005.

Brunetti, G. and A. Camuffo (2000), *Del Vecchio e Luxottica. Come si diventa leader mondiali*, Torino: Isedi.

Brusco, S. (1982), 'The emilian model: Productive decentralisation and social integration', *Cambridge Journal of Economics*, **6**, 167–84.

Brusco, S. (1989), *Piccole imprese e distretti industriali*, Torino: Rosenberg and Sellier.

Brusco, S. (1990), 'The idea of the industrial district: Its genesis', in F. Pyke, G. Becattini and W. Sengenberger (eds), *Industrial districts and inter-firm cooperation in Italy*, Geneva: International Institute for Labor Studies 10–19.

Brusco, S. (1991), 'La genesi dell'idea di distretto industriale', in F. Pyke, G. Becattini and W. Sengenberger (eds), *Distretti industriali e cooperazione fra imprese in Italia*, Studi e Informazioni, **34**, Firenze: Banca Toscana.

Buckley, J.P. and M. Casson (1989), 'La teoria dell'internazionalizzazione dei mercati nell'impresa multinazionale', in G. Balcet (ed), *Economia dell'impresa multinazionale*, Torino: Giappichelli Editore, 105–40.

Burgelman, R.A. (1983), 'Corporate entrepreneurship and strategic management: Insights from a process study', *Management Science*, **29** (12), 1349–64.

Bursi, T., G. Marchi and G. Nardin (1997), 'Trasformazioni organizzative nell'impresa distrettuale: Alcune premesse sulla definizione dell'unità di analisi', in R. Varaldo and L. Ferrucci (eds), *Il distretto industriale tra logiche di impresa e logiche di sistema*, Milano: Franco Angeli, 107–48.

Burt, R.S. (1992), *Structural holes: The social structure of competition*, Cambridge, (MA): Harvard University Press.

Cainelli, G., D. Iacobucci and E. Moranti (2006), 'Spatial agglomeration and business groups. New evidence from Italian industrial districts', *Regional Studies*, **40** (5), 507–18.

Camagni, R. (1991), 'Introduction: From the local 'milieu' to innovation through cooperation networks', in R. Camagni (ed), *Innovation networks: Spatial perspectives*, London: Belhaven Press, 1–9.

Camuffo, A., A. Furlan, P. Romano and A. Vinelli (2004), 'Crescere e creare valore nei settori maturi. Il caso Geox', *Economia & Management*, **6**, 111–24.

Cantillon, R. (1931), *Essay on the nature of general commerce*, London: Macmillan.

Carree, M.A. and A.R. Thurik (2003), 'The impact of entrepreneurship on economic growth', in D.B. Audretsch and Z.J. Acs (eds) *Handbook of Entrepreneurship*, Kluwer Academic Publishers, 437–71.

Cassia, L., M. Fattore and S. Paleari (2006), *Entrepreneurial Strategy. Emerging Businesses in Declining Industries*, Cheltenham (UK) and Northampton (MA): Edward Elgar.

Casson, M. (1982), *The entrepreneur. An economic theory*, Oxford (UK): Martin Robertson.

Castillo, J.J. (1989), 'El distrito industrial de la ceramica de Castellon', *Revista de Treball*, **11**, 93–104.

Castronovo, V. (1980), *L'industria italiana dall'ottocento a oggi*, Milano: Franco Angeli.

Cawthorne, P. (1995), 'Of networks and markets: The rise and rise of a south Indian town, the example of Tirippur's cotton knitwear industry', *World Development*, **23** (1): 43–56.

Chandler, A.D. (1962), *Strategy and structure: Chapters in the history of the industrial enterprise*, Cambridge (MA): MIT Press.

Church, R. (1993), 'The family firm in industrial capitalism: International perspectives on hypothesis and history', *Business History*, **35** (4), 17–43.

Ciciotti, E. (1993), *Competitività e territorio. L'economia regionale nei Paesi industrializzati*, Roma: NIS.

Cillo, P. and G. Troilo (2002), 'Il ruolo del senso di appartenenza nell'evoluzione dei distretti industriali. Una proposta metodologica', *Finanza, Marketing e Produzione*, **20** (1), 63–93.

Coda, V. (1988), *L'orientamento strategico dell'impresa*, Torino: UTET.

Cohen, M.D. and D.A. Levinthal (1990), 'Absorptive capacity: A new perspective on learning and innovation', *Administrative Science Quarterly* **35**, 128–52.

Coleman, J.S. (1988), 'Social capital in the creation of human capital', *American Journal of Sociology*, **94**, 95–120.

Collins, M. (1999), *Alessi*, London: Carlton Books Limited.

Cooke, P. (1999), 'The co-operative advantage of regions', in T. Barnes and M. Gertler (eds), *The new industrial geography: Regions, regulation, and institutions*, London: Routledge, 54–73.

Cooke, P. (2001), 'Regional innovation systems, clusters, and the knowledge economy', *Industrial and Corporate Change*, **10** (4), 945–74.

Corbetta, G. (1990), 'I sistemi formali di pianificazione strategica', in G. Invernizzi, M. Molteni and G. Corbetta (eds), *Management imprenditoriale*, Milano: Franco Angeli, 81–130.

Corò, G. and E. Rullani (eds) (1998), *Percorsi locali di internazionalizzazione. Competenze e autorganizzazione nei distretti industriali del nord-est*, Milano: Franco Angeli.

Corò, G. and R. Grandinetti (1999), 'Evolutionary patterns of Italian industrial districts', *Human Systems Management*, **18** (2), 117–29.

Corò, G., P. Gurisatti and A. Rossi (1998), 'Il distretto sport system di Montebelluna', in G. Corò and E. Rullani (eds), *Percorsi locali di internazionalizzazione. Competenze e auto-organizzazione nei distretti industriali del Nord-Est*, Milano: Franco Angeli.

Covin, J.G. and D.P. Slevin (1991), 'A conceptual model of entrepreneurship as firm behavior', *Entrepreneurship Theory and Practice*, **16**, 7–25.

D'Aveni, R.A. (1994), *Hypercompetition*, New York: Free Press.

Daft, R.L. and R.H. Lengel (1986), 'Organizational information requirements, media richness and structural design', *Management Science*, **32**, 554–71.

Davidsson, P. (1989), *Continued entrepreneurship and small firm growth*, Doctoral dissertation, Stockholm: EFI/ Stockholm School of Economics.

Davidsson, P. (1991), 'Continued entrepreneurship: ability, need and opportunity as determinants of small firm growth', *Journal of Business Venturing*, **6**, 405–29.

Davidsson, P., F. Delmar and J. Wiklund (2002), 'Entrepreneurship as growth; growth as entrepreneurship', in M. Hitt and D. Ireland (eds) *Strategic entrepreneurship: Creating a new mindset*, Oxford: Blackwell Publishers, 328–42.

Day, G.S. and D.B. Montgomery (1999), 'Charting new directions for marketing, *Journal of Marketing*, **63** (2), 3–13.

De Toni, A.F. and A. Tracogna (2005), *L'industria del caffè*, Milano: Il sole 24 ore.

Dei Ottati, G. (1986), 'Distretto industriale, problemi delle transazioni e mercato comunitario: prime considerazioni', *Economia e Politica Industriale*, **51**, 93–121.

Dei Ottati, G. (1987), 'Il mercato comunitario', in G. Becattini (ed), *Mercato e forze locali: il distretto industriale*, Bologna: il Mulino, 117–42.

Dei Ottati, G. (1994), 'Cooperation and competition in the industrial district as an organizational model', *European Planning Studies*, **2**, 463–83.

Dei Ottati, G. (1996), 'Economic changes in the district of Prato in the 1980s: Towards a more conscious and organised industrial district', *European Planning Studies*, **4** (1): 5–52.

Delmar, F. (1997), 'Measuring growth: Methodological considerations and empirical results', in R. Donckels and A. Miettinien (eds), *Entrepreneurship and SME research: On its way to the next millennium.* Aldershot (UK) and Brookfield (VA): Ashgate, 190–216.

Dematteis, G. (1994), 'Possibilità e limiti dello sviluppo industriale', *Sviluppo Locale*, **1** (1), 10–30.

Denrell, J., C. Fang and S.G. Winter (2003) 'The economics of strategic opportunity', *Strategic Management Journal*, **24** (10), 977–90.

Dess, G.G., R.D. Ireland, S.A Zahra, S.W. Floyd, J.J. Janney and P.J. Lane (2003), 'Emerging issues in corporate entrepreneurship', *Journal of Management*, **29** (3), 351–78.

Dosi, G., F. Malerba, O. Marsili and L. Orsenigo (1997), 'Industrial structures and dynamics: Evidence, interpretations and puzzles', *Industrial and Corporate Change*, **6** (1), 3–24.

Drucker, P.F. (1985), 'The discipline of innovation', *Harvard Business Review*, **63** (3), 67–72.

Dutton, J.E. and R.B. Duncan (1987), 'The influence of the strategic planning process on strategic change', *Strategic Management Journal*, **8** (2), 279–95.

Eisenhardt, K.M. (1989), 'Building theories from case study research', *Academy of Management Review*, **14**, 532–50.

Eisenhardt, K.M. and B.N. Tabrizi (1995), 'Accelerating adaptive processes: Product innovation in the global computer industry', *Administrative Science Quarterly*, **40**, 84–110.

Eisenhardt, K.M. and J.A. Martin (2000), 'Dynamic capabilities: What are they?', *Strategic Management Journal*, **21**, 1105–21.

Elster, J. (1983), *Explaining technical change*, Cambridge: Cambridge University Press.

Enright, M.J. (1992), 'Why local clusters are the way to win the game', *World Link*, **5**, 24–5.

Enright, M.J. (1993), 'The geographic scope of competitive advantage', in E. Dirven, J. Groenewegen, and S. van Hoof (eds), *Stuck in the region? Changing scales of regional identity*, Utrecht: Netherlands Geographical Studies 155, 87–102.

Enright, M.J. (1996), 'Regional Clusters and economic development: A research agenda', in U. Staber, N.V. Schaefer and B. Sharma (eds),

Business Networks: Prospects for regional development, New York: De Gruyter, 190–213.

Evans, D.S. (1987), 'Test of alternative theories of firm growth', *Journal of Political Economy*, **95**, 657–74.

Ferrucci, L. and R. Varaldo (1993), 'La natura e la dinamica dell'impresa distrettuale', *Economia e Politica Industriale*, **80**, 73–98.

Friedman, D. (1988), *The misunderstood miracle*, Itacha (NY): Cornell University Press.

Fuà, G. and C. Zacchia (1983), *Industrializzazione senza fratture*, Bologna: il Mulino.

Galunic, D.C. and S. Rodan (1998), 'Resource recombination in the firm: Knowledge structures and the potential for Schumpeterian innovation', *Strategic Management Journal*, **19**, 1193–201.

Garofoli, G. (1991a), *Modelli locali di sviluppo*, Milano: Franco Angeli.

Garofoli, G. (1991b), 'Local networks, innovation and policy in Italian industrial districts', in E. Bergman, Maier, G. and Todtling, F. (eds), *Regions reconsidered. Economic networks, innovation and local development in industrialized countries*, London: Mansell, 119–40.

Garofoli, G. (1992), *Economia del territorio. Trasformazioni economiche e sviluppo regionale*, Milano: Etas.

Gartner, W.B. (1985), 'A conceptual framework for describing the phenomenon of new venture creation', *Academy of Management Review*, **10** (4), 696–706.

Gartner, W.B. (1990), 'What are we talking about when we are talking about entrepreneurship?', *Journal of Business venturing*, **5**, 15–28.

Garud, R., C. Hardy and S. Maguire (2007), 'Institutional entrepreneurship as embedded agency: An introduction to the special issue', *Organization Studies*, **28** (7), 957–69.

Gereffi, G., J. Humphrey and T. Sturgeon (2005), 'The Governance of Global Value Chains', *Review of International Political Economy*, **12** (1), 78–104.

Gerschenkron, A. (1965), *Economic backwardness in historical perspective*, Cambridge (MA): Belknap Press of Harvard University Press.

Ginsberg, A. and A. Buchholtz (1989), 'Are entrepreneurs a breed apart? A look at the evidence', *Journal of General Management*, **15** (2), 32–40.

Giuliani, E. and M. Bell (2005), 'The micro-determinants of meso-level learning and innovation. Evidence from a Chilean wine cluster', *Research Policy*, **34** (1), 47–68.

Glasmeier, A. (1994), 'Flexible regions? The institutional and cultural limits to districts in an era of globalisation and technological paradigm shifts', in A. Amin and N. Thrift (eds), *Globalisation, institutions and regional development in Europe*, Oxford: Oxford University Press, 118–46.

References

Goodman, E. and J. Bamford (eds) (1990), *Small firms and industrial districts in Italy*, London: Routledge.

Grabher, G. (1993), 'The weakness of strong ties: The lock-in of regional development in the Ruhr area', in G. Grabher (ed), *the embedded firm: On the socioeconomics of industrial networks*, London: Routledge, 255–77.

Granovetter, M. (1973), 'The strength of weak ties', *American Journal of Sociology*, **78** (6), 1360–80.

Granovetter, M. (1995), 'The economic sociology of firms and entrepreneurs', in A. Portes (ed), *The economic sociology of immigration*, New York, Russel Sage Foundation, 128–65.

Grant, R. (1996), 'Toward a knowledge-based theory of firm', *Strategic Management Journal*, **17**, 109–22.

Greiner, L.E. (1972), 'Evolutions and revolutions as organizations grow', *Harvard Business Review*, **50** (4), 37–46.

Guerrieri, P., S. Iammarino and C. Pietrobelli (eds) (2001), *The global challenge to industrial districts: small and medium-sized enterprises in Italy and Taiwan*, Cheltenham (UK) and Northampton (MA): Edward Elgar.

Gupta, A.K. and V. Govindarajan (2000), 'Knowledge flows within multinational corporations', *Strategic Management Journal*, **21**, 473–96.

Guth, W.D. and A. Ginsberg (1990), 'Corporate entrepreneurship', *Strategic Management Journal*, **11**, 5–15.

Hall, P. and A. Markusen (1985), *Silicon landscapes*, Boston: Unwin and Hyman.

Hamel, G. and C.K. Prahalad (1994), *Competing for the future*, Cambridge (MA): Harvard Business School Press.

Hannan, M. and J. Freeman (1989), *Organizational ecology*, Cambridge (MA): Harvard University Press.

Hargadon, A. and R.I. Sutton (1997), 'Technology brokering and innovation in a product development firm', *Administrative Science Quarterly*, **44**, 82–111.

Hayek, F.A. (1945), 'The use of knowledge in society', *American Economic Review*, **35**, 519–30.

Hayek, F.A. (1978), 'Competition as a discovery procedure', in F.A. Hayek (ed), *New studies in philosophy, politics, economics and the history of ideas*, Chicago: University of Chicago Press, 179–90.

Helfat, C.E. (1997), 'Know how and asset complementarity and dynamic capability accumulation: The case of R&D', *Strategic Management Journal*, **18**, 339–60.

Hellgren B. and L. Melin (1993), 'The role of strategists' way-of-thinking in strategic change processes', in G. Johnson, L. Hendry and I. Newton (eds),

Strategic thinking: Leadership and the management of change, New York: Wiley, 251–71.

Henderson, R. and I. Cockburn (1994), 'Measuring competence? Exploring firm effects in pharmaceutical research', *Strategic Management Journal*, **15**, 63–84.

Herrigel, G. (1993), 'Power and the redefinition of industrial districts: The case of Baden-Württemberg', in G. Grabher (ed), *The embedded firm*, London: Routledge, 227–51.

Herrigel, G. (1996), *Industrial constructions: The sources of German industrial power*, New York: Cambridge University Press.

Hitt, M.A. and T.S. Reed (2000), 'Entrepreneurship in the new competitive landscape', in G.D. Meyer and K.A. Heppard (eds), *Entrepreneurship as strategy: Competing on the entrepreneurial edge*, Thousand Oaks: Sage, 23–47.

Hitt, M.A., D.R. Ireland, M.S. Camp and D.L. Sexton (2002), *Strategic entrepreneurship: Creating a new mindset*, Oxford: Blackwell Publishing.

Hitt, M.A., D.R. Ireland, M.S. Camp and L.D. Sexton (2001), 'Integrating entrepreneurship and strategic management actions to create firm wealth', *The Academy of Management Executive*, **15** (1), 49–63.

Holstein, J.A. and J.F. Gubrium (1997), 'Active interviewing', in D. Silvermann (ed), *Qualitative research*, London: Sage, 113–29.

Hornaday, J.A. and J. Aboud (1971), 'Characteristics of successful entrepreneurs', *Personnel Psychology*, **24**, 141–53.

Humphrey, J. and H. Schmitz (2002), 'How does insertion in global value chains affect upgrading in industrial clusters?', *Regional Studies*, **36** (9), 1017–27.

Iansiti, M. and K. Clark (1994), 'Integration and dynamic capability: Evidence from product development in automobiles and mainframe computers', *Industrial and Corporate Change*, **3**, 557–606.

Illeris, S. (1992), 'The Herning-Ikast textile industry: An industrial district in West Jutland', *Entrepreneurship and Regional Development*, **4**, 73–84.

Innocenti, R. (ed) (1985), *Piccola città e piccola impresa. Urbanizzazione, industrializzazione e intervento pubblico nelle aree periferiche*, Milano: Franco Angeli.

Invernizzi, G. (1988), 'Genesi e valenza della tensione allo sviluppo imprenditoriale interno', in G. Invernizzi, M. Molteni and A. Sinatra (eds), *Imprenditorialità interna. Lo sviluppo di nuove attività nelle imprese*. Milano: Etas, 95–126 .

Invernizzi, G., M. Molteni and A. Sinatra (eds) (1988), *Imprenditorialità interna. Lo sviluppo di nuove attività nelle imprese*, Milano: Etas.

Invernizzi, G., M. Molteni and G. Corbetta (eds) (1990), *Management imprenditoriale*, Milano: Franco Angeli.

Jansen, J.J.P., F.A.J. Van den Bosch and H.W. Volberda (2005), 'Managing potential and realized absorptive capacity: How do organizational antecedents matter?', *Academy of Management Journal*, **48**, 999–1015.

Jaworski, B.J. and A.K. Kohli (1993), 'Market orientation: Antecedents and consequences', *Journal of Marketing*, **57**, 53–70.

Jennings, D.F. and G.T. Lumpkin (1989), 'Insights between environmental scanning activities and Porter's generic strategies: An empirical analysis', *Journal of Management*, **18** (4), 791–804.

Jick, T.D. (1979), 'Mixing qualitative and quantitative methods: Triangulation in action', *Administrative Science Quarterly*, **24**, 602–11.

Kanter, R.M. (1985), 'Supporting innovation and venture development in established companies', *Journal of Business Venturing*, **1**, 47–60.

Kaplan, S.R. and P.D. Norton (2000), Balanced scorecard. Tradurre la strategia in azione, Torino: ISEDI.

Kazanjian, R.K. and R. Drazin (1989), 'An empirical test of stage of a growth progression model', *Management Science*, **35** (12), 1489–503.

Kazanjian, R.K., R. Drazin and M.A. Glynn (2002), 'Implementing strategies for corporate entrepreneurship: A knowledge-based perspective', in A.M. Hitt, D.R. Ireland, M.S. Camp and D.L. Sexton (eds), *Strategic entrepreneurship: Creating a new mindset*, Oxford: Blackwell, 173–200.

Kim, L. (1998), 'Crisis construction and organizational learning: Capability building in catching-up at Hyundai Motor', *Organization Science*, **9**, 506–21.

Kinnear, T. (1999), 'A perspective on how firms relate to their markets', *Journal of Marketing*, **63** (2), 112–14.

Kirzner, I.M. (1973), *Competition and entrepreneurship*, Chicago: The University of Chicago Press.

Kirzner, I.M. (1982), 'Uncertainty, discovery, and human action: A study of the entrepreneurial profile in the Misesian system', in I.M. Kirzner (ed), *Method, process and Austrian economics: Essays in honour of Ludwig von Mises*, Lexington (MA): D.C. Heath, 139–59.

Kirzner, I.M. (1997), 'Entrepreneurial discovery and the competitive market process: An Austrian approach', *Journal of Economic Literature*, **35**, 60–85.

Knight, F.H. (1921), *Risk, uncertainty and profit*, New York: Harper & Row.

Knorringa, P. (1995), *Economics of collaboration in producer-trader relations: Transaction regimes between market and hierarchy in the Agra footwear cluster, India*, Amsterdam: Free University Amsterdam.

Koestler, A. (1966), *The act of creation*, London: Hutchinson.

Kogut, B. and U. Zander (1992), 'Knowledge of the firm, combinative capabilities and the replication of technology', *Organization Science*, **3**, 383–97.

Kogut, B. and U. Zander (1996), 'What do firms do? Coordination, identity and learning', *Organization Science*, **7**, 502–18.

Kristensen, P. (1994), 'Spectator communities and entrepreneurial districts', *Entrepreneurship and Regional Development*, **6**, 177–98.

Krugman, P.R. (1991), *Geography and trade*, Cambridge (MA): MIT Press.

Lane, P.J. and M. Lubatkin (1998), 'Relative absorptive capacity and interorganizational learning', *Strategic Management Journal*, **19**, 461–77.

Lawson, C. (1998), 'Towards a competence theory of the region', *Cambridge Journal of Economics*, **23** (2), 151–66.

Lazerson, M. (1993), 'Factory or putting-out? Knitting networks in Modena' in G. Grabher, *The embedded firm. On the socioeconomics of industrial networks*, London: Routledge, 203–26.

Lazerson, M. and G. Lorenzoni (1999), 'The firms that feed industrial districts: A return to the Italian source', *Industrial and Corporate Change*, **8** (2), 235–66.

Lazzeretti, L. and D. Storai (2002), 'An ecology-based interpretation of district 'complexification': The Prato district evolution from 1946–1993', in F. Belussi, G. Gottardi and E. Rullani (eds), *The Technological evolution of industrial districts*, Dordrecht: Kluwer.

Lenox, M. and A. King (2004), 'Prospects for developing absorptive capacity through internal information provision', *Strategic Management Journal*, **25**, 331–45.

Liao, J. and H. Welsch (2003). 'Social capital and entrepreneurial growth aspiration: A comparison of technology- and non-technology-based nascent entrepreneurs', *Journal of High Technology Management Research*, **14** (1): 149–70.

Lipparini, A. (1995), *Imprese, relazioni tra imprese e posizionamento competitivo*, Milano: Etas Libri.

Lipparini, A. (1997), 'Sistemi territoriali e comunità interorganizzative', in A. Lomi (ed), *L'analisi relazionale delle organizzazioni. Riflessioni teoriche ed esperienze empiriche*, Bologna: il Mulino, 271–308.

Lipparini, A. and A. Lomi (1999), 'Interorganizational relations in the Modena biomedical industry: A case study in local economic development', in A. Grandori (ed), *Interfirm networks. Organization and industrial competitiveness*, London: Routledge, 120–50.

Lipparini, A., F. Cazzola and P. Pistarelli (1998), 'Le risorse e le competenze alla base della crescita sostenuta. Il caso Illycaffè S.p.A.', *Economia & Management*, **3**, 21–32.

Livesay, H.C. (ed) (1995), *Entrepreneurship and the growth of the firms*, Aldershot (UK) and Brookfield (US): Edward Elgar.

Lorenzoni, G. and C. Baden-Fuller (1995), 'Creating a strategic center to manage a web of partners', *California Management Review*, **37** (3), 146–63.

Lorenzoni, G. and O. Ornati (1988), 'Constellation of firms and new ventures', *Journal of Business Venturing*, **3**, 41–57.

Low, M. and I.C. MacMillan (1988), 'Entrepreneurship: Past research and future challenges', *Journal of Management*, **14** (2), 139–61.

Lumpkin, G.T. and G.G. Dess (1996), 'Clarifying the entrepreneurial orientation construct and linking it to performance', *Academy of Management Review*, **21** (1), 135–72.

Lynskey, M.J (2002), 'Introduction', in M.J. Lynskey and S. Yonekura, *Entrepreneurship and organization – The role of the entrepreneur in organizational innovation*, Oxford: Oxford University Press, 1–57.

Malerba, F. and L. Orsenigo (1996), 'The dynamics and evolution of industries', *Industrial and Corporate Change*, **5** (1), 51–87.

Malipiero, A., F. Munari and M. Sobrero (2005), 'Focal firms as technological gatekeepers within industrial districts: Knowledge creation and dissemination in the Italian packaging machinery industry', *DRUID Working Paper*, 5, Copenhagen Business School.

Mansfield, E. (1985), 'How rapidly does industrial technology leak out?', *The Journal of Industrial Economics*, **34**, 217–24.

Markusen, A. (1996), 'Sticky places in slippery space: A typology of industrial districts', *Economic Geography*, **72**, 293–313.

Marshall, A. (1920), *Industry and trade*, Macmillan.

Marshall, A. (1950), *Principles of Economics*, London: Macmillan.

Marsili, O. (2002), 'Technological regimes and sources of entrepreneurship', *Small Business Economics*, **19** (3), 217–31.

Maskell, P. (2001), Towards a knowledge-based theory of the geographical cluster, *Industrial and Corporate Change*, **10** (4), 921–43.

Maskell, P. and A. Malberg (1999), 'Localized learning and industrial competitiveness', *Cambridge Journal of Economics*, **23** (2), 167–86.

McClelland, D. (1961), *The achieving society*, Princeton (NJ): Van Nostrand.

McGrath, R.G. and I.C. MacMillan (1992), 'More like each other than anyone else? A cross-cultural study of entrepreneurial perceptions', *Journal of Business Venturing*, **7** (5), 419–29.

McGrath, R.G. and I.C. MacMillan (2000), *The entrepreneurial mindset*, Cambridge (MA): Harvard Business School Press.

McGrath, R.G., I.C. MacMillan and S. Scheinberg (1992), 'Elitists, risk-takers, and rugged individualists? An exploratory analysis of cultural differences between entrepreneurs and non-entrepreneurs', *Journal of Business Venturing*, **7**, 115–35.

McGrath, R.G., S. Venkataraman and I.C. MacMillan (1994), 'The advantage chain: Antecedents to rents from internal corporate ventures', *Journal of Business Venturing*, **9** (5), 351–69.

Mendini, A. (1996), *Thirty colours. New colours for a new century*, Bussum: V+K Publishing.

Meyer, G.D. and K.A. Heppard (2000), *Entrepreneurship as strategy: Competing on the entrepreneurial edge*, Thousand Oaks: Sage.

Micheal, S., D. Storey and H. Thomas (2002), 'Discovery and coordination in strategic management and entrepreneurship', in A.M. Hitt, D.R. Ireland, M.S. Camp and D.L. Sexton (eds), *Strategic entrepreneurship: Creating a new mindset*, Oxford: Blackwell Publishing, 45–66.

Miles, M.B. and A.M. Huberman (1994), *Qualitative data analysis*, Thousand Oaks (CA): Sage.

Miller, D. (1983), 'The correlates of entrepreneurship in three types of firms', *Management Science*, **29** (7), 770–91.

Miller, J. and B. Glassner (1997), 'The 'inside' and the 'outside'. Finding realities in interviews', in D. Silvermann (ed), *Qualitative research*, London: Sage, 99–112.

Minoja, M. (2002), *Impresa distrettuale e competizione globale*, Milano: Egea.

Mintzberg, H. (1973), 'Strategy making in three modes', *California Management Review*, **16** (2), 44–53.

Mintzberg, H., B. Ahlstrand and J. Lampel (1998), *Strategy safari: A guided tour through the wilds of strategic management*, London: Prentice Hall.

Molteni, M. (1988), 'Fasi e ruoli nello sviluppo imprenditoriale interno', in G. Invernizzi, M. Molteni and A. Sinatra (eds), *Imprenditorialità interna. Lo sviluppo di nuove attività nelle imprese*, Milano: Etas, 71–94.

Molteni, M. (1990), 'Direzione e proprietà di fronte al cambiamento', in G. Invernizzi, M. Molteni and G. Corbetta (eds), *Management imprenditoriale*, Milano: Franco Angeli, 17–80.

Moon, Y., V. Dessain and A. Sjoman (2004) 'Alessi, evolution of an Italian Design Factory', *Harvard Business School case collection*.

Moorman, C. and A.S. Miner (1997), 'The impact of organizational memory on new product performance and creativity', *Journal of Marketing Research*, **34**, 91–106.

Morris, M.H. and D.F. Kuratko (2002), *Corporate Entrepreneurship*, Fort Worth (TEX): Harcourt College Publishers.

Morris, M.H. and D.L. Sexton (1996), 'The concept of entrepreneurial intensity: Implications for company performance', *Journal of Business Research*, **36**, 5–13.

Morrison, A. (2004), 'Gatekeepers of knowledge' within industrial districts: Who they are, how they interact', *CESPRI Working Paper*, 163, Bocconi University.

Mowery, D.C. and J.E. Oxley (1995), 'Inward technology transfer and competitiveness: The role of national innovation systems', *Cambridge Journal of Economics*, **19**, 67–93.

Mumford, M.D. (2000), 'Managing creative people: Strategies and tactics for innovation', *Human Resources Management*, **10**, 313–51.

Nahapiet, J. and S. Ghoshal (1998), 'Social capital, intellectual capital, and the organizational advantage', *Academy of Management Review*, **23**, 242–66.

Nelson, R.R. and S.G. Winter (1982), *An evolutionary theory of economic change*, Cambridge (MA): Harvard University Press.

Neustadt, R.E. and E.R. May (1986), *Thinking in time: The uses of history for decision makers*, New York: Free Press.

Nonaka, I. (1994), 'A dynamic theory of organizational knowledge creation', *Organization Science*, **5** (1), 14–37.

Normann, R. (1977), *Managing for growth*, New York: Wiley.

Novello, P. (2000), 'Reti di imprese e distretti industriali. Le implicazioni per la domanda di prodotti e servizi finanziari', *Piccola Impresa/Small Business*, **13** (2), 125–40.

Nuti, F. (ed) (1992), *I distretti dell'industria manifatturiera in Italia*, Milano: Franco Angeli.

Osborn, A.F. (1957), *Applied imagination*, New York: Scribner.

Owen-Smith, J. and W.W. Powell (2004), 'Knowledge networks as channels and conduits: The effects of spillovers in the Boston biotechnology community', *Organization Science*, **15** (1), 5–21.

Paci, M. (1982), *La struttura sociale italiana*, Bologna: Il Mulino.

Parri, L. (1993), 'Le trasformazioni dei distretti industriali italiani: Successi e difficoltà tra privato, associativo e pubblico', *Piccola Impresa/Small Business*, **6** (2), 43–72.

Penrose, E. (1959), *The theory of the growth of the firm*, London: Basil Blackwell.

Peterson, R. and S. Berger (1971), 'Entrepreneurship in organizations: Evidence form the popular music industry', *Administrative Science Quarterly*, **16**, 97–107.

Pettigrew, A. (1973), *The politics of organizational decision-making*, London: Tavistock.

Pettigrew, A. (1979), 'On studying organizational cultures', *Administrative Science Quarterly*, **24**, 570–81.

Pettigrew, A. (1990), 'Longitudinal field research on change: Theory and practice', *Organization Science*, **1** (3), 267–91.

Pettigrew A., H. Thomas and R. Whittington (2002). Strategic management: The strengths and limitations of a field, in A. Pettigrew, H. Thomas and R. Whittington (eds), *Handbook of strategy and management*, London: Sage, 3–30.

Pilotti, L. (1997), 'I sistemi locali industriali del nordest: Apprendimento, conoscenza, istituzioni', *Sviluppo Locale*, **4** (5), 64–122.

Pinchot, G. (1985), *Intrapreneuring: Why you don't have to leave the corporation to become an entrepreneur*, New York: Harper & Row.

Pine, B.J. and J.H. Gilmor (1999), *The experience economy. Work is theatre & every business a stage*, Boston: Harvard Business School Press.

Piore, M.J. (1990), 'Work, labour and action: Work experience in a system of flexible production', in F. Pyke, G. Becattini and W. Sengenberger (eds), *Industrial districts and inter-firm cooperation in Italy*, Geneva: International Institute for Labor Studies, 52–74.

Piore, M.J. and C. Sabel (1984), *The second industrial divide*, New York: Basic books.

Poni, C. (1998), 'Confrontare due distretti industriali urbani: Bologna e Lyon nell'età moderna', in V. Giura (ed), *Gli insediamenti economici e le loro logiche*, Edizioni Scientifiche Italiane.

Porter, M.E. (1990), *The competitive advantage of nations*, New York: The Free Press.

Porter, M.E. (1998), *On competition*, Cambridge (MA): Harvard Business School Press.

Porter, M.E. (2000), 'Location, competition and economic development: Local clusters in a global economy', *Economic Development Quarterly*, **14** (1), 15–34.

Portes, A. (1998), 'Social capital: Its origins and applications in modern sociology', *Annual Review of Sociology*, **24**, 1–24.

Prahalad, C.K. and G. Hamel (1990), 'The core competence of the corporation', *Harvard Business Review*, **68** (3), 79–91.

Provasi, G. (1995), 'Lumezzane: Terra di imprenditori', *Working Paper, Social Sciences Dept.*, Brescia University.

Pyke, F. and W. Sengenberger (1992), *Industrial districts and local economic regeneration*, Geneva: International Institute for Labor Studies.

Pyke, F., G. Becattini and W. Sengenberger (eds) (1990), *Industrial districts and inter-firm cooperation in Italy*, Geneva: International Institute for Labor Studies.

Rabellotti, R. (1997), *External economies and cooperation in industrial districts,* Basingstoke (UK): Macmillan.

Rabellotti, R. and H. Schmitz (1999), 'The internal heterogeneity of industrial districts in Italy, Brazil and Mexico', *Regional Studies*, **33** (2), 97–108.

Ressico, A. (1999), 'Struttura ed evoluzione di un distretto industriale piemontese: La produzione di casalinghi nel Cusio', *CERIS Working Paper CERIS, 8, CNR*.

Rindfleisch, A. and C. Moorman (2001), 'The acquisition and utilization of information in new product alliances: A strength-of-ties perspective', *Journal of Marketing*, **65**, 1–18.

Ronstadt, R. (1988), 'The corridor principle', *Journal of Business Venturing* **1**, 31–40.

Sabel, C. (2001), 'Diversity, not specialization: The ties that bind the (new) industrial district', paper presented at the conference *Complexity and Industrial Clusters: Dynamics and Models in Theory and Practice*, Milan, June 19–20.

Salaman, G. and D. Asch (2003), *Strategy and capability. Sustaining organizational change*, Oxford: Blackwell Publishing.

Salvato, C. (2003), 'The role of micro-strategies in the engineering of firm evolution', *Journal of Management Studies*, **40** (1), 83–108.

Salvato, C. (2006), *Micro-foundations of organizational adaptation. A field study in the evolution of product development capabilities in a design firm*, JIBS Dissertation Series No 033, Jonkoping, Sweden: Jonkoping International Business School.

Salvato, C., U. Lassini and J. Wiklund (2006), 'Dynamics of external growth in SMEs: A process model of acquisition capabilities emergence', in J. Katz, D. Shepherd, J. Wiklund and D. Dimov, *Advances in Entrepreneurship, Firm Emergence and Growth*, Vol. 9, Oxford: Elsevier Sciente, 237–75.

Sammarra, A. and F. Belussi (2006), 'Evolution and relocation in fashion-led Italian districts: Evidence from two case-studies', *Entrepreneurship & Regional Development*, **18** (6), 543–62.

Sammarra, A. and L. Biggiero (2001a), 'Identity and identification in industrial districts', *Journal of Management and Governance*, **5**, 61–82.

Sammarra, A. and L. Biggiero (2001b), 'Identity, trust, and co-operation in localized production networks', paper presented at *17th EGOS Colloquium*, Lyon, July 5–7.

Sandberg, W.R. (1992), 'Strategic management's potential contributions to a theory of entrepreneurship', *Entrepreneurship Theory and Practice*, **16** (3), 73–90.

Santarelli, E. and E. Pesciarelli (1990), 'The emergence of a vision: The development of Schumpeter's theory of entrepreneurship', *History of Political Economy*, **22**, 677–96.

Sapelli, G. (1989), *L'Italia inafferrabile*, Venezia: Marsilio.

Sapelli, G. and F. Carnevali (1994), *L'impresa – storia e culture*, Roma: NIS.

Sarasvathy, D., H. Simon and L. Lave (1998), 'Perceiving and managing business risks: Differences between entrepreneurs and bankers', *Journal of Economic Behavior and Organization*, **33**, 207–25.

Sathe, V. (2003), *Corporate entrepreneurship. Top managers and new business creation*, New York: Cambridge University Press.

Saxenian, A. (1991), 'The origins and dynamics of production networks in Silicon Valley', *Research Policy*, **20** (5), 423–38.

Saxenian, A.L. (1994), *Regional advantage: Culture and competition in Silicon Valley and Route 128*, Cambridge (MA): Harvard University Press.

Say, J.B. (1971), *A Treatise on political economy or the production, distribution and consumption of wealth*, New York: Augustus M. Kelley.

Schendel, D.E. (1990), 'Introduction to the special issue on corporate entrepreneurship', *Strategic Management Journal*, **11**, 1–3.

Schmitz, H. (1995), 'Small shoemakers and fordist giants: tales of supercluster', *World Development*, **23**, 9–28.

Schollhammer, H. (1982), 'Internal corporate entrepreneurship', in C.A. Kent, D.L. Sexton and K.H. Vesper (eds), *Encyclopedia of entrepreneurship*, Englewood Cliffs (NJ): Prentice-Hall, 209–29.

Schumpeter, J.A. (1934), *The theory of economic development*, Cambridge (MA): Harvard University Press.

Schumpeter, J.A. (1942), *Capitalism, socialism and democracy*, New York: Harper & Row.

Sciascia. S, L. Naldi and F. Alberti (2008), 'Hypercompetition and the entrepreneurial orientation of SMEs', *International Journal of Technology Management* (forthcoming).

Scott, A. (1998a), 'Flexible production systems and regional development: The rise of new industrial space in North America and Western Europe', *International Journal of Urban and Regional Research*, **12**, 171–86.

Scott, A. (1998b), *New industrial space*, London: Pion.

Seale, C. (2004), 'Quality in qualitative research', London: Sage Publications.

Sengenberger, W., G. Loveman and M.J. Piore (eds) (1990), *The re-emergence of small enterprises: Industrial restructuring in industrialised countries*, Geneva: International Institute of Labour Studies.

Sexton, D.L. (1980), 'Characteristics and role demands of successful entrepreneurs', paper presented at the *40th Academy of Management Meeting*, Detroit, August.

Sforzi, F. (1987), 'L'identificazione spaziale', in G. Becattini (ed), *Mercato e forze locali: Il distretto industriale*, Bologna: il Mulino.

Sforzi, F. (1989), 'The geography of industrial district in Italy', in E. Goodman and J. Bamford (eds), *Small firms and industrial districts in Italy*, London: Routledge, 153–73.

Sforzi, F. (1990), 'The quantitative importance of Marshallian industrial districts in the Italian economy', in F. Pyke, G. Becattini and W. Sengenberger (eds), *Industrial districts and inter-firm cooperation in Italy*, Geneva: International Institute for Labor Studies, 75–107.

Sforzi, F. (1991), *I distretti industriali marshalliani nell'economia italiana*, in F. Pyke, G. Becattini and W. Sengenberger (eds), *Distretti industriali e cooperazione fra imprese in Italia*, Firenze: Banca Toscana.

Sforzi, F. (2002), 'The industrial district and the 'new' Italian economic geography', *European Planning Studies*, **10** (4), 439–47.

Shane, S. (1996), 'Hybrid organizational arrangements and their implications for firm growth and survival: A study of new franchisors', *Academy of Management Journal*, **39** (1), 216–34.

Shane, S. (2000), 'Prior knowledge and the discovery of entrepreneurial opportunities', *Organization Science*, **11**, 448–69.

Shane, S. (2003), *A general theory of entrepreneurship. The individual–opportunity nexus*, Cheltenham (UK) and Northampton (MA): Edward Elgar.

Shane, S. and S. Venkataraman (2000), 'The promise of entrepreneurship as a field of research', *Academy of Management Review*, **25** (1), 217–226.

Shapero, A. (1975), 'The displaced, uncomfortable entrepreneur', *Psychology Today*, **9** (6), 83–8.

Sharma, P. and J.J. Chrisman (1999), 'Toward a reconciliation of the definitional issues in the field of corporate entrepreneurship', *Entrepreneurship Theory and Practice*, **23** (3), 11–27.

Simon, H.A. (1985), 'What we know about the creative process', in R.L. Kuhn (ed), *Frontiers in creative and innovative management*, Cambridge (MA): Ballinger, 3–20.

Simon, H.A. (1991), 'Bounded rationality and organizational learning', *Organization Science*, **2**, 125–34.

Sinatra, A. (1988), 'Da manager a imprenditore interno', in G. Invernizzi, M. Molteni and A. Sinatra (eds), *Imprenditorialità interna. Lo sviluppo di nuove attività nelle imprese*, Milano: Etas, 7–34.

Smith, A. (1937), *The Wealth of Nations*, New York: The Modern Library.

Smith, K.G and D. DeGregorio (2002), 'Bisociation, discovery and entrepreneurial action', in A.M. Hitt, D.R. Ireland, M.S. Camp and D.L. Sexton (eds), *Strategic entrepreneurship: Creating a new mindset*, Oxford: Blackwell, 129–50.

Solinas, G. and D. Baroni (2001), 'I sistemi locali manifatturieri in Italia 1991 – 1996', in G. Becattini, M. Bellandi, G. Dei Ottati and F. Sforzi (eds), *Il caleidoscopio dello sviluppo locale. Trasformazioni economiche nell'Italia contemporanea*, Torino: Rosenberg and Sellier, 395–417.

Spender, J.C. (1996), 'Making knowledge the basis of a dynamic theory of the firm', *Strategic Management Journal*, **17**, 45–62.

Staber, U. (1996), 'The social embeddedness of industrial district networks', in U. Staber, N.V. Schaefer and B. Sharma (eds), *Business networks prospects for regional development*, Berlin: Walter de Gruyter, 148–74.

Staber, U. (1997), 'An ecological perspective on entrepreneurship in industrial districts', *Entrepreneurship and Regional Development*, **9**, 45–64.

Staber, U. (1998), 'Inter-firm co-operation and competition in industrial districts', *Organization Studies*, **19** (4), 701–24.

Staber, U. (2001), 'Spatial proximity and firm survival in a declining industrial district: The case of knitwear firms in Baden-Wurttemberg', *Entrepreneurship and Regional Development*, **35** (4), 329–41.

Stevenson, H.H. and D.E. Gumpert (1985), 'The heart of entrepreneurship', *Harvard Business Review*, **85** (2), 85–94.

Stevenson, H.H. and J.C. Jarillo (1990), 'A paradigm of entrepreneurship: Entrepreneurial management', *Strategic Management Journal*, **11**, 17–27.

Stevenson, H.H., H.I. Grousbeck, M.J. Roberts and A.V. Bhide (1999), *New business ventures and the entrepreneur*, Burr Ridge (IL): Richard D. Irwin.

Stevenson, H.H., M. Roberts and H. Grousbeck (1989), *New business ventures and the entrepreneur*, Homewood (IL): Irwin.

Stopford, J.M. and C.W.F. Baden-Fuller (1994), 'Creating corporate entrepreneurship', *Strategic Management Journal*, **15**, 521–36.

Storper, M. and A. Scott (1989), 'The geographical foundations and social regulation of flexible production complexes', in J. Wolch and M. Dear (eds), *The power of geography: How territory shape social life social reproduction*, Boston: Unwin and Hyman, 21–40.

Sutton, J. (1998), *Technology and market structure, theory and history*, Cambridge (MA): MIT Press.

Tallman, S., M. Jenkins, N. Henry and S. Pinch (2004), 'Knowledge, clusters, and competitive advantage', *Academy of Management Review*, **29** (2), 258–71.

Teece, D.J., G. Pisano and A. Shuen (1997), 'Dynamic capabilities and strategic management', *Strategic Management Journal*, **18**, 509–33.

Timmons, J.A. (1978), 'Characteristics and role demand of entrepreneurship', *American Journal of Small Business*, **3**, 5–17.

Tinacci Mossello, M. (1990), *Geografia Economica*, Bologna: il Mulino.

Trigilia ,C. (1990), 'Tre equivoci della piccola impresa', paper presented at the *4th La piccola impresa Symposium*, Bologna, April 26–27.

Trigilia, C. (1986), *Grandi partiti e piccole imprese*, Bologna: il Mulino.

Tsai, W. (2001), 'Knowledge transfer in intraorganisational networks: Effects of network position and absorptive capacity on business unit innovation and performance', *Academy of Management Journal*, **44**, 996–1004.

Tsai, W. and S. Ghoshal (1998), 'Social capital and value creation: The role of intrafirm networks', *Academy of Management Journal*, **41**, 464–76.

Tushman, M.L. (1977), 'Special boundary roles in the innovation process', *Administrative Science Quarterly*, **22**, 587–605.

Ucbasaran, D., P. Westhead and M. Wright (2001), 'The focus of entrepreneurship research: Contextual and process issues', *Entrepreneurship Theory and Practice*, **25** (4), 57–80.

Ugolini, M. (1995), *La natura dei rapporti tra imprese nel settore delle calze per donna*, Padova: CEDAM.

Vaccà, S. (1986), 'L'economia delle relazioni tra imprese: Dall'espansione dimensionale allo sviluppo per reti esterne', *Economia e Politica Industriale*, **51**, 3–42.

Vagaggini, V. (1990), *Sistema economico e agire territoriale*, Milano: Franco Angeli.

Venkataraman, S. (1997), 'The distinctive domain of entrepreneurship research: An editor's perspective', in J. Katz and J. Brockhaus (eds), *Advances in entrepreneurship, firm emergence and growth*, Greenwich (CT): JAI Press, 791–805.

Vernon, R. (1989), 'L'ipotesi del ciclo di prodotto nel nuovo contesto internazionale', in G. Balcet (ed), *Economia dell'impresa multinazionale*, Torino: Giappichelli Editore, 81–104.

Vesper, K.H. (1984), 'Three faces of corporate entrepreneurship: A pilot study', in J.A. Hornaday, F.A. Tarpley, J. Timmons and K.H. Vesper (eds), *Frontiers of entrepreneurship research*, Wellesley (MA): Babson College, 294–320.

Viesti, G. (2000), *Come nascono i distretti industriali*, Bari: Laterza.

Visconti, F. (1996), *Le condizioni di sviluppo delle imprese operanti nei distretti industriali*, Milano: Egea.

Visconti, F. (2001), 'I percorsi di sviluppo delle piccole e medie imprese operanti nei distretti industriali', *Piccola Impresa/Small Business*, **1**, 27–48.

Visconti, F. (2002), *Il governo dei distretti industriali*, Milano: EGEA.

Viteritti, A. (2000), 'La costruzione dell'identità in un distretto industriale: il biomedicale di Mirandola', *Studi organizzativi*, **3**, 193–219.

Von Hippel, E. (1988), *The sources of innovation*, New York: Oxford University Press.

Wall, S.T. (2005), 'The protean organization: Learning to love change', *Organizational Dynamics*, **34** (1), 37–46.

Weber, A. (1929), *Theory of the location of industries*, Chicago: University of Chicago Press.

Weber, M. (1947), *The theory of social and economic organization*, Oxford: Oxford University Press.

Weick, K.E. and K.H. Roberts (1993), 'Collective mind in organizations: Heedful interrelating on flight desks', *Administrative Science Quarterly*, **38**, 357–81.

Wernerfelt, B. (1984), 'A resource-based view of the firm', *Strategic Management Journal*, **5**, 171–80.

Whitford, J. (2001), 'The decline of a model? Challenges and response in the Italian industrial districts', *Economy and Society*, **30** (1), 38–65.

Wigren, C. (2003), *The Spirit of Gnosjö - The grand narrative and beyond*, JIBS Dissertation Series No 017, Jonkoping, Sweden: Jonkoping International Business School.

Wiklund, J. (1998), *Small firm growth and performance: Entrepreneurship and beyond*, JIBS Dissertation Series No 003, Jonkoping, Sweden: Jonkoping International Business School.

Winter, S.G. (1984), 'Schumpeterian competition in alternative technological regimes', *Journal of Economic Behaviour and Organization*, **5**, 287–320.

Yin, R.K. (1989), *Case study research. Design and methods*, London: Sage.

Zagnoli, P. (1991), *I rapporti tra imprese nei settori ad alta tecnologia: il caso della Silicon Valley*, Torino: Giappichelli.

Zahra, S.A. (1991), 'Predictors and financial outcomes of corporate entrepreneurship: An exploratory study', *Journal of Business Venturing*, **6**, 259–85.

Zahra, S.A. (1993), 'A conceptual model of entrepreneurship as firm behavior: A critique and extension', *Entrepreneurship Theory and Practice*, **17** (4), 5–21.

Zahra, S.A. (ed) (2005), *Corporate entrepreneurship and growth*, Cheltenham (UK) and Northampton (MA): Edward Elgar.

Zahra, S.A. and G. George (2002), 'Absorptive capacity: A review, reconceptualization, and extension', *Academy of Management Review*, **27**, 185–203.

Zahra, S.A. and G.G. Dess (2001), 'Entrepreneurship as a field of research: Encouraging dialogue and debate', *Academy of Management Review*, **26** (1), 8–10.

Zook, C. and J. Allen (2001), *Profit from the core: Growth strategy in an era of turbulence*, Cambridge (MA): Harvard University School Press.

Zucchella, A. (2006), Local cluster dynamics: Trajectories of mature industrial districts between decline and multiple embeddedness, *Journal of Institutional Economics*, **2** (1), 21–44.

Index